# A Philosophical History of Police Power

Also Available from Bloomsbury

*On Resistance*, Howard Caygill
*The Ethics of Resistance*, Drew M. Dalton
*Resistance, Revolution and Fascism*, Anthony Faramelli

# A Philosophical History of Police Power

Melayna Kay Lamb

BLOOMSBURY ACADEMIC
LONDON • NEW YORK • OXFORD • NEW DELHI • SYDNEY

BLOOMSBURY ACADEMIC
Bloomsbury Publishing Plc, 50 Bedford Square, London, WC1B 3DP, UK
Bloomsbury Publishing Inc, 1359 Broadway, 12th Floor, New York, NY 10018, USA
Bloomsbury Publishing Ireland, 29 Earlsfort Terrace, Dublin 2, D02 AY28, Ireland

BLOOMSBURY, BLOOMSBURY ACADEMIC and the Diana logo
are trademarks of Bloomsbury Publishing Plc

First published in Great Britain 2024
This paperback edition published in 2025

Copyright © Melayna Kay Lamb, 2024

Melayna Kay Lamb has asserted her right under the Copyright,
Designs and Patents Act, 1988, to be identified as Author of this work.

For legal purposes the Acknowledgements on p. x constitute
an extension of this copyright page.

All rights reserved. No part of this publication may be: i) reproduced or transmitted in any form, electronic or mechanical, including photocopying, recording or by means of any information storage or retrieval system without prior permission in writing from the publishers; or ii) used or reproduced in any way for the training, development or operation of artificial intelligence (AI) technologies, including generative AI technologies. The rights holders expressly reserve this publication from the text and data mining exception as per Article 4(3) of the Digital Single Market Directive (EU) 2019/790.

Bloomsbury Publishing Inc does not have any control over, or responsibility for, any third-party websites referred to or in this book. All internet addresses given in this book were correct at the time of going to press. The author and publisher regret any inconvenience caused if addresses have changed or sites have ceased to exist, but can accept no responsibility for any such changes.

A catalogue record for this book is available from the British Library.

A catalog record for this book is available from the Library of Congress.

ISBN: HB: 978-1-3502-0404-1
PB: 978-1-3502-0408-9
ePDF: 978-1-3502-0405-8
eBook: 978-1-3502-0406-5

Typeset by Deanta Global Publishing Services, Chennai, India

For product safety related questions contact productsafety@bloomsbury.com.

To find out more about our authors and books visit www.bloomsbury.com
and sign up for our newsletters.

*For Norah and Maria*

# Contents

| | |
|---|---:|
| List of figures | ix |
| Acknowledgements | x |
| | |
| Introduction | 1 |
|     Sovereign police? | 5 |
|     The end of *Oikonomia?* | 12 |
|     Anti-Blackness and *an-archic* police power | 14 |
|     The argument | 17 |
|     The structure | 20 |
| | |
| Prologue: Foucault, Smith and disappearing police | 22 |
|     Archaeology and order | 24 |
|     Biopolitics, discipline and order | 29 |
|     From *Polizei* to 'the police' | 32 |
|     Order: Physis or nomos? | 38 |

## Part I  Divine & sovereign order

| | |
|---|---:|
| 1  Sovereignty and fear: Hobbes and the production of order | 45 |
|     The political animal vs. the wolf | 49 |
|     (Dis)order, teleology and the life of the state | 54 |
|     Living and living well | 56 |
|     The splitting of power | 62 |
|     Conclusion | 66 |
| | |
| 2  Hegel and police: On the relation between universal and particular | 68 |
|     The Hegelian state | 70 |
|     Hegel's *Polizei* | 72 |
|     Fichte's police | 77 |

| | | |
|---|---|---|
| | Hegel on Fichte's police | 78 |
| | *Polizei*, police, police-power | 81 |
| | Violence, nature and Hegel's emergency | 85 |

## Part II  Police order

| | | |
|---|---|---|
| 3 | Law, sovereignty and the exception: Benjamin and modern police | 95 |
| | Schmitt's sovereign | 96 |
| | The transcendent made immanent: Benjamin's response | 101 |
| | Violence and critique | 105 |
| | Benjamin's police | 108 |
| | Force-of-law | 111 |
| 4 | The *an-archy* of order: Agamben and the police | 116 |
| | Divided power and *Oikonomia* | 118 |
| | Fate, government and collateral effects | 121 |
| | The signature of order | 125 |
| | The *an-archic* character of police power | 132 |
| | Potentiality, exceptionality, police | 134 |
| 5 | da Silva: Nature, necessity and violence | 138 |
| | The racial and the modern | 140 |
| | Police power and colonial boomerangs | 144 |
| | Revisiting the state of nature | 150 |
| | Time and anti-Black violence | 155 |

| | |
|---|---|
| Concluding remarks | 161 |
|   'No drugs were found' | 161 |
| Notes | 167 |
| References | 197 |
| Index | 212 |

# Figures

1  Abraham Bosse with input from Thomas Hobbes, 1651  63

# Acknowledgements

This book started life as a PhD thesis under the supervision of Bob Brecher without whose support there would have been no PhD. I am deeply indebted to Lars Cornelissen and Jishnu Guha who provided much valuable commentary and editorial support for my thesis. Thanks also to German Primera, Bettie Vasileva, and Joel Roberts Quinn Lester for insightful comments and illuminating conversations regarding this work. I'd also like to thank Gabriel Burne, Greg Brown, Emma Harrisson, Gab Wulff, Gari Gomez, Megan Archer, Jacopo Condo and Giovanni Marmont for their help with editing and supporting me over the finish line with the PhD. Thank you to Alice Butler for the years we spent together in the British Library and for always picking me up at the hardest moments.

Much appreciation goes to Liza Thompson and the editors at Bloomsbury for their patience and hard work in making this into a book. My thanks also to Will White for the art that appears on the cover of this book.

I'd like to express gratitude to Illan Rua Wall and Howard Caygill who provided invaluable comments during the viva examination and for championing my work in this area. A huge thank you also goes to James Martel who saw me shakily present the penultimate chapter of this book and whose encouragement, enthusiasm and insightful comments ever since have ensured that I didn't lose faith in the work or myself as an academic. Thank you as well to James Trafford for reading an early chapter draft and providing excellent comments and reading suggestions.

# Introduction

How to think police power? How to grasp it? How to critique it? This task – though necessary – is far from straightforward. As Walter Benjamin identified in 1921, police power is 'formless, like its nowhere tangible all-pervasive, ghostly presence in the life of civilized states' (1978: 287). No less true today than it was then, the atmosphere we find ourselves in is one where the brutal face of police power shows itself so frequently, yet is paradoxically so elusive when one tries to take hold of it. It is, in other words, difficult to have a *theory* of police power as such, yet thinking it remains more urgent now than ever. This book is not a history of the institution of the police – though it does reflect on police practices. Neither is it a protracted etymology – though it does reflect on its conceptual beginnings. It is, rather, what I have termed a philosophical history. A reappraisal of how Western political philosophy has thought (and not thought) police seems to me necessary, given how crucial and unique police power is, and paradoxically, how marginal its place has been in the Western canon of political philosophy.

One of the questions that reoccurs upon even a cursory glance at the institution of the police is how, even when there is much evidence (video or otherwise) that police killed or hurt an unarmed person who did not present and could not have presented a physical threat, does the law absolve them? I do not wish to recount here all the police killings that have taken place in the UK and the United States in recent times; as Fred Moten and Stefano Harney put it, Michael Brown is only the most recent name of an 'ongoing event of resistance to, and resistance before, socioecological disaster' (2015: 82) and thus Michael Brown is '(aka Eric Garner, aka Trayvon Martin, aka Eleanor Bumpurs, aka Emmitt Till, aka an endless stream of names and absent names)' (2015: 84). To focus on spectacular cases of police violence, undertaken with impunity, is, in the words of Steve Martinot and Jared Sexton, to reduce the 'paradigm to the non-paradigmatic' (2003). In this way, they write, 'whenever one attempts to speak about the paradigm of policing, one is forced back into a discussion of particular events – high profile homicides and their related courtroom battles, for instance. The spectacular event camouflages the operation of police law as contempt, as terror, its occupation of neighbourhoods' (2003). Part of the task at hand is thus to resist the urge to focus on individual instances of police violence that in themselves cannot reveal the structure of police power but nevertheless point towards one of the central arguments of this book that police power in modernity is incapable of being called to order by or through the law.

I do not wish to claim that police on both sides of the Atlantic are exactly the same, nor that police power has remained entirely consistent with its older form. What I do suggest is that there is a *logic of police power* that can be grasped by attending to the philosophical and metaphysical grounds of political thought. In this regard, this book is also not an addition to the ever-expanding Foucauldian literature on police.[1] The primary reason for this, which I will unpack in more detail in the prologue, is that while there is much important work being done on *policing* as it relates to strategies of normalization and biopolitical power, this does little to shed light on either the power or function of *the police* in modern-day Western states. That is to say, an expanded concept of police and 'policing' as it relates to Foucault's 'governmentality' that became popular in certain ranks of political theory in the 1990s does not attend theoretically to the problem of the relationship of police power to sovereignty and law.[2] In light of this, I take my cue from Agamben, who in a striking yet brief essay, entitled 'Sovereign Police', writes the following:

> The point is that the police – contrary to public opinion – are not merely an administrative function of law enforcement; rather, the police are perhaps the place where the proximity and the almost constitutive exchange between violence and right that characterizes the figure of the sovereign is shown more nakedly and clearly than anywhere else. (2000: 68)

This claim, however, remains underdeveloped and mostly unexplored not only in Agamben's own work but in much work on sovereignty more generally. That police officers are involved in death-dealing, that they can *kill and it not be considered a crime*, is not a contingent or incidental characteristic of their power.[3] This places the institution of police in a significant place in any theorization of power.[4] That this is the power that characterizes *sovereignty* has been argued by, for example, both Foucault and Agamben, Achille Mbembe and others.⁵ Indeed, we find this notion throughout the history of Western thought on sovereignty: to take one example, Ernst Kantorowicz cites John of Salisbury in 1159 as writing 'that the Prince, although he be not bound by the ties of Law, is yet Law's servant as well as that of Equity; that he bears a public person, and that *he sheds blood without guilt*' (my emphasis added, 1957: 95). Insofar as he acts for the good of the public, and not his own private gain, the sovereign can shed blood 'in his capacity as judge; for what he does as the ordinary he does as "the minister of the public utility" and for the benefit of the common weal' (1957: 95). What is transmitted through the Middle Ages, then, is the configuration of the sovereign as above the law, acting 'for the love of justice herself, and not for the fear of punishment' (1957: 95).⁶ While there is not scope here fully to elaborate on the transmission of this particular strand of thought, we find centuries later in William Blackstone's *Commentaries on the Laws of England* (1765) – a foundational text on common law – that government is the result of the formation of civil society, necessary 'to preserve and keep that society in order' (2011: 51). Here Blackstone argues that 'the supposition of *law* therefore is, that neither the king nor either the house of parliament (collectively taken) is capable of doing any wrong' and further that the law also ascribes to kings 'absolute perfection' and as such finds them incapable of doing wrong (2016: 159).

And yet, *and yet*, while political philosophers have obsessed over questions of sovereignty, few have considered or even noted the critical place of police within those questions. Police violence can then be easily passed over, chalked up to rogue cops, rotten apples, *aberrations* from a norm of orderly conduct – spectacular, yet particular, instances of violence that raise no need for theoretical reflection.⁷ This blind spot is, I think, not accidental. Indeed, in order for theories of sovereignty and the law (especially liberal ones) to cohere, police power must be relegated and reduced to something so banal, something so unexceptional, as to be barely worth mentioning. That is, police must be reduced to something like the execution of the law, or a purely technical, administrative institution that does nothing but carry out remedial tasks necessary for the day-to-day functioning of a society. To take but one example from Montesquieu: 'the business of the Police consists in affairs which arise every instant, and are commonly of a trifling nature: there is then but little need of formalities' (2001: 519). In short, what I argue is that police (the idea and the institution) pose a profound, yet mostly unacknowledged, problem for theories of sovereignty and law.[8]

Most prominently, the recognition that police power has a relationship to sovereignty unsettles one of the most central tenets of received theories of sovereignty: that sovereign power is the power of *one*.[9] It is the singular that founds the universal – that lies at the foundation of the political as such. It is also the highest power – it stands over and above right and cannot be subject to it (lest it no longer be supreme and therefore no longer sovereign): 'the sovereign having the legal power to suspend the validity of the law, legally places himself outside the law' (Agamben 1998: 15). This point has been scrutinized by many seeking to uncover the economy of this power; how is it that right rests on something outside of itself? What is a power that is supreme and unaccountable and yet the very foundation of law?[10] If, as I am arguing, police can kill and it not be considered a crime then this poses a problem for the mythology of sovereignty in that their power rests on the very same theoretical foundations as that of sovereignty. And yet, sovereign power cannot reside in multiple places: 'This great Authority being Indivisible' (Hobbes 1996: 128) as Hobbes puts it, as a 'Kingdome divided in it selfe cannot stand' (Hobbes 1996: 127). The mythology of sovereign power presupposes that sovereign power itself is not divisible, cannot be 'dispersed' and fragmented into thousands of other agents, for then sovereignty itself – its idea and its concept reliant as it is on being unified and one – would be undermined.[11]

It is in light of this that I claim that theories of sovereignty that do not account for police necessarily run into aporias and contradictions. The intervention this book therefore makes is to recentre the police through a reconsideration of Western metaphysics and political thought on questions of sovereignty and the exception. Seeing police as either the implementation of a sovereign will or the enforcement of law places the police in a secondary, derivative locus; a power that is, in Agamben's terminology, *founded* and not *founding*. By attending to the ways in which police is not secondary and derivative, but rather a founding power, we can begin to unravel the ways in which police power is, in modernity, the an-archic condition of possibility for sovereignty itself. In order to understand the shifting relations between sovereignty and police, however, something must be said about the uses of the term 'police'. This is not, however, a search for an *origin* of the term nor the delineation of a strict definition of police, but rather points to another hypothesis, that the various *uses* of the concept can tell us something about police power and its relationship to sovereignty.

## Sovereign police?

The history of the concept of police is an unsettled one. The word 'police' was not officially used in Great Britain until 1714, referring then to the ten 'Commissioners of Police' in Scotland (OED 1989). However, prior to this, the corresponding concept had already begun to take shape on the continent, in particular, in Germany[12] and France in the fifteenth century, eventually giving rise to a form of governing that was the 'legislative and administrative regulation of the internal life of a community to promote general welfare and the condition of good order . . . and the regimenting of social life' (Neocleous 2000: 1). The term *Polizei* became a 'structural principle of the absolutist order' and was ultimately used to centralize the state 'at the expense of aristocratic and municipal civil society' (Caygill 1989: 105). It was a centralizing, integrating power, a crucial aspect of the development of the modern state. The 'science of police' (*Polizeiwissenschaft*) of the seventeenth and eighteenth centuries is to be distinguished from the statutes of *Polizei*, which were aimed at the 'institution and maintenance of order' (Knemeyer 1980: 173). *Polizeiwissenschaft*, on the other hand, 'puts forward theories which are concerned with the detailed conditions for the institution and/or maintenance of order, and in consequence has to grapple with the objective of the state itself, and the forms of activity considered requisite for the establishment of order' (Knemeyer 1980: 173). Between these two formulations we can discern a distinction between a more general *Polizei* and the 'science of police' that would determine more precisely the objects to which *Polizei* is directed; its material, technical aspects.[13]

'Police' during the eighteenth century thus contains within it the idea of a common good that is to be attained via the creation and sustaining of a certain kind of *order*. As one commentator puts it: 'the application of a mechanistic view of the world to the sphere of government and the belief in a voluntaristic state direction for maximising the potential of society entailed active intervention and supervision on the part of prince and administrators' (Raeff 1983: 1229). The creation of 'good order' meant a concern not only with security but also with welfare, and thus *Polizei* was indistinguishable from 'domestic administration' (Knemeyer 1980: 182).[14] Initially at least, *Polizei* was a broad notion, encompassing a vast array of activities pertaining to the normative ordering of society and this in itself was seen to be linked to a moral, ethical order that could not be separated from the more general prosperity of the state.[15] In this way, for the theorists of *Polizeiwissenschaft*, the state was 'conceived as a giant oikos' (Caygill 1989: 109) and police ordinances were aimed at managing the 'household' in a 'patriarchal model of social organisation' (Caygill 1989: 109). This form of state was one in which there was no distinction between state and civil society or a separate realm known as 'the economy'. Police, then, was the name given to sovereign power *acting directly on its subjects in the name of good order*. As the prominent theorist of *Polizei*, Von Justi, writes: 'The law-giving power in police affairs, since the internal arrangement of the state chiefly rests upon it, can unquestionably be exercised by no one but the sovereign power, the destiny of which is to administer the affairs of the state for the promotion of common happiness' (in Small 1909: 451). Police is here considered and treated along with *Oekonomie (oikonomia)* (Small 1909: 437), and it is why, as Tribe notes, 'German historians have long accepted the idea that the economic discourse of the 17th and early 18th centuries was "neo-Aristotelian"' (2015: 32).

Police and *oikonomia* are also considered together by Blackstone, who sees civil society as a scene of self-interest and, as a result of this, of conflict. This in turn means that 'there must be a controlling power somewhere lodged; and wherever or whatever it is, that is *Government*' (Blackstone 2016: 650). This is absolutely crucial and it is possible to draw some preliminary conclusions, namely that civil society was conceived of as necessitating government for the purpose of *order*. The specificities of government and order are unclear, but they are made to seem indissolubly linked; wherever a 'controlling power' resides with the objective of keeping 'order', one will find government. In Book 4, Chapter 13, of the *Commentaries*, Blackstone describes offences 'against public police and oeconomy' that are defined as 'the due regulation and domestic order of the kingdom: whereby the individuals of the state' are conceived of as 'members of a well-governed family' (2016: 783). We thus find in Blackstone not only a conception of a separation of state and civil society, but civil society is considered as being in need of 'ordering', where citizens must be governed 'like family'.

Two things are especially striking here. First, that *Polizei* was the name given to a limitless range of things to be regulated in the name of good order.[16] Second, that this was in itself indissolubly linked to *oeconomy* or *oikonomia*. It is precisely the recognition of these matters that has led various scholars to locate police in relation to economy. Exemplary in this regard, and showing the historical and theoretical terrain on which it has grown, is the work of Mark Neocleous and, in particular, *The Fabrication of Social Order*. Here Neocleous is concerned to demonstrate

> the centrality of the historically massive police operation on the part of the state to the consolidation of the social power of capital and the wage form: as order became increasingly based on the bourgeois mode of production, so the police mandate was to fabricate an order of wage labour and administer the class of poverty. (2000: xii)

While agreeing on many counts, I see my argument as departing from his analysis in a number of important ways. While I go on to discuss this in detail, for now it should be noted that I see order, not as the order of bourgeois capitalist social and wage relations, but rather, following Agamben, as expressing the aporetic and paradoxical relationship between transcendent and immanent realms of power that Western political philosophy has simultaneously split and held together in the form of a relation. That police was initially the name given to 'the management of the societal household' (Dubber 2005: 47) for the end of order, requires reflection on *oikonomia*, and its origins in Aristotelian thought.[17] To this end, a brief introduction to Agamben's *The Kingdom and the Glory*, which carries out a detailed genealogy of *oikonomia*, will follow. It is here that Agamben theorizes the split between sovereignty and government, and the attempt, by Western political thought, to cover over this split through recourse to the concept of *order*. This helps to form the analytical lens which informs my readings of Hobbes and Hegel. Therefore, while a more detailed discussion appears in the penultimate chapter, given that I will mobilize Agamben's concepts at certain points both in the first and second half of this book, I shall offer an overview here.

## Oikonomia

*Oikonomia*, or the management of the household as it appears in Aristotle, is defined in contradistinction to the realm of the *polis*; as such, we find a scission between the house and the city, or *oikonomia* and politics. Aristotle articulates a qualitative distinction between the government of free men and the government of the household in opposition to those who would argue that ruling a household is just a difference in numbers to ruling a polis (2013, 1252a7: 54). He goes on to argue that 'rule in a household is monarchical, since every house has one ruler', while the 'rule of a statesman is rule over free and equal persons' (2013, 1255b16: 74). This notion, in its beginnings, thus points to a non-political realm, one that requires a different modality of governance from that of the *polis*.[18] At the very foundation of Western political thought there is a split between the *oikos* and the *polis*; and it is this that is crucial for the development of a mode of governing that was a mode of groundless praxis, contingent actions, not subject to the rules of the *polis*. As Agamben writes, it is activities that are 'decisions and orders that cope with problems that are each time specific and concern the functional order (*taxis*) of the different parts of the *oikos*' (2011: 17–18). Indeed, matters of household governance 'lie beyond the realm of justice' (Dubber 2005: 5) and in this sense are not concerned with rules and laws as such. The task of the householder in this paradigm of *oikonomia* is to maximize the welfare of the household, and in so doing they may have recourse to what they see fit in order to attain this outcome (Dubber 2005: 43). This constitutes a realm of contingency and a managerial form of governance that is, as it were, *ex nihilo* – not referencing law or justice for its necessity but order *alone*. As Aristotle writes, 'a master's knowledge consists in knowing how to put his slaves to *use*' (2013, 1255b30: 75, emphasis in original). It is thus not epistemic knowledge that is useful here, but activity: the term 'head of the family', Aristotle writes, 'does not refer to a science but to a certain way of being' (in Agamben 2011: 17).

That *oikonomia* leaves the sphere of Aristotelian thought and is taken up by, among others, the Stoics who use it to express governing 'the whole from the inside' (Agamben 2011: 19) and the Church Fathers, is what Agamben seeks to interrogate. While the inflections might slightly differ, Agamben argues that the meaning of *oikonomia* across these fields remains consistent with an 'activity ordered for a purpose' (2011: 26). In particular, this idea of *oikonomia* has been identified by Agamben as being taken up by Christian theologians in order to solve the problem of the Trinity; it is crucial for an understanding of government and order that will follow. For such theologians, the problem was one of finding a way to articulate the Trinitarian doctrine while simultaneously holding on to the idea that God is one. In so doing they were trying to avoid 'a fracture of monotheism that would have introduced a plurality of divine figures, and polytheism with them' (2011: 53). The way Christian theologians tried to solve this problem was through recourse to the notion of *oikonomia*, that is, by articulating a split between God's being (one) and his action (the Trinity). Via the Stoics, this idea is taken up by Tertullian: 'the Trinity derives from the father by intermingled and connected in degrees in no way threatening the monarchy but protecting the quality of the economy' (in Zartaloudis 2010: 63) and further that 'The Trinity itself is a *dispensation*, an *oikonomia* as an internal disposition of the divine substance. It does not threaten unity, but administers it' (Zartaloudis 2010: 63).

The main issue, then, was that God, in terms of his substance, is absolutely one, but that, in terms of his *oikonomia* – that is to say in the way in which he manages the divine house and life – he is three. Hence we arrive at the paradox of the government of the world. The world must be governed, and yet God, as transcendent, cannot be both being *and* praxis if he is to remain unitary. In this way, '*oikonomia* renders possible a reconciliation of the transcendent God, at the same time one and Trinitarian, in order to remain transcendent, assumes an *oikonomic praxiology* and founds an immanence of government as praxis where the mystery of sovereignty coincides with the history of humanity' (Zartaloudis 2010: 65). What is divided is not God's being, but God's *action* in the world. We thus come to a division between a divine transcendent order, and an immanent, domestic order that is *of the world*:

> we have shown that the first seed of the division between the Kingdom and the Government is to be found in the Trinitarian oikonomia, which introduces a fracture between being and praxis in the deity himself. The notion of *ordo* in medieval thought – and especially in Thomas Aquinas – is only able to suture this division by reproducing it inside itself as a fracture between a transcendent and immanent order (and between *ordinatio* and *executio*). (Agamben 2011: 111)

In terms of the theological foundations of a split between two planes, transcendence and immanence, there is the conceptual solution that they become joined together through the notion of divine providence. This becomes not only a theological issue but a philosophical one, or as Zartaloudis has it: 'providential government is theology's and philosophy's attempt to answer the scission evident in classical ontology between being and praxis, a transcendent and an immanent good, *theologia* and *oikonomia*' (2010: 81). *Oikonomia* comes to refer to the pole of action, the government of things in their immanent realm, as opposed to the realm of the transcendent. *Oikonomia* and order are then the conceptual solutions to the problem of the split between God's being and action, enabling a relationship that keeps the two in constellation with each other, without either collapsing them into identity or positing an absolute separation. While Aristotle himself has no notion of providence, for Agamben, nevertheless, providence 'is the name of the "oikonomia" insofar as the latter presents itself as the government of the world' (2011: 111).

What is important to highlight here in terms of the understanding of the providential paradigm is that the transcendent register of power is 'never given by itself and separated from the world, as in Gnosis, but is always in relation to immanence' (Agamben 2011: 141). Therefore, government is that which 'results from this functional correlation' (Agamben 2011: 141). Indeed, as Agamben has put it, in the providential apparatus the '[t]wo levels are strictly entwined, so that the first founds, legitimates, and makes possible the second, while the second concretely puts into practice in the chain of causes and effects the general decisions of the divine mind' (Agamben 2011: 141). From this perspective, then, neither the immanent pole of government nor the transcendent pole of sovereignty is given by themselves: government is both *ordinatio* and *executio*. The Trinitarian fracture between being and action and the attempt at its reconciliation through providence required two different registers – transcendent/immanent – to be articulated in a bipolar machine. *Oikonomia*, in this sense, is nothing but the 'functional relation between a glorified transcendental power (that appears but cannot be used) and an immanent *praxis* (that is invisible and yet effective)' (Zartaloudis 2010: 85).

Aristotle also conceives of a distinction between transcendence and immanence, where transcendence is defined by 'separation and autonomy', while the figure of immanence is 'that of order, that is the relation of every thing with other things' (Agamben 2011: 80). Agamben's analysis of Aristotle finds that transcendence and immanence are 'not simply distinguished as superior and inferior, but rather articulated together', which, Agamben writes, constitutes a 'machine that is, at the same time, cosmological and political' (Agamben 2011: 80). While transcendence is separate, immanence is order, which is to say, concerned with *relations*. Indeed, in Aristotle the order of the world and its unity is compared not to the city but to the *household* (Aristotle 2004: 385). Expressed in this way, order becomes a fundamental concept, one that exposes, in the history of political thought, two different registers, that of transcendent and immanent order, as well as the accompanying attempt to resolve the tension between the two. It is through this concept of order that the possibility of a divine being can retain its unity in being and transcendence while simultaneously acting in the world. Not only this, but 'order is the apparatus that makes possible the articulation of the separate substance with being, of God with the world. *Taxis* names their aporetic relation' (Agamben 2011: 84). Significantly, then, order is a relational concept that not only refers to the relations of things to a higher entity, and to the relations between these things themselves, but also, and perhaps more importantly, that enables the mediation of these two different orders: the transcendent and the immanent. Where this gets more complicated is, as Agamben writes, the fact that order (that is a figure of relation) 'becomes the way in which the separate substance is present and acts in the world' (2011: 83).

What is crucial here is that in *oikonomia*, order and providence we find metaphysical and philosophical solutions to the problem of the divided character of power, implying that there is the *being* of power, its substance and the way this power acts in the world. This gets transposed, Agamben argues, into the fracture between sovereignty and government, whereby government is supposedly derived from sovereignty as a merely administrative power, concerned with governing things in their heterogeneity and multiplicity but towards a common end. Power, Agamben writes, 'every power, both human and divine – must hold these two poles together, that is, it must be, at the same time, kingdom and government, transcendent norm and immanent order' (2011: 82).[19]

The connection I noted earlier between police and *oikonomia* thus acquires even further significance here. As Caygill has noted, the concept of *Polizei* undergoes a shift after the end of the Thirty Years War in 1648. Police ordinances were a series of measures designed to 'meet immediate and specific social problems which were not covered by existing law or custom' (Caygill 1989: 105). Prior to the Thirty Years War, these had taken the form of 'ad-hoc, reactive measures' (Caygill 1989: 105), while afterwards police ordinances were used as a means for achieving specific ends, thus were a mechanism to mould the social order in a certain shape so as to promote security and welfare

(Caygill 1989: 105). This form of ordinance, then, was not merely reactive, but proactive and interventionist where the common good, that is the wealth and order of the state, were to be promoted and achieved by conscious design. The state, it was thought, could be perfected through interventionist measures. Thus we find, in the history of the concept of *Polizei* itself, an oscillation between an understanding of order that is related to power reacting to contingent events and one that is the outcome and implementation of an order that is *designed*.

Three points therefore emerge that are crucial for my argument. First, there is a split between transcendence and immanence, between ontology and praxis, whereby the immanent is a realm of contingent activity not referencing an episteme or higher law, and in this way it is groundless. This in itself stems from the split between the household and the *polis* that Aristotle conceptualizes in an oppositional relation. Second, when this is taken up by the Church Fathers in their articulation of providence, the second, immanent, realm is conceived as the activity of ordering that is the government of the world. This means that God's being and action split apart, yet this does not affect the unitary singular being of God. Third, this providential paradigm becomes salient once displaced into the political realm for the relationship between sovereignty and government, with government a praxiological, immanent power that supposedly derives from sovereignty, but where in fact the relation is far more complex. Indeed, as I will go on to show with regard to police power, rather than a power of administration or enforcement, police power is not the execution of the law or implementation of a sovereign will but a non-epistemic form of power, a groundless ground. Having looked at Agamben's investigation into *oikonomia* I'll now turn to the commonplace understanding of the development of police in the transition to modernity.

## The end of *Oikonomia*?

It is often argued that during the course of the nineteenth century and into the twentieth, political economy became detached from the model of the household (Tribe 2015: 42) and it is this that saw the undermining and eventual disappearance of *Polizeiwissenschaft* and the police state.[20] Concomitantly, over the course of the eighteenth century it is thought the concept of police began to undergo a series of shifts in meaning and the objects to which it referred narrowed substantially, in line with a shift in state administration which was reduced through the excision of the Eudaemonian sphere. So, on the one hand, there is a continental notion of police, originating in France and Germany, concerned with ordering the realm according to the dictates of the peace and happiness of its citizens (Tribe 1995: 12). On the other, we find a later, more modern, notion of police as a 'regular uniform patrol of public space coupled with *post hoc* investigation of reported or discovered crime or disorder' (Reiner 2010: 5). It is argued that this is the result of a 'struggle over the function of the police and the *restriction* of their activities' (emphasis added, Knemeyer 1980: 186). It is with the decline of absolute sovereignty and the 'police state' that we see the ascendance, supposedly, of the 'rule of law':

> that the domestic and international rule of law replaces an older reliance on both state and, to a lesser degree popular sovereignty, is a commonplace of 20th-century liberal constitutional thought. In its most basic form, the rule of law, as opposed to the rule of men, allegedly supplants the naked and arbitrary force of a willful sovereign power or majority mob. (Rasch 2004: 91)

It is this thinking that sees police 'relegated to the backwater of a very narrowly conceived "police studies" . . . being reduced to the study of crime and law enforcement' (Neocleous 2006: 17). Police exist, in this narrative, to enforce laws, to apply them or to prevent people from transgressing them and catch those who do. Indeed, it is here we find a break between an older, broad notion of police and a more modern, limited, notion that comes to be synonymous with the institution concerned with law enforcement. This in itself is linked, as I will show in the prologue, with the notion of a 'natural order' that no longer needs sovereign intervention, and is in fact imperilled by it. Rather than take this narrative for granted, one of the aims of this book is to show that an *oikonomic* – that is, not referencing anything outside of itself and particularistic – form of governing has not disappeared and is to be found precisely in the figure of police. However, I argue also that police is not *reducible* to government; it is not simply concerned with an immanent ordering but is in fact also in a complex, aporetic relationship with sovereignty. Indeed, while Agamben has prepared the theoretical terrain from which to investigate the divided character of power, he does not extend this investigation to police power specifically, and it is this that the present study attends to.

Agamben's methodology in this regard is useful though much misunderstood. As Matthew Abbott has argued, Agamben (in contrast to Foucault) 'is more primarily concerned with the historically contingent and quasi-transcendental conditions of the biopolitical as such' (Abbott 2012: 29), and thus what has been read as sweeping remarks about the 'West' in general should be understood in the context of Agamben's 'political ontology' – a radical interrogation of the metaphysical-political economies of power that structure Western political forms. Politics and ontology, Agamben writes, 'are in solidarity because they have need of one another to actualize themselves' (2015: 132). In order to understand the way in which police power operates in modernity in its (un)relation to law and sovereignty, I argue that Agamben's political ontology marks a path to being able to highlight the metaphysical grounds operative within political structures. This is why the present study is not concerned with the historical specificities of *the police* as *institution* in different geographical and temporal contexts but tackles a different problem, which is also Agamben's problem: that of 'thinking our political situation in terms of its metaphysical heritage' (Abbott 2012: 25).

## Anti-Blackness and *an-archic* police power

As I write, news has just broken of another unarmed Black man, killed by police, this time in Streatham, South London . His name was Chris Kaba and he was twenty-four years old. To speak of police power is necessarily to speak of anti-Blackness and white supremacy. The events of 2020 did not inaugurate this fact but merely confirmed what was already known by many – that those that the police kill and it not be considered a crime are disproportionately Black.[21] The subsequent conviction of Derek Chauvin – the police officer who murdered George Floyd – does not negate this because Chauvin's conviction was an exception, both in the sense that he was found guilty and also in the sense that he was one individual, found guilty of murdering another individual. The police were not on trial for the death of yet another Black person and, of course, nor could they be.

To understand the logic of police power means that shock, amazement or surprise at the violence that goes unchecked, and indeed the subsequent trials that usually find no law to have been transgressed, is untenable. Not only this, but shock, surprise or amazement is a very part of the fabric that ensures this cycle of death and absolution keeps going. For Biko Mandela Gray, echoing the writings of Walter Benjamin[22],

> 'surprise' is a *temporal* structure of absolution; 'surprise' allows for one to make 'progress', to look to the past in order to change the present for a 'better' future . . . it produces – or manufactures – a novelty, an event, out of an ongoing structure of violence in order to prompt violent and empty 'progressive' reforms. (2022: 3)

The question of the temporal looms large in all of this because *it keeps happening*. We cannot talk about anti-Black police violence in the past tense because it is with us now, but also because we cannot attribute causal sequentiality to these events to make sense of them. The law operates to violently impose a linear sequence of events, a progression, so as to pinpoint a victim, a perpetrator, a violent act, and a consequence of the violent act. The logic follows something like this: this person had this bad intention which led them to doing this bad thing which led to a victim being harmed.. In the trial that followed the beating of Rodney King, frame-by-frame stills of the footage taken of the beating were 'mounted on clean white illustration board' with each 'micromoment . . . broken down into a series of frozen images' (Crenshaw and Peller 1993: 58) which were then interpreted on their own. Witnesses were questioned about them; given the posture of King, could the police have reasonably considered him a threat? As Crenshaw and Peller put it: 'The videotape images were physically mediated by the illustration board, and in the same moment of disaggregation were symbolically mediated by the new narrative backdrops of the technical discourse of institutional security and the reframing of King as a threat rather than a victim' (Crenshaw and Peller 1993: 59). Here, time is broken down and weaponized, deconstructed into tiny, minuscule moments of activity in order to retroactively secure the activity of the police to legality. Each frame follows the previous in a line of images that are then interpreted on their own: 'a police approved technique of restraint complete with technical names for each baton strike' (Crenshaw and Peller 1993: 59). We might see this as a very literal and visual symbol of a deeper process at work in the law and in the trial form more generally, breaking down events into slices of time that are thoroughly decontextualized so as to make harm and justice about smaller and smaller components of time, space and people. Calvin Warren limns this temporal architecture of time that is metaphysical and argues that the attempt to treat anti-Black violence as an object 'left behind' is in itself a form of domination:

> if metaphysical time relies on the stability of cause (beginning) effect (end), teleology (the calculation of cause and effect), past, present and future, then part of the enterprise of pain is to stuff an event-horizon into the temporal categories of metaphysical reason. Thus, something that exceeds and defies metaphysical time is subjected to its logic; without this violent subjection we cannot know the event. (2016: 57)

It is this stability of metaphysical time and linearity that the law wishes to impose on this event in order to make it knowable. Making it 'knowable' means dominating it, or as Warren has it, to 'invade it thoroughly to extract as much information as possible' (2016: 57). The effect this produces is to precisely obscure actual knowledge of these events and the political structures that mean they keep happening. Yet even those critical accounts that would accept anti-Black violence as part of a wider structure struggle to articulate analysis that contains adequate explanatory force.

For example, that anti-Black police violence is connected to the global machinations of capital but cannot be *reduced* to the needs of capital is a point evaded by scholars who would posit police power as primarily existing to protect capital and private property. This point is captured by many Black studies scholars who insist on the gratuitous nature of anti-Black violence that far exceeds any disciplining mechanism capitalism might make use of in order to extract profit. Indeed, the idea that the machinations of police violence can be reduced to the 'needs' of capital or the protection of private property is challenged by the sheer scale and intensity of anti-Black violence meted out by police officers across various times and spaces. How would one begin to understand the killing of Amadou Diallo – who was shot forty-one times by police officers in the Bronx, New York – simply by reference to capitalism or private property? We are confronted with the extreme inadequacy of concepts such as 'exploitation' and 'discipline' time and time again. In order to make sense of this scholars have articulated the concept of 'gratuitous violence' which distinguishes between the violence of exploitation and 'metaphysical violence'.[23] For Frank Wilderson and Patrice Douglass, this violence is 'peculiar, in that, whereas some groups of people might be the recipients of violence, after they have been constituted *as people,* violence is a structural necessity to the constitution of blacks' (2013: 117). In other words, a consideration of anti-Black violence forces a reckoning with metaphysical violence – that is 'beyond thinking direct relations of violence as a tractable force by instead engaging the infinite refractions of violence at the level of being and existence within the world' (2013: 119). This takes us very far away from notions of violence which presume that violence occurs only at the level of individuals on the solid ground of 'the political' but rather forces a reckoning with a notion of violence in terms of political ontology.

Relatedly, we also cannot understand anti-Black police violence in terms of crime and punishment, 'law-enforcement' or any other such liberal mythology about police power. The nature of anti-Black police violence is such that no crime needs to have been committed for the violence to be called just and necessary. No transgression of the legal order need to have taken place. Nor can this violence be considered 'punishment' in the liberal sense of the term, as no crime has been committed, no trial has been held and no sentence has been passed. There is no specific action to which anti-Black police violence is a response – and in this way it possesses an atemporal structure – it cannot be categorized into cause and effect. For Wilderson, 'modernity marks the emergence of a new ontology because it is an era in which an entire race appears, people who, a priori, that is prior to the contingency of the "transgressive act" (such as losing a war or being convicted of a crime), stand as socially dead in relation to the rest of the world' (2010: 18). The concept of social death, drawn from Orlando Patterson (1982), encapsulates the form of violence that goes beyond 'economic' violence or retributive violence. To be sure, this is a violence that cannot be contained within, nor delimited to standard concepts and explanations of police and state violence, or sovereign or judicial power. What follows is then an attempt to grapple with this *an-archic* police power at the level of political ontology, which is also, and necessarily, an engagement with anti-Black violence.

## The argument

Four main lines of argument are put forward in this book. First, I unsettle the presumed relation between natural/artificial order that is crucial for the histories of the sovereign state. In very broad terms I challenge the idea that, around the start of the nineteenth century, an absolutist era interventionist sovereign who must overcome natural disorder is replaced by a non-interventionist liberal sovereign who must allow natural order to flourish. This is intrinsically linked to, and forms the groundwork for, the challenge I present to received narratives of police power, which see it as a formerly broad interventionist, positive power that, with the shift from the police state to the liberal state, gets replaced with a limited, negative, repressive power under the modern state.

Second, I argue that via order, police is that which mediates transcendence and immanence, universal and particular and sovereignty and government while being reducible to neither. In relation to the first strand, there is a tendency to see transcendence, and indeed transcendent sovereignty, pushed aside in favour of an immanent, governmental mode under the liberal state. I challenge this through my analysis of Smith and Schmitt and Benjamin, showing that liberalism does not excise sovereign transcendence in favour of immanence, but rather reconfigures the relation between them.

Third, I engage with arguments surrounding the 'colonial origins' of policing that has been so frequently cited in explanation for anti-Black police violence and also for police 'brutality' more generally. Related to the argument that sees an 'unbounded' police power emerge under absolutism, to be replaced in modernity with a limited police power, I undertake a reading of Denise Ferreira da Silva, whose work, I argue, helps to illuminate the inadequacy of this formulation. In particular, I analyse the way in which anti-Black police violence is always already justified on the grounds of necessity and self-defence, something that is intrinsically linked to the 'natural' violence of the state of nature. As this book argues, the state of nature is a construction that cannot be considered 'external' to sovereign and police power and thus we cannot be content with a formulation of police power that sees it as becoming excessive in an 'elsewhere'.

Relatedly, I show that a concern with police power is always already a concern with the exception. For Hegel this is precisely the moment in which police power becomes unbounded, and where anything and everything may become a concern of the police – as Hegel insists, no objective lines can be drawn to circumscribe the emergency, or the powers used in the face of it in advance. Later on we shall see how the philosophical stakes of the exception are variously articulated by Benjamin, Schmitt and Agamben – all of whom recognize its significance for the political as such. However, that they either do not or only briefly touch on police power and its relation to the exception leaves open the space into which my book intervenes.

All of this is to say that the presumed relationship between police and law; that police enforce, uphold or implement the law cannot be maintained once we see police power in its proper locus – that is, as concerned with *order* and in a complex and overlapping relationship with sovereign power. I argue that once it is understood that police are neither executing, transgressing or making law (though they may at times carry out these functions) we are in a better position to see that it is the power to *suspend* the law while bearing its force that marks police power out as being exceptional and ultimately *an-archic* in character. This configuration marks police out not as sovereignty itself, but rather that police power is the *an-archic groundless ground* for sovereignty.

These strands are not presented separately but emerge throughout the chapters as I engage with different thinkers. It is the method of a philosophical history that enables me to grasp and unravel these different strands that as such do not appear in a linear historical progression. In so doing I draw on Benjamin, Agamben, Wilderson, da Silva and Warren, who, in different ways, present exhortations to resist the temptation to see history as a sequence of unfolding events linked causally. With an attentiveness to signatures in particular, we can begin to acknowledge how and in what ways the present shapes the past, how politics does not derive from metaphysics and how praxis is not secondary to ontology. In other words, we are able to grasp that what is usually presented as secondary or derivative is in fact a founding power itself. This methodological approach and argumentative strategy has led me to not only put the philosophers studied into conversation with each other but also question the dominant interpretations of these thinkers and indeed the widely shared axioms routinely mentioned in those interpretations. This has enabled me to challenge the ways in which the history of police has been thought through key binaries: transcendent/immanent, natural/artificial and positive/negative. In utilizing a philosophical-historical approach this book is not concerned to find the *origins* of the police in either linguistic or historical terms but rather to create a space where it is possible to think differently about the ontology of power.

## The structure

The prologue to this book attends to the work of Michel Foucault and Adam Smith. As I discussed earlier in the introduction much of the critical theory that exists on police orbits Foucault's work. Indeed, Foucault prepared the terrain from which to examine the 'police state' and *Polizeiwissenschaft* that critical histories of police must attend to through his careful excavation of the thought of thinkers of *Polizei* such as Von Justi. Second, Foucault's work on biopolitics, discipline and security has inspired much literature pertaining to the role of *policing* in contemporary society in an expanded sense. That is to say policing appears alongside and through various institutions – education, health and punitive – that serve a normalizing function. It is for this reason that an engagement with Foucault appears as a prologue to the main book, for it is necessary in order to clear the way for a philosophical history of police, to first break free of, and then move beyond some of the axioms around police that stem from Foucault's work.

This book then unfolds in two parts. The first, comprised of two chapters, undertakes an analysis of what has traditionally been seen as the move from 'divine' order to 'sovereign' order or the move from natural to artificial order. Chapter 1 is concerned with the transition from 'natural' to 'artificial' order that supposedly takes place between Aristotle and Hobbes. Rather than take this transition for granted, I interrogate the ways in which Hobbes's 'artificial order' is not devoid of nature, and indeed, Aristotle's 'natural' order is not devoid of artifice. In so doing I argue that while Hobbes superficially attacks Aristotle, his criticisms cannot be taken simply at face value and should rather be interrogated for what they allow Hobbes to claim – that is, that order is the consequence of sovereignty. This then provides the groundwork for the claim that it is the sovereign who can use the fear of natural violence to legitimize sovereign violence in the name of order, which is contingent and precarious.

Chapter 2 draws on Hegel, who explicitly sees police as mediating the spheres of universal and particular. This is crucial for underlining the divided character of power and how police becomes, in modernity, a critical concept in establishing a relation between universal and particular as well as transcendent and immanent. This chapter also attends to the aporias and contradictions Hegel necessarily runs into as a result of distinguishing his own concept of police from that of his contemporary, Fichte. If Fichte sees police as an all-encompassing constraining power, in which everyone is surveilled all the time, Hegel sees the need to denounce this. Yet Hegel himself cannot escape this unconstraining of police power when he considers the 'emergency'.

The second part, comprised of three chapters, tackles a different sort of order – what I am calling 'police order'. Chapter 3 is where I argue police power in modernity becomes dislocated from sovereignty and law – producing its own legitimating grounds that functions in a similar way to the state of exception. Thinking with Schmitt, Benjamin and Agamben I analyse the move, supposedly found in liberalism, from transcendence to immanence, and how this relates to police power. I think through the relationship of police to law with Benjamin and argue how, once we see that it is police who are charged with maintaining and securing order, their power becomes unconstrained. Articulating police power in terms of its exceptional, decisionistic character, I find that police power in modernity is structurally incapable of being held to account by the law in a way analogous to, but not reducible to, sovereign power.

Chapter 4 analyses Agamben's work more closely to argue that once police are charged with creating or maintaining *order* we find that the power of police, which is usually thought of as a power of administration, is in reality no such thing. Rather, by attending to the divided character of power and the way in which sovereignty and government are related to each other via the concept of order, I argue that police project order, the law and the public as that which their power derives from, but which in reality is a *mythological* projection that obscures the fact that police produce their own legitimating grounds. That is to say, in modernity, police power does not come from the application of the law or the implementation of a sovereign will but is fundamentally *an-archic* (that is to say, not deriving from origin or command) in character.

Chapter 5 engages with the work of Denise Ferreira da Silva to challenge critical accounts of police power that sees its 'excessive' and violent origin in the colonial encounter. In addition to challenging the presupposition that an 'unbounded' police power is the preserve of premodernity, this book also challenges the narrative that an unbounded police power finds its origins in the colonial encounter to later be exported back to the metropole. These accounts fall short of explanatory weight when it comes to anti-Black police violence and its repetition across different times and different spaces. da Silva's work I argue offers a path beyond an analysis of police violence which sees it as a colonial remnant or 'boomerang' that in itself cannot explain the production of race difference and its relationship to police power.

# Prologue

## Foucault, Smith and disappearing police

As I briefly touched on in the introduction a commonplace understanding of police sees an older broader notion contrasted with a more modern limited notion. This in itself is tied, I argue, to an understanding of *order* that had previously been thought to be something that needed to be produced, which, under the pressures of liberal thought and political economy, becomes recast as something *natural*. This understanding of police and order stems in large part from Foucault's work. His highly regarded and influential work on police has done much to recentre the concept, yet, as I will show, his presuppositions have remained largely unquestioned. It is for this reason that the present piece focuses on Foucault and his theorization of police and order, and ultimately, why the book does not take for granted his presuppositions.

My aim is not to present a reading of Foucault as such, rather it is to posit that while order and police play a critical role for Foucault in the transition from the classical period to modernity, his analysis of these concepts remains limited and beholden to the idea of an epistemic break that occurs at the threshold of modernity. In doing this, though he presents a nuanced, and at times contradictory, picture of the continuities and discontinuities between the classical and the modern, he over-emphasizes certain (modern, governmental) aspects of power at the expense of (older, sovereign) others. Indeed, one is left with the impression that one aspect of power (biopolitical) is independent and autonomous with respect to sovereign power. Once this impression is given, the way is opened for the serious problem that Mark Neocleous has identified with regard to Foucauldian scholarship on the police that 'for all their discussions of policing as a form of governmentality, Foucauldians barely mention the police institution itself, to the extent that one begins to think policing and the police have nothing connecting them at all' (2000: x).

I want to suggest that, though this problem does indeed emerge, a separate but related issue also arises when the police is subsumed under the banner of *policing*. When police is read in terms of a biopolitical register, or at the level of 'ordering' (to which I'll return), the concept of order has a positive content returned to it. However, as I will argue with regard to Agamben, order functions precisely as a concept devoid of any positive content (or in Agamben's terminology it is a 'signature'). It also neglects the dimensions of police power that I will highlight as unbounded and *an-archic*: in other words, Foucault's analysis of power, though attending to an immanent (as opposed to transcendent) register, nevertheless remains wedded to a functional oppositional divide between 'artificial' and 'natural' order.

In the first and second sections, I will present what I argue are two contrasting and contradictory accounts that Foucault presents in *The Order of Things* and his writings on biopolitics. While in *The Order of Things* he argues that a break occurring in the nineteenth century signals the transition to modernity from a previous episteme, in his writings on biopolitics we find a thesis that does not emphasize a break but rather sees the birth of biopolitics in the European 'police states' that were present during the seventeenth and eighteenth centuries. The significance of the discrepancy in the two timelines, is, as I will argue, to be found in the presumption that it is the conception of order that impacts on political organization, that the impact is just one way. Therefore I suggest that Foucault's archaeology in *The Order of Things* has theoretical implications at the level of political organization, and more specifically for the concept of police, that can lead to two divergent but equally theoretically vacuous understandings of police. The first is one in which police is equated with 'policing' writ large and the second is an understanding of the police as a limited institution simply concerned with 'repressing disorder'. The aim of the present piece is to show why both of these understandings should be rejected in turn. This in itself pivots on how one understands the concept of order.

Foucault's interrogation of order is one that is anchored to an epistemological register. He argues that in the classical period order was understood as being natural – there was an essential order to nature. This understanding is transformed in the transition to modernity, which first sees the elimination of this conception of the natural order and then a reintroduction of a natural order of a different kind. The significance of the differing conceptions of order for politics is highlighted by Foucault, but ultimately he does not question the distinction between 'natural' and 'non-natural' order that his archaeology traces. Throughout the course of this book however, I will argue that we cannot take for granted any understanding of order as being either 'natural' or 'artificial', but rather must come to terms with the way in which it confounds the oppositional relation between those categories.

## Archaeology and order

In *The Order of Things* Foucault undertakes an 'archaeology' of the human sciences. In doing this he tracks the epistemic breaks he sees as occurring between the classical era and modernity. It is the 'silence' (Robinson 2016: 134) between the classical period and the modern that Foucault probes through his archaeology, contending that both periods are characterized by distinct epistemes that are discontinuous, and this as a result of the loss of the classical conception of order. The classical episteme was grounded in a conception of a 'general order of identities and differences' that it was the function of knowledge to bring to light. Under these conditions, 'the constant, fundamental relation of knowledge, even empirical knowledge to a universal mathesis justified the project of a finally unified corpus of learning' (Foucault 2002: 268). Indeed, it was a search for order that underlay the project of knowledge itself 'as the ground and foundation of a general science of nature' (Foucault 2002: 292). On this view, there was a 'divinely arranged chain of being' (Dreyfus and Rabinow 1983: 27) that, when brought to light, could be represented in tables wherein everything that exists could be placed. In this sense, there was a 'visible order with a permanent grid of distinctions' (Foucault 2002: 273). Things must be placed in position, compared with other things and their place in the general order identified (Foucault 2002: 60). Crucial here is that order is *representable*.

It is the classical period that sees the advent of 'general grammar, natural history and the analysis of wealth' which for Foucault are dependent on a 'universal science of order' (2002: 63). Though there is a science of order, accessible to knowledge, the relationship of nature to order at this point is not straightforward. Order was not a 'visible harmony of things or their observed arrangement, regularity or symmetry' (2002: 237), rather it is 'the particular space of their being that which, prior to all effective knowledge, established them in the field of knowledge' (2002: 237). Order was not a *visible* natural 'harmony' between things – or the absence of any kind of disorder. Indeed, Foucault argues that there is a 'disorder' in the appearance of nature which is 'due to its own history, to its catastrophes, or perhaps merely to its jumbled plurality, which is no longer capable of providing representation with anything but things that resemble one another' (2002: 77–8). It was up to what Foucault calls 'imagination' to 'reconstitute order' (2002: 77–8):

> order is at one and the same time that which is given in things as their inner law, the hidden network that determines the way they confront one another, and also that which has no existence except in the grid created by a glance, an examination, a language; and it is only in the blank spaces of this grid that order manifests itself in depth, as though already there, waiting in silence for the moment of its expression. (Major-Poetzel 1983: 153)

We can thus discern three layers of order in the classical episteme. First there is an 'essential' order that exists between things; second, there is the appearance of disorder and the confusion of their 'interpenetrating jumble'; and third, order is reconstituted through things being ordered by the imagination in representative tables. This classical conception of order is disrupted and then displaced over two stages 'which are articulated one upon the other more or less around the years 1795–1800. In the first of these phases, the fundamental mode of being of the positivities does not change; men's riches, the species of nature, and the words with which languages are peopled, still remain what they were in the classical age' (Foucault 2002: 240).

The first of these stages is illustrated by Foucault through the thought of Adam Smith. His thought encapsulates the beginnings of the epistemic break that Foucault identifies, yet Smith remains anchored to the classical episteme that, in his view, has not yet been transcended. The break that Adam Smith represents is indeed that he 'formulates a principle of order, but one that is irreducible to the analysis of representation' (Foucault 2002: 244). Smith is seen as transforming order, but only the *third* layer of order identified above, that is, the ability to *represent* order. This takes the form of a criticism of physiocratic doctrine, which was 'associated with a specific technical proposal, Quesnay's economic "Table", a device intended to permit a sovereign to monitor the totality of economic processes within the state' (Gordon 1991: 15).[1] For Foucault, it is the impossibility of this table, the idea that economic processes are ordered, but ultimately un-representable and unknowable in their totality, that are the first signs of an impending break with the classical episteme.

However, though Smith's thought contains some modifications of this classical episteme, it ultimately remains anchored to it, in that 'it does not refute its fundamental conditions of possibility; it has not yet touched the mode of being of a natural order' (Foucault 2002: 251). In short, the first layer of order identified above is untouched by Smith and this is why, for Foucault, a second stage is required before the epistemic break is able to finally take place. Indeed, it is the first layer of order – essential, natural order; *the order of physis* – that must be moved. As the classical episteme is displaced, Foucault writes:

> the project of a general taxonomia disappears; the possibility of deploying a great natural order which would extend continuously from the simplest and most inert of things to the most living and the most complex disappears; and the search for order as the ground and foundation of a general science of nature also disappears. (Foucault 2002: 292)

When this occurs, Foucault argues, 'The visible order with its permanent grid of distinctions is now only a superficial glitter above an abyss' (Foucault 2002: 273). The essential order that exists in nature and that appears as disorderly, only to be made orderly again by the imagination, is now transformed into an 'abyss'. This is linked to the insertion of a limit to man's knowledge (and this in turn is a result of the thought of Immanuel Kant). Fundamentally, there is now an unknowable abyss beneath knowledge that cannot, as it were, be brought to the surface. However, this limit to knowledge is not, as has been argued elsewhere, 'something that is an externally imposed limit, but is somehow a limit to man's knowledge imposed or decreed by man himself' (Dreyfus and Rabinow 1983: 29). In this way, man is now 'in place of the king' and the idea of a divinely arranged 'chain of being' (Dreyfus and Rabinow 1983: 27) is undone. This chain of being in turn had been intrinsically linked to a conception of nature which was not only orderly, but good. The Aristotelian legacy that had seen order as a fundamental good and attributed this to nature (that was still seen to be operative with Adam Smith) is only moved in the second stage that Foucault identifies.

Within modernity, Foucault tells us, nature 'can no longer be good' (2002: 302). The break with the classical metaphysic of order is seemingly complete. Nature is no longer conceived as having an essential order (though it may have appeared disorderly) but is 'wild once more' (2002: 302). The seeming severing of the link between a positive view of nature and order marks the passage from one episteme to the other. Indeed, for Foucault, this transformation is not merely a break with the classical metaphysic but the end of metaphysics as such. It is the end of metaphysics which enables, on his reading, the 'appearance of man' (2002: 346). This manifestation of man, of life as such, is tied to a particular ontology for Foucault: 'in relation to life, beings are no more than transitory figures, and the being that they maintain, during the brief period of their existence, is no more than their presumption, their will to survive' (2002: 303).² There is then a link between a loss of the classical conception of order as natural and nature as good and a modern conception of order which sees life as survival and nature no longer as good.³ In turn, it is the displacement of these notions that sees the rise of a different form of politics and political organization – one apparently no longer concerned with happiness and virtue – but rather with life as such.

As Dreyfus and Rabinow note:

> traditionally in Western culture, political thinking was concerned with the just and the good life. Practical reason sought to change character, as well as communal and political life, based on a larger metaphysical understanding of the ordered cosmos. Christian versions, like those of Saint Thomas were in a line with Aristotle. Thomas was concerned with an order of virtue that was anchored in an ontotheoretical world view. Politics served a higher goal. This higher goal rested on a larger order, which could be known. Political thinking was that art which, in an imperfect world, led men toward the good life, an art which imitated God's government of nature. (1983: 136)

In their analysis of Foucault's work, Dreyfus and Rabinow highlight the order of *physis* that underlay a certain type of politics. Accordingly, the epistemic break Foucault identifies as dismantling this view would also have effects at the level of the political. The question remains: if there is a loss of the classical conception of *physis* as order, an essential order that it was the task of knowledge to bring to light, what are the consequences of this loss for the political? While Foucault does not tackle this in *The Order of Things*, it is here, I argue, that biopolitics enters the frame. Foucault's biopolitics is a distinctly *modern* form of power which aims at making life *live* (Foucault 1984: 136). The advent of biopolitics is, however, in itself tied to the transformations in epistemology that we find in *The Order of Things*. Indeed, as David Tarizzo has argued in an explicit linking of the epistemological transformations in modernity with biopolitics,

> During the 1970s, Foucault will in fact argue that in the Modern Age a new form of power spreads, one that is detached from the law of the sword, from the classical code of sovereignty, in order to take charge of life as such. Its motto is no longer Take life or let live but Make live and let die . Power, that is, now targets life itself, a life to be cultivated, empowered, directed, and regulated. That said, what are the conditions of possibility of this modern apparatus of power? One, the most important, had been identified by Foucault ten years earlier. It is precisely the emergence of life, together with labour and language, as an epistemic historical a priori. Foucault makes the point very clear: before modernity, life did not exist, just as a science of life itself, biology, did not exist. Only with the rise of modernity do a knowledge about life and a power over life appear simultaneously, a biology and a biopolitics whose lethal connections we had better analyze and understand. (2017: 19)

What is crucial is that biopolitics is here simultaneously presented as something distinctly modern and made possible by the epistemic transformations Foucault tracks in *The Order of Things* and is also framed in opposition to sovereign power. Leaving aside this latter point for a moment, it is clear that the processes Foucault tracks as beginning in the nineteenth century do indeed make an appearance much earlier. If biopolitics is also seen as dependent on an epistemic a priori – the appearance of life as such in modernity – this aporia comes clearly to light. With a new 'untamed ontology' (Tarizzo 2011) the condition of the possibility of biopolitics is seemingly set. Interestingly, however, while in *The Order of Things* the break between the classical and the modern is explicitly formulated as discontinuous, when we turn to Foucault's writings on biopolitics we find the nascent biopolitical form of power in the police state. Thus, what is seemingly a precondition or condition of possibility for biopolitics – namely the human sciences and in particular the appearance of 'life' and biology – happens long after the police state and *raison d'état* were the dominant modes of political organization.[4] As Dreyfus and Rabinow argue:

the job of the police was the articulation and administration of techniques of bio-power so as to increase the state's control over its inhabitants. While the 17th and 18th century French police were part of the juridical administration, they dealt with individuals not as juridical subjects but as working, trading, living human beings (*this dimension was treated archaeologically in the order of things*). (emphasis added 1983: 139)

Indeed, when we turn to Foucault's genealogical investigation of biopolitics and liberalism we find that the ethical order outlined earlier is dispensed with under *raison d'état* and the police state, which sees the increase in the force of the state as the end goal, rather than a *telos* of ethics, virtue or justice. In *The Political Technology of Individuals*, Foucault tells us, 'It [police] wields its power over living beings as living beings, and its politics therefore has to be a biopolitics' (2002a: 416). For Foucault, individuals were henceforth seen in their capacity as increasing the power of the state and thus the embryonic human sciences became the way in which the knowledge of this force and power was produced (2002a: 416). This is where Foucault sees the birth of biopolitics, and it is to this I shall now turn.

## Biopolitics, discipline and order

For Foucault, changes taking place at the level of power and institutions as the transition to modernity was made required a new analysis, one no longer so concerned with sovereignty and 'the state' as traditionally conceived. The insertion of life into modern techniques of power constitutes for Foucault the defining characteristic of modern power. Life, which had previously not been a concern in terms of *living* as such, thus comes into being as David Tarizzo points out, modernity and the invention of the modern notion of life are coterminous (2011) in Foucault. Life is now considered a force that, though unknowable in terms of representation, is knowable and calculable in terms of its contribution to the power of the state. Seen in this way life is not a scientific category, but rather an 'epistemological indicator' (Esposito 2004: 30). Indeed, we can begin to see that which life indexes are the transformations that occur in the nineteenth century as outlined in *The Order of Things*. That is to say, the loss of the classical conception of order in which life is in a chain of being, divinely placed, means that 'the continuous relation which had placed man with the other beings of the world was broken. Man, who was once himself a being amongst others, is now a subject among objects' (Dreyfus and Rabinow 1983: 28).

The stakes of this conception of life for political power only become clear, however, in a range of other texts. In *The History of Sexuality Volume 1*, for example, Foucault sets out his stand concerning modern techniques of power, contending that

> since the classical age the West has undergone a very profound transformation of these mechanisms of power. 'Deduction' has tended to be no longer the major form of power but merely one element among others, working to incite, reinforce, control, monitor, optimize, and organize, the forces under it: a power bent on generating forces, making them grow and *ordering* them, rather than one dedicated to impeding them, making them submit or destroying them. (emphasis added, 1984: 136)

We see here the clear distinction between a negative form of power of submission and destruction and a positive *ordering* power. If sovereign power is conceptualized as a negative, oppressive power, biopolitics by contrast is positive – making life *live* rather than a violent force capable of taking life away.[5] This is confirmed several times in Foucault himself, for whom 'it is no longer a matter of bringing death into play in the field of sovereignty, but of distributing the living in the domain of value and utility' (1984: 144). To put this in the terms discussed in my argument, Foucault reads modernity as the triumph of an immanent realm of power – normalization as opposed to the juridical,[6] discipline and biopower[7] as opposed to sovereignty – over the transcendent. This process is closely linked with the rise of 'disciplinary power' and techniques which make their appearance in the seventeenth and eighteenth centuries. This form of power 'had very specific procedures, completely new instruments, and very different equipment. It was . . . absolutely incompatible with relations of sovereignty. This new mechanism of power applies primarily to bodies and what they do rather than to the land and what it produces' (Foucault 2004: 35).

That this form of disciplinary power is also tied to the appearance of the human sciences (those that Foucault cites as appearing in modernity occurring at the beginning of the nineteenth century in *The Order of Things*) is made clear in *Society Must Be Defended*:

the discourse of discipline is alien to that of the law; it is alien to the discourse that makes rules a product of the will of the sovereign. The discourse of disciplines is about a rule: not a juridical rule derived from sovereignty, but a discourse about a natural rule, or in other words a norm. Disciplines will define not a code of law, but a code of normalization, and they will necessarily refer to a theoretical horizon that is not the edifice of law, but the field of the human sciences. And the jurisprudence of these disciplines will be that of a clinical knowledge (Foucault 2004: 38)

This appears to confirm what has become known as the 'expulsion thesis' (Golder and Fitzpatrick 2009) where Foucault has been taken as saying that law is superseded by the norm and processes of normalization. Relatedly, sovereign power is thought to be eclipsed by biopolitics. However, as Golder and Fitzpatrick discuss in *Foucault's Law*, there is evidence that both supports and complicates the idea that Foucault sees law as eclipsed or expelled from modernity, as biopolitics and disciplinary power are extended. In their words; 'on the one hand he would seem to counterpose the old forms of sovereignty and law to the new modalities of power (indicating that the latter are outstripping the former); on the other he would seemingly gesture towards their interaction or mutual interaction' (2009: 23). Moreover, Roberto Esposito sees this tension in Foucault as an 'irresolution', where what Foucault refers to is a 'copresence of opposing vectors' that can't be read in terms of 'contemporaneity or succession' (2004: 39). So, while Golder and Fitzpatrick and Esposito read this tension as productive in different ways and we can't simply read biopolitics as *replacing* sovereign power in Foucault, the tension nevertheless exists and becomes particularly acute regarding police.

Despite this nuance we can add to Foucault's account, there is present a hypothesis of *discontinuity*, not only between the modern and classical as beginning in the nineteenth century that we see in *The Order of Things*, however, but also between biopower and sovereign power, positive and negative power. The crucible of this new form of modern, positive power is the police state. Police, or *Polizei*, is configured along a positive vector of power – a power of *ordering*. For Foucault, 'In the eighteenth century, sex became a "police" matter – in the full and strict sense given the term at the time: not the repression of disorder, but an ordered maximisation of collective and individual forces' (1984: 24). Here, police is considered as being concerned with ordering and maximizing and this is counterposed to the repression of 'disorder'. Or, as

Roberto Esposito has it, if 'the meaning of the term *politik* remains the negative one of the defense from internal and external enemies, the semantics of *Polizei* is absolutely positive, it is ordered to favour life in all its magnitude, along its entire extension through all its articulations' (2004: 37).[8]

As we have seen, police (*Polizei*) on this reading is a concern with life as such (Gordon 1991: 10) and Foucault identifies this with a form of power which is not strictly legal or concerned with law but rather regulation. It is sovereign power 'acting directly on his subject but in non-judicial form' (Foucault 2007: 339) and even more, police is a 'permanent *coup d'État*' which functions on its own terms, and, definitively – 'police is not justice' (Foucault 2007: 339). Discernible here are the beginnings of the powers that Foucault sees as coming to dominate modern life – regulatory, disciplinary and crucially non-judicial. However, despite these clear assertions, Foucault then modifies this account of police to declare that though police regulations may not be judicial, they are 'nevertheless juridical' and further, 'although it is completely different from the judicial institution, police employs instruments and modes of action that, morphologically if you like, are not radically different from those of justice' ( Foucault 2007: 340). The significance of this somewhat contradictory account – the non-judicial but nevertheless juridical, the not-justice but justice-like form of police regulations – attests to the unique place of police not only linguistically but institutionally. Where this poses a problem, however, is that this contradictory picture then resumes a more rigidly dual either/or character once Foucault begins his discussion of political economy and liberalism. If the police state for Foucault had seen 'the marginalization of the distinction between government by law and government by decree' (Gordon 1991: 11) then the ascent of liberalism seemingly reverses this.

## From *Polizei* to 'the police'

The idea of a 'natural order' to things, that appear disorderly, but are in fact united by a common end (though one which is imperceptible to an individual) is seen as turning point for not only for the metaphysics of order but also the conceptual and institutional life of police.[9] It is a thought commonly attributed to Adam Smith where, ostensibly, the turn from 'police' to 'the police' is made. Whereas police in his *Lectures on Jurisprudence* had taken a broad, all-encompassing function, including the setting of food prices, by the publication of the *Wealth of Nations*, police is referred to only in a negative capacity, as the 'wrong form of government'. The idea that the state and, more specifically, police had to be expelled from the market in order for the 'natural' order of exchange to emerge is seemingly born here, alongside the idea that order is no longer linked to *sovereignty* but to *wealth* – or is the outcome of exchanging individuals rather than sovereign power.[10]

Indeed, it is the reintroduction of the idea of natural order, which had supposedly disappeared with Hobbes, that necessitates the reduction of police to the function of executing or upholding the law only. This is, as has been argued elsewhere, the liberal view of police,[11] which, by virtue of its focus on an immanent order – not politically regulated – remains blind to the locus of police power which must, for the theory to work, be subsumed under the law.[12] It is with the advent of liberalism and liberal thought that we are to find a new principle of government – one that aims at 'limiting and rationalizing the exercise of political power in the operations of the freedom and rationality of those who are to be governed' (Burchell 1991: 139). This in turn necessitates the '[l]egal regulation of state activities and governmental intervention through "general and equal" laws [that] exclude exceptional, particular and individual forms of intervention by the state' (Burchell 1991: 139). In other words, *Polizei* had to vanish into 'the police'.[13]

The idea that Smith's concept of police changed from the *Lectures on Jurisprudence* to the Wealth of Nations has been marked out as crucial in understanding the shift from *Polizei* to 'the police'. Indeed, his first conceptualization of police is not unaligned with this notion of police seen in Germany and can be found in his 1763 *Lectures on Jurisprudence*:

> the design here is to give each one the secure and peaceable possession of his own property . . when this end, which we may call the internall peace, or peace within doors, is secured, the government will be desirous of promoting the opulence of the state. This produces what we call police. Whatever regulations are made with respect to the trade, commerce, agriculture, manufactures of the country are considered as belonging to the police. (1978: 5)

As we can see, police for Smith does not have only justice and the prevention of crime as its concern, but also 'bon Marché or the cheapness of provisions, and having the market well supplied with all sorts of commodities' (1978: 5). Crucially, however, Smith also points out the function the state has of ensuring that the rich are maintained in the 'possession of their wealth against the violence and rapacity of the poor and by that means preserve that usefull inequality in the fortunes of mankind which *naturally* and *necessarily* arises from the various degrees of capacity, industry and diligence in the different individuals' (emphasis added, 1978: 338). Once again, civil society (as we will see is also the case with Hegel) is configured as a scene of potential disorder coming from disparities in wealth. This disorder cannot be finally resolved given the inevitability of inequality and its seemingly 'natural' basis, but can only be guarded against.

According to the commonplace argument I'm here concerned with, there is a shift between these *Lectures* and the *Wealth of Nations* in terms of Smith's conceptualization of police power and its function (Neocleous 2000, 1998b). In *Wealth of Nations* police measures are described as 'foolish' (1976: 137). Police regulations, where they exist, are cited as keeping the market price 'a good deal above the natural price' (1976: 77) and as such constitute the wrong form of government. Vivienne Brown reads the shift in Smith's usage of the concept police from a generally positive, self-describing term used to denote policies that increase the opulence of the state, to one which stands in for an idea of 'state economic regulation to which the *Wealth of Nations* is opposed' (1994: 154). Indeed, she continues, 'the different use of the word "police" in WN signals a different discursive structure for WN, where the state is no longer assigned the responsibility for pursuing any "object of police", whether that object is constituted by the cheapness and plenty of provisions, or by the promotion of towns or agriculture' (994: 155). For Brown, this shift in usage indicates a deeper discursive and epistemic shift reflecting the independence of an economic realm, which is no longer subject (or should no longer be subject) to sovereign power: 'the crucial difference lies instead in the autonomy of the conception of progress to be found in WN, an autonomy that makes economic progress a self-regulating and independent process' (1994: 160). It is now that we can begin to discern how the narrative surrounding the liberal state is born – there is a natural order to things that should not be disturbed by the intervention of government. The state's function, on this reading, is to be limited to safeguarding life and property as well as being excised from the market. Indeed, the market must 'regulate itself free from state power and police' (Neocleous 1998b: 446). Or as it has been put elsewhere, we encounter the 'epistemological and practical disqualification of sovereignty over economic processes' (Burchell 1991: 134).

In relation to Foucault, there is a notion that Smith's ideas of natural order led him to reject the tenets of *Polizeiwissenschaft* in favour of a different mode of government, that is, liberalism. For Foucault, the work of political economists in general, and Smith's work in particular, represent a direct negation of the ideas of cameralism and the positing of a new art of government freed from totalizing police ordinances and sovereign power (2008: 279). The infamous 'invisible hand' makes its appearance as the clearest expression of what might be meant by 'natural order' in the liberal paradigm – an order that arises not from human design (as with *Polizei*) but from the interplay of human actions.

What happens to the political when one takes this view? The configuring of a 'natural order' that is characterized by its opacity, that is, that the workings of this natural order must remain obscure to those who try and render it visible to the rational eye, has led to the view that it is this particular metaphysic of order which sees (artificial) government restricted in its scope of activities. When one takes this view, the operations of government are always already posited as being outside of, or external to, this 'natural' order which mustn't be disturbed. This comes from the proposition that social order (naturally) grows out of the market. However, it should be noted that this idea is not to be found in Smith himself. Indeed, as Keith Tribe has amply demonstrated, '[u]nderlying the apparently blind workings of the "market mechanism" and the "invisible hand" there was an elaborated framework concerning ethics, politics and social order' (1988: 150) that is found in the *Theory of Moral Sentiments*.[14]

What to make, then, of the claim that it is in Smith that the (Hobbesian) link between order and sovereignty is broken, no longer a function and consequence of sovereignty but of wealth? Or, as the Ordoliberals argue, that it is in Smith and classical liberalism that order is configured as being the outcome of the liberty of private individuals exchanging with each other and not, as they would have it, its precondition?[15] ? It will be helpful to turn to another shift that has been noted in Smith's work that operates parallel to the shift in the conceptualization of police discussed earlier in this chapter. It is the idea that from the *Theory of Moral Sentiments* to the *Wealth of Nations* Smith's concept of order undergoes a radical change – from an order that is politically regulated to one that emerges spontaneously (Caygill 1989: 91). This has been construed as a crucial transformation in a metaphysics of order *and* the form of government and politics emergent. If the necessity of an artificial, politically administered order constituted the understanding of society that the police states operated under, then it is supposedly with Smith that the idea of a spontaneous, natural order that, crucially, coincides with the shift from *Polizei* to 'the police', emerges.

The idea that Smith's view of order moves from an artificially regulated one to a 'naturally' occurring one is unsettled by the transformations that Viner tracks from the *Theory of Moral Sentiments* to the *Wealth of Nations*. While in the former, natural order is conceived as 'harmonious', universal and very much 'under divine guidance' (1927: 206), in the latter this natural order shows its cracks and crevices, its imperfections and defects (1927: 208).[16] Viner attributes this change in perspective partly to the fact that, in the *Wealth of Nations*, Smith's concerns were *particular* rather than general. The *Wealth of Nations* on this view was not a piece of literature expounding universal laws but instead a study into particular operations of wealth creation that are in themselves not automatically orderly. That the creation of wealth is not directly tied to government can go some way in explaining the confusion surrounding Smith's ideas of order and the 'system of natural liberty'. There has been a tendency, rather, to focus only on Smith's rejection of 'police' measures at the expense of everything else he has to say not only in the *Theory of Moral Sentiments* but also in the *Wealth of Nations* itself. The point is that Smith's notion of nature does not exclude government or even governmental intervention.[17]

When police are conceived in terms of interference or non-interference in the economy we are left with a common narrative which holds that while *Polizei* signified the operations of the state that interfered in the economy itself, by setting food prices for example, the advent of political economy means the recasting of *Polizei* as 'the' police, an institution concerned with detecting infractions of the law. Axiomatic to these discussions is the idea that the invocation of a 'natural order' to things means that government activities have to be restricted and reduced for order to be established. This narrative is misleading, however, for it presumes that the most significant thing about *Polizei* was the way in which 'interference' in the economy was managed, while 'the' police are noted for lacking this quality or this responsibility. The way is then set for the idea that politics is to be limited by economics (Campesi 2016:

149)¹⁸, a proposition that cannot be so readily maintained when one reflects on police power.¹⁹

It is the police state which Foucault sees as being undermined with the advance of political economy, and in particular Adam Smith and the *économistes*. What is carried over from the police state is supposedly a positive ordering power at the level of the population and the increasing of the state's force, but what changes is the epistemological presuppositions around *order*. While *raison d'état* replaced a medieval natural order with an 'absolute artificiality' (Foucault 2007: 349), with the *économistes*, naturalness reappears; but this time it is the 'natural' equilibrium of prices that is 'opposed precisely to the artificiality of politics, of *raison d'État* and police' (Foucault 2007: 349). Furthermore, 'It is not the naturalness of processes of nature itself, as the nature of the world, but processes of a naturalness specific to relations between men, to what happens spontaneously when they cohabit, come together, exchange, work and produce' (Foucault 2007: 349).²⁰ If the modern liberal state is underpinned, as Foucault is wont to demonstrate through Adam Smith, by the idea of a spontaneous order that cannot be represented, indeed cannot be *known*, then the direct political consequence of this is that police should only interfere to repress any disorder that occurs. This is due to what has been termed by some a 'critique of state reason' (Gordon 1991: 15) – a new limit being placed on what the state can know and limits to the areas in which it should interfere. Police then becomes equated with artificial order, and liberalism and political economy with the reintroduction of a 'natural' one; however, this naturalness is one that should be left to itself. In Foucault, then, we find that the artificiality/natural distinction is maintained and used as an analytical grid to map the changes from the 'police state' to the modern liberal state. The presupposition of the 'natural' processes related to exchange means that the 'artificial' construction of the police state that took its form as *intervention* was undone.²¹

The problem that comes to the fore here is that the *physis/nomos* distinction, rather than being interrogated and questioned, is reiterated. The natural order of medieval politics is replaced with the *nomos* of *raison d'état* and then nature re-enters the scene (albeit differently) with the advent of political economy, which sees a 'natural order' to exchange and trade. It is at this precise moment that police will be concerned with the 'elimination of disorder' (Foucault 2007: 354) and an 'apparatus or instrument for ensuring the prevention or repression of disorder, irregularity, illegality and delinquency' (Foucault 2007: 353). These are 'simply negative functions', and, furthermore, police will simply be the 'instrument by which one prevents the occurrence of certain disorders' (Foucault 2007: 354). Police, in other words, becomes a negative power, in direct opposition to its previous incarnation as a positive one.[22] Ordering then occurs in and through a multiplicity of institutions, norms and disciplinary techniques that have little to do with what Foucault sees as the repression of 'disorder'. The way is then opened for 'policing' and 'the police' to be seen as separate – with 'policing' seen as a concern with 'ordering' the population and 'the police' as dealing with 'disorder'.[23] It is precisely this view that I aim to challenge in this book. Indeed, it is my contention that modernity, far from seeing the predominance of one pole over the other, or as adhering to any sort of positive/negative power in the sense outlined earlier, sees the intensification of their *indistinction*.

## Order: Physis or nomos?

One of my concerns is to show how the presumption of a metaphysics of order that determines political form has led to a particular way of conceiving of the history of police, and indeed political institutions that are presented as necessary (and natural) for there to be social order. The concept of order has been shown to have a long history and critical place in Western thought – moving from Aristotle to Christian theology and political theorists of sovereignty and the political. It is thought that order across time and space has been variously conceived as being either a 'natural' phenomenon, or, alternatively as requiring human artifice – institutions, laws or *nomos*.[24] The 'order' of nature was seen as analogous to, or reflected by, the order of society and thus how one is conceived has an impact on the other. As Cedric Robinson argues with regard to Greek philosophy:

> the human body was also *physis*, that is, in its consciousness and its physiology. So just as the cosmology of *physis* as a metaphysics would result in a mathematical and geometric political philosophy when applied to the affairs of men, so too that same metaphysics when conceived in a different set of analogies would manifest itself in aesthetic anatomy and a concern with psychic harmony, balance and symmetry . . . thus one could

conceptualise a semblance in the deterioration of the *polis* reflected in the deterioration of the body or the mind. (2016: 142)

For Robinson, it is with the Greeks that the association of order and *archē* (rule, leadership) is formed (2016: 144) due to the discovery of the 'capacity for chaos' contained in the mind and body, and even numbers were reflected in, or analogous to, the capacity for the disintegration of order in the polis (2016: 142–4).²⁵ Thus Aristotle's understanding of order – though anchored in a view of nature – is not 'natural' in the sense of being inevitable. Though the *polis* may precede and take precedence over the individual, this does not entail that order spontaneously arises within it. His recognition that all existing 'cities are imperfect' (Castoriadis 1984: 288) attests to this, and furthermore, in his view, the high probability of conflict arising in the polis leads to seeing the rule of law as a remedy. In this way, law and *nomos* are not antithetical to the natural order of things but are in fact necessary for order itself in the *polis*. The medieval onto-theological world view of natural order, as Agamben, Dreyfus and Rabinow and others have noted, is a specifically Aristotelian legacy. Yet, as is hopefully becoming clear, the opposition or division between nature and artifice, *physis* and *nomos*, is far from straightforward. Indeed, as Cornelius Castoriadis argues:

> In this foundation, it is not so easy, either at the start or the finish to separate the question of fact – quid facti – from the question of right – and here there can be neither a straightforward identification, nor an absolute separation and opposition between nature/spontaneous finality/norm/life regulating itself in conformity with its eternal destination, which is *physis* and the mutable, contingent, arbitrary convention/institution which is *nomos*. (1984: 320)

Political societies are 'natural' for Aristotle in as far as man is a 'political animal': however this cannot be separated and disentangled from *nomos*. Furthermore, and in relation to Aristotle: 'Virtue is man's telos, his 'natural end' but it is not 'natural' in the sense that men 'for the most part' and spontaneously manage to attain it' (Castoriadis 1984: 322). We see here a confounding of the oppositional distinction between *physis* and *nomos*. My contention is that 'order' can be posited as being man's *telos*, his natural end, but this does not mean 'natural' in the sense that it exists inevitably. Indeed, the institutions which must create or maintain 'order' are naturalized in so far as order is posited as the 'natural' end of human societies. Thus, even when order is conceived as being a result of human artifice, 'nature' is not eviscerated from the narrative, rather it re-enters the stage as being either the characteristic of the *telos* (order is the natural end) – or, indeed, characteristic of the necessity of institutions due to the 'natural' violence that engulfs the state of nature.[26]

I argue that when the natural/artificial distinction is presupposed rather than questioned, this has implications for the conceptualization of police that follows. It forces a view of police which is either too narrow – police merely and negatively uphold an already existing order by repressing disorder, that is to say policing and 'the police' are separated – or too broad, in which the police as an institution gets lost. Police in the latter sense become a preoccupation with panopticism,[27] disciplining (*policing*), managing flows and thus becomes something all-pervasive and in this sense intangible.[28] 'The police' disappears into *policing* and there is a privileging of a supposedly positive, productive power of 'ordering' that is biopolitical. In a particularly striking example of this Paul Veyne, articulating the distinction between the old, sovereign, deductive powers with more modern, productive ones uses the example of a traffic cop

> who 'channels' the spontaneous movement of traffic so it will flow smoothly: that is his job, as a result, drivers proceed in safety; this is called the welfare state and it is the one we live in. It is not at all like the Old regime, where a prince encountering traffic on the road would have imposed his own right of passage and left it at that. (1997: 151)[29]

Furthermore, it highlights that once this jump is made, once police is associated with a biopolitics of ordering necessarily seen in opposition to sovereign power the way is left open to neglect the way in which police power relates to sovereignty and law (i.e. those things which it is presumed biopolitics is not). The images conveyed and language used are necessarily not that of the supposedly archaic deductive sovereign power of taking life. To read modernity as the triumph of the norm, of managed flows and networks, of 'channelling' and police as part of this is to miss the exceptional, decisionistic, *an-archic* character of police power I forward in this book. That is to say that, if biopolitics is more about calculation, then the incalculable, gratuitous and contingent remains unaccounted for. Conversely, if one sees police power as merely 'repressing disorder' if and when it occurs then we presume that it is already known what disorder is, and, relatedly, that police uphold and maintain an 'order' of which the content is known in advance. Both accounts fall short in analysing contemporary police power. Police violence cannot be seen as an aberration from the 'norm' of biopolitics. It must be placed at the centre of what the police is as an institution and also, conceptually and historically, what the police are for. Similarly, the way in which police *produce* their own legitimating grounds, their projection of a transcendent law or sovereign power, and indeed, projection of order – as their own mythological legitimation – should also not be missed when naming their 'repressive' negative function.

In short, if it is presumed that the form of political organization follows from a particular metaphysics of order, we lose sight of the way in which the metaphysics of order changes, depending on the form of political organization that predominates. What I refer to in the penultimate chapter as the self-referential legitimizing term *par excellence*, the concept of order, as a signature, means that what is supposedly founded – in this case, politics – is, in actuality, a founding power itself. Taking the police, we can see that police power projects a metaphysics of order that it supposedly derives from (i.e. the police are there to maintain or uphold order) but which in fact has no other content than the police power invoking it. Without interrogating this general economy of order, the concept of order itself must necessarily see some sort of positive content returned to it that in turn sees the form police power takes as being dependent on an underlying metaphysics of order – whether 'natural' or 'artificial'. Order as artificial leads to an expanded police power, all-encompassing and indistinct from an all-pervasive social control. A view of 'natural' order as predominant leads to a conception of police power as negative or restricted. It is this very distinction, however, that must be interrogated, and in so doing we can move away from any simplistic notion of police power as either negative or positive and from all the attendant problems that come with those characterizations.

Part I

# Divine & sovereign order

1

# Sovereignty and fear

## Hobbes and the production of order

What is the purpose of the state and what are its beginnings? What is the relationship of the state to the individual? How does sovereignty relate to law and justice? Does order exist among humans naturally? What place does violence have in and outside of the state? In tackling these questions Hobbes lays the theoretical foundations of police without recourse to the concept itself. This is alluded to by Carl Schmitt who (in reference to Hobbes) writes, 'The absolutism of the state, is accordingly, the oppressor of irrepressible chaos inherent in man or as Carlyle said in his drastic manner, *anarchy plus police*' (Schmitt 1996: 22, my emphasis). Here we have the notion that even within the absolutist state there is ('inherent in man') an anarchy that it is the task of police to oppress. Crucially, however, this 'chaos' is not and cannot be eliminated and thus the task of police is never complete. It is this conception which drives Schmitt to claim that the Leviathan, or, indeed, the order that is engendered by the Leviathan, is equivalent to police:

> In the civil stately condition all citizens are secure in their physical existence; there reign peace, security and order. This is a familiar definition of police. Modern state and modern police came into being simultaneously and the most vital institution of the security state is the police. (1996: 31)

Leaving aside for a moment the historical claim Schmitt makes here, the broader claim is that the state engenders order; and it is this which is the very definition of police. Of course, to equate Hobbes's theory of state with police is an anachronism.[1] This makes it all the more striking that Schmitt is not the only one to invoke the concept of police when discussing Hobbes's political theory: both Jacques Derrida (2009) and Mark Neocleous (2014) also resort to the term in order to provide an illustration of Hobbes's meaning when discussing sovereignty. Indeed, the implicit definition of police at work in all three interpretations of Hobbes is that the order that the sovereign engenders is equivalent to, or can be explained by, the concept of police. In particular, it seems that the theoretical constellation of concepts Hobbes makes use of – sovereignty, order and fear – can be rendered intelligible to a modern eye through the concept of police, and it is this issue that will be the focus of this chapter. The seemingly self-explanatory nature of this anachronism is in need of analysis, lest we take for granted what it presupposes – that is, that the concept of police naturally arises when one confronts Hobbes's problems, that of the violence thought to be inherent to man and how sovereign power can function to suppress it.

As I noted in the introduction to the book, Hobbes has been considered as *the* thinker of artificial order, over and against the Greek and medieval conceptions of order as *natural*. The Hobbesian idea of order has been characterized in the following way: 'society is no longer a transcendentally articulated reflection of something predefined, external and beyond itself which orders existence hierarchically. It is now a nominal entity ordered by the sovereign state which is its own articulated representative' (Collins 1989: 7). This, indeed, is how Hobbes himself understood his intervention in the philosophical tradition, believing that it was only in his time of writing that Aristotle's hegemony in political philosophy was breaking, the axioms of which he thought had not been questioned in 2,000 years (Riedel 1996: 105). Aristotle's conception of man as *zoon politikon* stands as the supposed arch-antithesis of Hobbesian man, the man who is naturally violent, individualistic and must be coerced into obeying the sovereign. On one side lie nature and a cosmological paradigm which ensures order from the heavens and stars down to earth. On the other lies the great artificial creation of Leviathan, the only thing capable of producing order out of the naturally disorderly world. Therefore, when Hobbes counterposes his own idea of man against Aristotle's the foundations are laid for the idea of a radical break with classical Greek and scholastic thought, and this is seen as marking the beginning of the transition to modernity and the modern state.[2]

As Adriana Cavarero has detailed, for the Greeks 'the entire visible world, from the movements of the heavens to the bodies of animals, bears witness to a "durable order of existence" whose origin is the supersensible order' and further 'this durable order may serve as a model or analogy for the political community, *insofar as that community is the material expression of the divine order that shapes it*' (emphasis added, 2002: 101). This is a conception of order which has a relationship to the *polis* that goes further than mere analogy. The order of the *polis* is, on this reading, a material expression of the wider, divine order that gives it its form. There is, in other words, an underlying metaphysic of order which ensures the form of the political community – politics as determined by natural order. It is then supposedly in the transition to modernity that this classical view of order is broken. Indeed, as Neocleous argues: 'by the mid-seventeenth century the idea of social order had been largely emancipated from cosmology and replaced by the *essentially Hobbesian* belief that order is constituted by the sovereign' (emphasis added, 2000: 7). The implications for the political are great. It is for this reason this chapter focuses on Hobbes for it is supposedly in Hobbes we find the transition from a natural/divine order to one that is 'produced' – a transition, moreover, which has been widely understood as inaugurating the modern phenomenon of police. This, then, is why any philosophical history of police must begin with the Hobbesian moment and its precise relation to the Aristotelian paradigm. By theorizing order as the highest political good (Aristotle) and the raison d'être of sovereignty (Hobbes), political philosophers have made order a central term animating political questions. Yet, in spite of this, Western political thought has done little to question order itself, instead busying itself with the question of how it may be upheld, fabricated or attained. This later becomes transmuted into the problem of police, which from its inception is conceived as imbricated with order.

One of the purposes of this chapter is to show that the break Hobbes makes with Aristotle is not nearly so radical as his pronouncements of the Greeks' 'vain philosophy' (1996: 459) maintain. I do not wish to claim that there is no novelty in Hobbes's conception of the state and order but rather to suggest that where one locates those novel aspects has significant consequences for the theorizations of the political that follow. Hobbes's own reductive presentation of Aristotle's thought enables him to present his thought as a radical negation of classical Greek thought, and in so doing to obscure the many continuities between the two. It is my contention that it is also Hobbes's stringent polemic against Aristotle that forms the substance of claims such as Derrida's, who, when analysing the 'prosthetic' nature of Hobbesian sovereignty, declares that 'the opposition between physis and nomos (nature and law) as opposition between physis and thesis (nature and convention or nature and positing) is here fully and decisively functional' (2009: 42). I will argue that this 'functional opposition' is not nearly as functional, or indeed oppositional, as Derrida's reading suggests.

In light of the above, however, the question arises as to the purpose of the state. Hobbesian order has been read as the *restraining* of what is natural: 'Hobbes understood that a world in flux was natural and that order must be created to restrain what was natural' (Collins 1989: 6). Even further, Collins argues, order was 'the negation of natural instincts and natural liberty' (Collins 1989: 29). Order (i.e. the order engendered by the Leviathan) is read here then as producing *stasis* in the face of *natural* movement and natural liberty and violence. In other words, we find the thesis that the artificial must restrain the natural, and order and nature come to be split. This relation is, however, more complex than might initially appear. By focussing on the 'artificial' order that Leviathan engenders as opposed to the 'natural order' of Aristotle and by presuming that it is a natural disharmony between universal and particular that determines the politics of the sovereign we miss the signatorial operations of order that confound the distinction between artificial and natural. Thus, my reading will show that even in Hobbes's civil state the natural and the artificial, the transcendent and the immanent, blend and interact, presupposing rather than negating one another. I will highlight two levels on which this interaction is apparent. First, even after Leviathan has been constituted, 'disunity' continues in the form of the dissolved multitude, which is the potential cause of civil war. Second, even in the Hobbesian state 'natural' violence is not eliminated but is to be found in the figure of the sovereign.

The chapter is structured as follows. First I will examine the 'natural order' found in Aristotle and the Greeks before going on to the way in which this has been posited as the antithesis of Hobbes's 'artificial order', in itself based on a series of claims around the positive anthropology found in Aristotle in distinction to the negative anthropology found in Hobbes. I challenge the insistence on a Hobbesian 'break' with Aristotle along three lines: first on the natural condition of man, second the endurance and life of the state and finally the question of just living and living well. In all three moments, I argue, the break is not so radical as has been previously suggested and that, relatedly, the oppositional distinction between 'natural' and 'artificial' order does little to shed light on the displacement of order from the theological to the political realm. I then use this as the theoretical terrain from which to study Hobbesian sovereignty itself. I find in Hobbes a dynamic, improvisational sovereign, one whose power cannot be constrained or subject to law. This, pushed to its extreme, means that the Hobbesian sovereign can kill without justice being harmed, due to the fact that the sovereign 'will' is the will of the people. It is this logic that, as I will go on to argue, is found later in the figure of police.

## The political animal vs. the wolf

Hobbes's negative anthropology, the natural violence he sees as inherent to man (*homo homini lupus*), is explicitly conceived in distinction to Aristotle's supposed positive anthropology – man as *zoon politikon*. Indeed, Hobbes regards Aristotle's view of the political animal as woefully inadequate. As he writes in *De Cive*:

> The greatest part of those men who have written aught, concerning commonwealths, either suppose or require us or beg us to believe that man is a creature born fit for society. The Greeks call him *zoon politikon*; and on this foundation they so build up the doctrine of civil society, as if for the preservation of peace, and the government of mankind, there were nothing else necessary than that men should agree to make certain covenants and conditions together, which themselves should then call laws. (1978: 110)

Hobbes repeatedly attacks Aristotle's mention of bees in *The Politics*, taking Aristotle as saying that bees are also political animals. In a six-pronged critique, Hobbes rails against the idea that these creatures which nonetheless 'live sociably with one another' (yet crucially without any coercive power) can be considered along the same lines as men. First, men are competitive, and second, they naturally will their own, private good rather than willing public or collective good. Third, they have no reason and thus cannot start a civil war by criticizing the government. Fourth, they cannot use their voice to trouble peace. Fifth, they 'cannot distinguish betweene Injury, and Dammage', and last, 'the agreement of these creatures is Naturall; that of men, is by Covenant only, which is Artificiall' (p. 119–120). Hobbes explicitly uses the artificial/natural distinction here in order to claim that man's political life, life lived in common, does not come from 'nature' but rather from the artificial covenant that creates the Leviathan:

art goes yet further, imitating that Rationall and most excellent work of Nature, Man. For by art is created that great LEVIATHAN, called a COMMONWEALTH or State, (in latine CIVITAS) which is but an Artificiall Man; though of greater stature and strength than the Naturall. For whose protection and defence it was intended; and in which the Soveraignty is an Artificiall Soul, as giving life and motion to the whole body; The Magistrates, and other Officers of Judicature and Execution, artificiall Joynts; Reward and Punishment (by which fastned to the seate of the Sovraignty, every joint and member is moved to performe his duty) are the Nerves. (Hobbes 1996: 9)

In his polemic against Aristotle in Leviathan, Hobbes goes on to argue that another one of the former's great errors was to claim 'that in a wel ordered Common-wealth, not men should govern, but the Laws' (1996: 471). This claim was grounded, Hobbes believes, in an overly optimistic view of human nature, which leads Aristotle to conclude, wrongly, that the rule of law is a sufficient condition for a well-ordered *polis*. Without the personalistic element of rule, Hobbes believes, there will be no order. Hobbes's overt criticisms of Aristotle's emphasis on the natural sociality of man and, indeed, on the natural order that characterizes the classical *polis*, have then contributed to the commonplace view that casts them as antipodes – Aristotle, the great thinker of natural order and positive human nature; Hobbes, the thinker of artifice, natural disorder and an extremely negative view of human nature. Even further, Hobbes is regarded by some as breaking hegemonic Aristotelianism and inaugurating a new era of the modern. Ferdinand Tönnies, for example, is described as emphasizing the 'revolutionary element' of Hobbes's thought which consisted of 'the principle on the state of nature, in the axiom of *homo homini lupus* which discards the classical idea of *zoon politikon* and the associated scholastic-natural right concept of an original community of peace and law among mankind' (in Riedel 1996: 101). For Laird, the upshot of this is that in Hobbes's account 'men did not naturally drift or tumble into orderly political government and subsequently describe that fact in speech and philosophy' (1942: 9).[3]

This reading is seemingly bolstered by Aristotle's comments on order which he explicitly conceives of as natural. In Aristotle nature was depicted as a 'hierarchical series of finite substances, each moving in an orderly fashion towards its *telos*' (Spragens 1973: 98). This depiction of nature led him to the conclusion that 'which is produced or directed by nature can never be anything disorderly: for nature is everywhere the cause of order' (Aristotle 1969: 252a). I argue that the significance of Aristotle's conception of order lies not so much in his characterization of it as 'natural' but rather in his identification of order with the 'highest good' (2004: 385) but also as a *relation* between things themselves, and between things and a higher order – which he uses the analogy of an army to explain (2004: 385). There is order among the soldiers but the soldiers also find their order in the relation to their leader. As Aristotle writes:

> We must consider also in which of two ways the nature of the universe contains the good, and the highest good, whether as something separate and by itself, or as the order of the parts. Probably in both ways, as an army does; for its good is found both in its order and in its leader, and more in the latter; for he does not depend on the order but it depends on him. And all things are ordered together somehow, but not all alike, both fishes and fowls and plants; and the world is not such that one thing has nothing to do with another, but they are connected. For all are ordered together to one end, but it is as in a house, where the freemen are least at liberty to act at random, but all things or most things are already ordained for them, while the slaves and the animals do little for the common good, and for the most part live at random; for this is the sort of principle that constitutes the nature of each. I mean, for instance, that all must at least come to be dissolved into their elements, and there are other functions similarly in which all share for the good of the whole. (2004: 385)

Order is thus fundamentally relational. There is an immanent order, the way in which things relate to each other domestically, and this immanent order is related to a wider order. Through the analogy of the army, Aristotle shows that the immanent order is dependent on a separate order, without which its own order would cease. Crucially, then order is not 'spontaneous' but dependent on a transcendent principle or *archē* and thus the move Hobbes supposedly makes in detaching order from nature is less decisive than appears at first glance. Indeed, for both, order is the proof that an antecedent point exists (the first mover for Aristotle and the sovereign for Hobbes) and is structuring the world.

Furthermore, we can see that Hobbes's reading of *The Politics*, according to which men 'naturally' drift or tumble into order and government, is not quite accurate. Indeed, that Aristotle is using the example of bees to demonstrate men's *difference* from – as opposed to similarity to – animals is evident when he argues 'obviously man is a political animal in a sense in which a bee is not, or any other gregarious animal' (1243a1 1992: 60). Aristotle's understanding of man is, in fact, not one in which human nature is spontaneously good: 'For as man is the best of all animals when he has reached his full development, so he is worst of all when divorced from law and justice' (1992: 61). Far from being guaranteed, then, in a way that anticipates Hobbes, man's 'best nature' is accomplished by and through political life – law and justice. This points towards the argument made here: that natural does not mean that the *polis* and what Aristotle considers to be 'good order' are an inevitability. Were this to be the case, then much of *The Politics* would be a mere description of what is, and extended discussions of government would certainly be unnecessary. Indeed, if order was natural, spontaneous and inevitable then questions of government such as the following would certainly not arise:

> what sort of matters ought to be supervised by many boards for different places, and which other sorts by a single official, whose authority is sovereign everywhere? I am thinking of such matters as keeping order in the market. Should there be a separate market-controller in every place, or one for everywhere? Should divisions be made according to the work or according to the persons? Is all regulation of good order a task for one man, or should there be a separate one for women and children? (Aristotle 1992: 283–4)

Order, then, as 'natural' but order also as something which must be cultivated, supervised and regulated. It is worth dwelling, I think, on what Hobbes's ultimately reductive and misleading presentation of Aristotle's thought allows him to do. He is able to claim that there is (contra Aristotle) nothing inevitable about the state or order and that they are consequently contingent and precarious. It also allows him to claim that order becomes the function and consequence of sovereignty. In so doing, disorder, anarchy, chaos and violence can be presented on one side of a line, with order and peace on the other side. Order becomes the proof and outcome of sovereign power and questions of justice disappear in that it is no longer a question of governing well – but more simply a question of government versus anarchy.[4] This however raises the question: What does this 'anarchy' of the state of nature consist of and how does it relate to sovereign power?

For Hobbes, there is no order among humans in 'mere nature': a world in which physical violence is ubiquitous and politics is absent. Life in the state of nature is extreme: 'solitary, poor, nasty, brutish and short'. The violence that saturates the state of nature is a consequence, Hobbes thinks, of man's natural equality: 'for as to the strength of the body, the weakest has strength enough to kill the strongest, either by secret machination, or by confederacy with others, that are in the same danger with himselfe' (1996: 87). Equality resides then in the capacity to kill and be killed, and it is this condition which constitutes the war 'of every man against every man' (1996: 88). However, Hobbes is clear that this condition of 'war' is not marked by continuous fighting but is rather a 'tract of time, wherein the Will to contend by Battell is sufficiently known: and therefore the notion of Time, is to be considered in the nature of Warre; as it is in the nature of Weather' (1996: 88). It is this all-pervasive state of a will to violence like the 'weather' that characterizes the state of nature and which requires that men come together in order to exit it.

In light of this there has been a tendency to see Hobbes's Leviathan as the 'permanent prevention of chaos and violence' (Palaver 1995: 63). This presupposes a 'fundamental opposition between the state of nature and the civil state' which 'puts war on the one side of the divide, and law on the other with the result that the moment originary violence is repressed by the institution, politics "quits the field" of violence' (Balibar 2015: 30). The consequences of reading the civil or the political state as coming chronologically after the natural state and standing opposed to it are powerful.[5] The fear and violence that characterizes the state of nature are supposedly overcome, cancelled out or held at bay and thus excluded from the commonwealth, which is characterized by peace and order. In this way order and nature come to be seen as split and it is this that ostensibly characterizes Hobbes's great break from the Greek tradition. As one commentator writes: 'the disorder of meer [*sic*] nature, standing as it does in such stark contrast to the orderliness of Aristotelian nature, helps to explain the radically creative force which Hobbes attributes to the word of the sovereign. Given the anarchy of meer nature, the voice of the sovereign must serve as the *logos* – the origin of order' (Spragens 1973: 108). However, the seemingly functional and oppositional relation between anarchy (the state of nature) and order (the state) that Hobbes inaugurates is rather more complex than appears at first glance.

## (Dis)order, teleology and the life of the state

For Aristotle not only is order conceived of as natural, but it is also conceived teleologically. Things move because they have a final cause: 'Since motion must always exist without interruption, there exists necessarily something first which causes motion, and this may be one or many; and a first mover must be immovable' (Aristotle 1969: 258b). Motion is attached fundamentally and essentially to a teleological end point: '[i]n that which has an end, a prior stage and the stages that follow are done for the sake of that end' (Aristotle 1969: 199a). Order thus meant movement towards, and because of, an end. Therefore, while Aristotle's idea of motion was conceived as a deviation from the goal and thus finite, Hobbes conceived of motion as infinite, with 'no order, no structure, no end, or limitation. It is endless, aimless motion' (Spragens 1973: 63). Motion as what constitutes the life of the state is not towards a final end, but is, instead, for the sake of continuation.

These differing conceptions of motion have been seen as then forming the underlying framework for the differing conceptions of the political that follow (Spragens 1973). In Aristotle part and whole exist harmoniously and that which does not must ultimately perish: 'If so whenever all the parts came together as if generated for the sake of something, the wholes which by chance were fitfully composed survived, but those which came together not in this manner, like the man-faced oxen mentioned by Empedocles, perished and still do so' (Spragens 1973: 198b). The city, Aristotle writes 'is thus prior by nature to the household and to each of us. For the whole must of necessity be prior to the part; for if the whole body is destroyed there will not be a foot or hand, unless in the sense that the term is similar ... but the thing itself will be defective' (Aristotle 2013: 1253a). The whole and part are naturally ordered and the *polis* exists prior to the citizen (Aristotle 2013: 1253a). Crucially, he argues, 'whatever is incapable of participating in the association which we call state, a dumb animal for example, and equally whatever is perfectly self-sufficient and has no need (e.g. a god), is not a part of the state at all' (1992: 61).[6]

For Hobbes, on the other hand, it is the application of the 'ontological primacy of sustained motion' (Spragens 1973: 66) into the political which ensures that the goal of the state is its continuation. In order for a community to have life, for Hobbes, it must move, and for there to be movement, there must be order:

Likewise if one asks: 'is a man when old and young the same being, *ens*, or matter in number? It is clear that because of the continual casting of [existing] body tissue and the acquisition of new, it is not the same material [that endures], and hence not the same body; yet because of the unbroken nature of the flux by which matter decays and is replaced, he is always the same man. The same must be said of the commonwealth. When any citizen dies, the material of the state is not the same, i.e. the state is not the same *ens*. Yet the uninterrupted degree [*ordo*] and motion of government that signalise a state ensure, while they remain as one, that the state is the same in number. (Hobbes 1976: 141)[7]

The question that Hobbes answers is this: How can something in which the parts or material change nevertheless still be considered the same thing? How can the state endure, given that the material that makes up the state, that is, its citizens, do not? The answer for Hobbes lies in the concept of order. Here we find Hobbes using the commonwealth as analogy, but the significance of it is no less stark. The *ordo* (order) of the state is its endurance, its life. That there is also posed here a connection between order and the 'motion of government' reveals the underlying core of Hobbes's political theory: that order must be constantly and continually produced for the state to survive.[8] Order, motion and praxis are entwined and it is this that constitutes, for Hobbes, the life of the state. As Caygill argues, 'Hobbes identifies life with order, and order with a continually produced unity; death is the dispersal following the inability to reproduce unity' (1989: 22).

To briefly summarize, then, in Aristotle, order is related to the *end* in the sense of the *telos*, and law is that which ensures the continuity of the *polis*. Law is in the service of order. In Hobbes, however, it is order that ensures the endurance of the commonwealth, and order is motion, activity.[9] The distinctive character of Hobbes's theory is not, as others would have it, that order comes to be viewed as artificial rather than natural. Rather, order becomes an incessant activity, and indeed the proof and product of a sovereign will. That the relation between universal and particular must be effected by the sovereign is a decisive turning point. Yet it remains to be seen how Hobbes conceives of this activity of order, and how, in turn, this relates to the function and goal of the state. As Foucault argues in *Security, Territory, Population*, sovereign power cannot simply posit entitlement as the justification for exercising its power. Indeed, sovereign power must, in order to be 'good', 'always propose an end' be that the 'common good' or the 'salvation of all' (2007: 98). What 'end' does Hobbes propose, and how does this relate to the endless motion of the state? This will be the focus of the following section.

## Living and living well

One of the key ways in which Hobbes, according to many of his interpreters, breaks with Aristotle is on the question of merely living and living well. Leo Strauss, for example, writes of the Aristotelian distinction between 'the reason of the genesis of the state and the reason of its being' (Strauss 1952: 33). For Strauss, Aristotle places a dividing line between 'common benefit' and 'peace and defence' (Strauss 1952: 33), or, in other words, between life and the good life. According to this interpretation, Hobbes's intervention is precisely to reduce or erase the category of living well and to make the commonwealth more simply about just living or mere survival. Fear of death becomes the motivation for the creation of the state *and* its raison d'être, and for Strauss this means that earlier concerns with 'common benefit' (1952: 33) disappear. On this reading, order is divorced from the 'good life' as such and becomes the most minimal condition for survival, from a concept loaded with positivity and divinity to one stripped back to the barest condition of existence.

What I wish to underscore here is that happiness and common benefit are not eviscerated from the Hobbesian narrative. While safety and preservation of life are the function and consequence of sovereignty, Hobbes makes it clear in chapter 13 of *De Cive* that by 'safety' we should understand not only the 'simple preservation of life (but to the extent that is possible) that of a happy life' (1998: 143). This notion of safety is reiterated in Leviathan, where he writes that safety means not just 'bare Preservation, but also all the other Contentments of life, which every man by lawfull industry, without danger, or hurt to the Common-wealth, shall acquire to himselfe' (1996: 231). That the reason of the genesis of the state – fear of death – and the reason of its being – safety – are still, if only by a hair's breadth, held apart by Hobbes must be taken as further evidence that he is closer to Aristotle than he himself would have us believe and furthermore that the function of the Leviathan in Hobbes is not reducible to the restraining of natural violence.

When one reads Hobbes's political philosophy in terms of an Aristotelian *telos*, however, the valence of Hobbes's theory changes. Without an appreciation of his a-teleological conception of motion we remain committed to the idea that the end point of the state is security, bare existence and the suppression of conflict. Indeed, we find evidence of this in Schmitt's thesis that 'the goal and terminus is security of the civil, stately condition' (1996: 31). Yet, where Hobbes writes 'goal' taken as 'objective' and 'intention' this does not mean the same as when it is taken as 'final point' or the 'terminus *ad quem* of the motion' (1976: 493). By collapsing goal and terminus, contrary to what Hobbes says himself, Schmitt can claim that all else is eclipsed in the Hobbesian political universe by security, which is in fact the end of all government. The notion that the state performs a *katechontic* function is applied to Hobbes,[10] which consists of 'the belief that a restrainer holds back the end of the world' and it is this that 'provides the only bridge between the notion of an eschatological paralysis of all human events and a tremendous historical monolith like that of the Christian Empire of the Germanic Kings' (Schmitt 2003: 60). The deferral of catastrophe and the end of the world is thought to be the secularized function of the Leviathan, which holds back civil war.[11]

The Schmittian reading of Hobbes as the thinker of the state as *katechon* renders the oppositional divide between (natural) anarchy and (artificial) order operative. By deferring catastrophe, by holding back civil war, the Leviathan is simultaneously presented as what makes politics possible at all; as Bredekamp argues, the *katechon* 'produces history' by deferring the coming of the Antichrist ('the lawless one') (1999: 253), thus fundamentally negating any 'positive goal' for the state, whose sole function is 'the restraining of the apocalyptic state of war' (Palaver 1995: 63). Indeed, the very mythology of sovereignty itself, which Schmitt wants to reanimate, presupposes the divide between anomie and law, disorder and order, war and peace, where sovereignty can be presented as keeping disorder in all of its forms at bay. Conversely, if these poles become indifferent, if there is anywhere a hint of undecideability and if the exception coincides with the norm, this dialectic becomes impossible, throwing the very function of sovereignty and its reason for being into crisis.[12] In short, the Schmittian project, which is to rescue the concept of sovereignty, *has* to understand Leviathan as fulfilling a *katechontic* function, and this explains, in part, why the Schmittian reading of Hobbes is so invested in the stark distinction between the (artificial) maintenance of order and the (natural) existence of violent disorder.

It is the desire to overcome the violence of the state of nature that supposedly compels men to make a covenant which suspends violence by investing it in the figure of the sovereign; they relinquish their right to use violence and transfer this to the sovereign 'to keep them all in awe' (Hobbes 1996: 88). In so doing the violence of the state of nature is suspended (but crucially not eliminated) and 'The Obligation of Subjects to the Soveraign, is understood to last as long and no longer, than the power lasteth, by which he is able to protect them' (Hobbes 1996: 153). The condition of war is turned into a time of 'peace'[13] only once a sovereign power has been instituted, and this men do as a result of their inclination to avoid violent death. The will to avoid death is, in fact, so strong that it becomes, for Hobbes, a natural law:

> For every man is desirous of what is good for him, and shuns what is evil, but chiefly the chiefest of natural evils, which is death; and this he doth by a certain impulsion of nature, no less than that whereby a stone moves downward. Therefore the first foundation of natural right is this, that every man as much as in him lies endeavour to protect his life and members. (1978: 115)

The fear that motivates the creation of the sovereign is the same, Hobbes thinks, as the fear that takes hold of people living in a state that is being conquered: the fear of death. This fear of death – which is as strong as gravitational pull – collapses the distinction between a sovereignty that is a result of a covenant and sovereignty that comes from conquest.[14] Whether we want sovereignty or not, whether we fought for it or not, and, indeed, whether we were subjected to it against our will or not, is irrelevant to Hobbes. There is an ambivalence to this process, however, which is highlighted when Hobbes writes, in the conclusion to Leviathan, that 'there is scarce a Common-wealth in the world, whose beginnings can in conscience be justified' (1996: 486). Hobbes thus contends explicitly that the violence which founds states[15] is almost always unjustifiable, as a result of which any appeal to this founding violence as a reason for men's continuing obedience is 'one of the most effectuall seeds of the Death of any State' (1996:486.).[16] The legitimacy of sovereignty therefore comes not from the manner in which a sovereign is instituted, but rather from the fact it exists at all. It is in what could be seen as Hobbes testing the outer limits of acceptability, and the pushing of his logic to the extreme, that leads Foucault to write that 'basically, it does not matter if we have a knife to our throats, or if what we want is explicitly formulated or not. For sovereignty to exist, there must be – and this is all there must be – a certain radical will that makes us want to live, even though we cannot do so unless the other is willing to let us live' (Foucault 2004: 96). It is this characterization that leads Foucault to categorize this form of sovereign power as the power to take life: the sovereign can 'either have people put to death or let them live' (Foucault 2004: 240). Foucault equates this form of power with the Leviathan, which is 'that model of an artificial man . . . a fabricated man, but also a unitary man who contains all real individuals' (Foucault 2004: 35).[17]

In short, it is fear that motivates not only the creation of the sovereign but also the subsequent observance by citizens of the sovereign's commands and laws. Indeed, it is the continual fear of 'penalty to follow' (Hobbes 1996: 203) the breaking of law – without which laws would be 'but vain words' (Hobbes 1996) – that compels men to obey. The move from the state of nature to the sovereign state is thus not a move that involves the elimination of fear but rather the move to a fear that is 'certain' (Esposito 2010: 25). The fear that holds the state together is, it would seem, a fear that is calculated, calculable and *expected*. This move – from total, incalculable fear to one which can be measured – is a defining moment. Yet this is, I argue, contradicted by what Hobbes says about the power of the sovereign, who is instituted as a 'representative' of the people. Indeed, to identify *with* the sovereign entails giving one's subjectivity entirely up to the sovereign (2010: 31). Furthermore, 'nothing the Soveraign Representative can doe to a subject, on what pretence soever, can properly be called Injustice or Injury; because every Subject is Author of every act the Sovraign doth' (Hobbes 1996: 148). By seeing the sovereign's actions as, logically speaking, belonging to each individual subject, the sovereign can do anything, even kill an innocent person, and this will not be considered unjust:

> and therefore it may, and doth often happen in Common-wealths, that a subject may be put to death, by the command of the Soveraign power; and yet neither doe the other wrong: As when *Jeptha* causes his daughter to be sacrificed: In which, and the like cases, he that do dieth, had Liberty to doe the action, for which he is neverthelesse, without Injury put to death. And the same holdeth also in a Soveraign Prince, that putteth to death an Innocent Subject. (Hobbes 1996: 148)

The Hobbesian logic is that one cannot – given that the sovereign's will is one's own – will against oneself. What we see, at the supposed foundation of modern sovereignty, is a logic in which sovereign power, as representative, cannot logically be called unjust. This leads to an unbounding of sovereign power, which even under normal circumstances can justifiably do anything given its power of representation. This applies not only to the sovereign's actions, but also to the laws promulgated by sovereign power: 'The law is made by the Soveraign Power, and all that is done by such Power, is warranted, and owned by every one of the people; and that which every man will have so, no man can say is unjust' (Hobbes 1996: 239). Sovereign power is what renders the concept of justice operative and thus sovereign power itself cannot be called unjust. So here lies the contradiction: the 'calculable' fear that is supposedly evoked once sovereign power is instituted, rather than the fear of anything and everything without, is in fact not calculable at all. Rather, a logic of identification of people and sovereign introduces a logic of power that is unbound, unrestricted and cannot be called unjust. Sovereign power, which is necessarily above or outside of right, cannot be under right.

As previously noted, the way in which order comes about among humans is through sovereignty: the 'artificiall person' that constitutes the sovereign is defined by 'imperium' (Caygill 1989: 27). The multitude-turned-people becomes a collective author that, while not authoring individual acts, nevertheless gives the sovereign the 'authority to improvise' (Caygill 1989: 27). As Quentin Skinner argues, Hobbes devises a theory of representation in which the sovereign can 'personate' in such a way that the words or actions of the representative can be validly attributed to the person (or thing) represented (1999: 6). However, 'once you have covenanted, you must leave it to your representative, who is now in possession of your right of action, to exercise it at his discretion when acting in your name' (1999: 9). In this sense the collective is not an 'author' in directly composing what the sovereign must say but designates the sovereign as its representative, whose will and words are not their own but who is nevertheless mandated to act in the name of all by the collective. Thus, at base we see the legitimation of an improvisational sovereign power, one where individuals cannot 'limit him in what and how far he shall represent them' (Hobbes 2014: 127).[18] The concept of the sovereign 'will' thus contains a gap between the will of the 'people' and the actions of the sovereign, whereby the latter does not necessarily derive directly from the former. Indeed, the activity of sovereign power finds its legitimation in the 'will' of the people but nevertheless has the power to exceed that will while acting in its name. As we will see later in this book, this is a logic that, far from disappearing under liberal democratic states, re-emerges in the figure of police.

The diseases[19] of the commonwealth do not and cannot stem from the sovereign himself, given that '[t]he Soveraignty is the soul of the Commonwealth; which once departed from the Body, the members doe no more receive their motion from it' (1996: 153). The machinations of the body politic are made operative by the 'soul' of the commonwealth, the sovereign, who for this reason cannot be the cause of disorder. Furthermore, given that the soul 'is in no way a part or organ of the body politic and is therefore not one element of its anatomy among many' (Caverero 2002: 173), it follows that disease is impossible here. The Hobbesian shift of gaze from sovereign to multitude means that the question is no longer which form of government is best (Aristocracy? Democracy? Monarchy?); rather, the focus is now on the multitude, for it is with them and their 'ignorance and passion' that the 'Intestine Discord' (1996: 153) that the cause of society's diseases lie.[20] 'Natural' violence and disorder are ever-present as that which the state may use or convert, or ultimately succumb to in the case of civil war. Indeed, that the state of nature is not a *pre-political* condition finds confirmation when Hobbes argues that though the state of nature might not have been a reality: '[h]owsoever, it may be perceived what manner of life there would be, where there were no common power to feare; by the manner of life which men that have formerly lived under a peacefull government, use to degenerate into, in a civill Warre' (Hobbes 1996: 89–90).[21]

In light of the above we can now make better sense of the way in which, in the Hobbesian model, sovereignty does not entail the restraining of 'natural' violence or the 'natural' wolf that man is in the state of nature. Rather, 'natural' violence and disorder are ever-present as threat and as raw material constitutive of, and used by the state.[22] This very problem is taken up by Agamben, for whom the *physis/nomos* distinction is critical for Western politics and thought – yet, crucially, is always marked by indistinction. For him, the 'Sophistic polemic against *nomos* in favour of nature. . . can be considered the necessary premise of the opposition between the state of nature and the "commonwealth" which Hobbes posits as the ground of his conception of sovereignty' (1998: 35). The violence of the state of nature then legitimates and is the cause of 'the absolute power of the sovereign'; in this way 'sovereignty thus presents itself as an incorporation of the state of nature in society, or, if one prefers, as a state of indistinction between nature and culture, between violence and law, and this very indistinction constitutes specifically sovereign violence' (1998: 35). I will examine the stakes of this construction of the state of nature and natural violence specifically with regard to race and anti-Blackness in the final chapter, but for now it should be noted that sovereignty, the state and the *polis* cannot be straightforwardly read as being 'artificial' in the sense of being opposed to, or devoid of, nature. Rather, it is (the state of) nature that is not only a legitimating myth but also that which characterizes and is constitutive of sovereign power itself – that is, a power without constraint. In other words, it is the supposed violence of nature that at once legitimates unconstrained sovereign power and exists in the sovereign himself – 'who is the only one to preserve its natural *ius contra omnes*' (1998: 35).[23] The indistinction between *physis* and *nomos* is, following Agamben, intrinsically linked to sovereign violence and power. What I wish to add is that this, in turn, is indissolubly linked to order.[24]

## The splitting of power

The topology of Hobbes's rendering of sovereignty can be illuminated by studying the frontispiece to Leviathan (Figure 1). While different versions of the image exist, the fundamental symbols remain the same. Significantly, it is believed that the engraved frontispiece was produced under the direct supervision of Hobbes himself (Springborg 1995: 354). The frontispiece depicts a huge sovereign standing *outside* and behind an almost empty city. We are thus presented with a riddle: 'a city devoid of its inhabitants and that of a State situated outside its geographical borders' (Agamben 2015: 33). The Leviathan, which is composed of the 'people' that came into existence upon instituting the sovereign, must exist outside of the place which it governs. The city, although it appears empty at first glance, is in fact not. It contains some barely visible tiny figures. Agamben credits Francesca Falk with establishing 'that the two figures standing near the cathedral are wearing the characteristic beaked mask of plague doctors' (2015: 37). The other figures are armed guards:

> like the mass of plague victims, the unrepresentable multitude can be represented only through the guards who monitor its obedience and the doctors who treat it. It dwells in the city, but only as the object of the duties and concerns of those who exercise sovereignty. (2015: 37–8)

Sovereignty and Fear

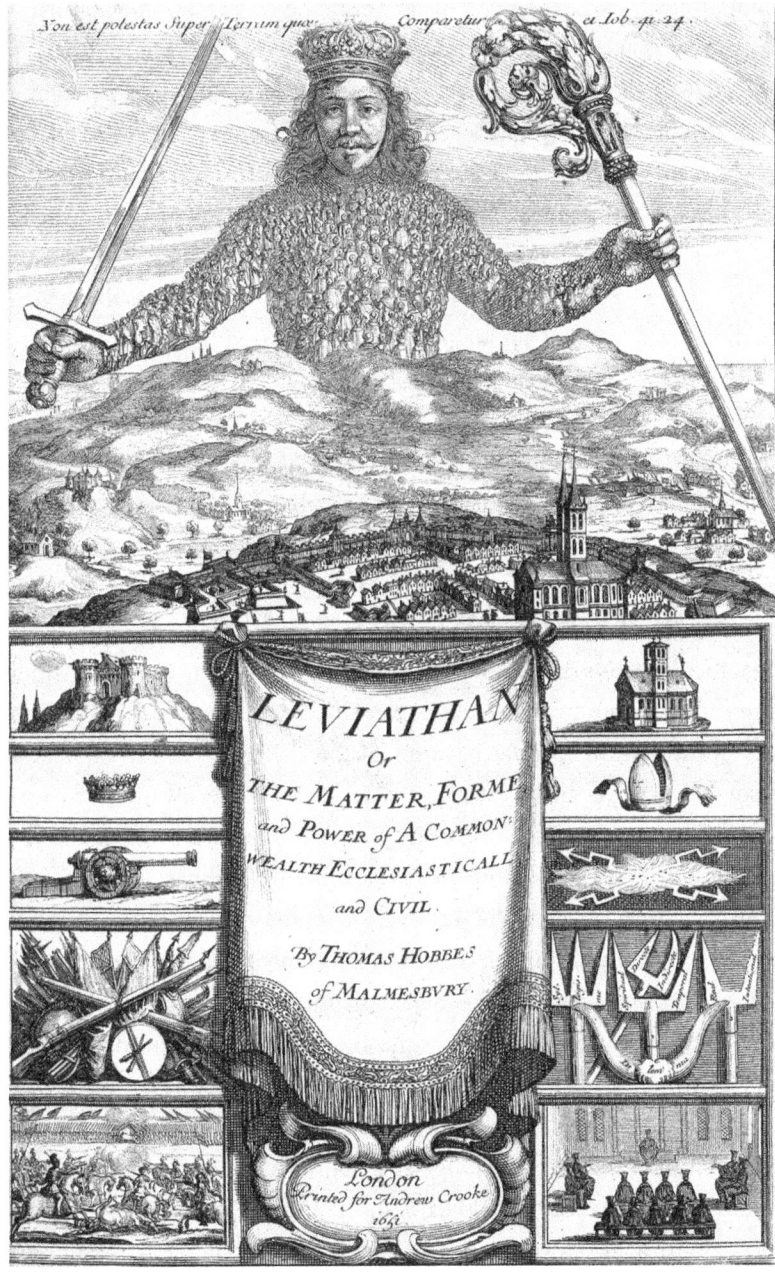

**Figure 1** Thomas Hobbes, Leviathan, Crooke, London Frontispiece of the First Edition, 1651.

Agamben posits this moment as announcing the 'biopolitical turn that sovereignty was about to take' and in doing so goes against Foucault's reading, which reduces the Leviathan's sovereign function to the right over life and death. For Foucault, biopolitics stands in direct contrast to sovereign power – it is 'incompatible' with, and opposite to sovereignty in every way (2004: 35–36).[25] What to make, then, of these very different readings – one which sees in Hobbes's Leviathan a mechanism of power that is the precise opposite of the one that came to dominate in modernity, and the other that sees the Leviathan as the beginning of it? The danger, I believe, in reading Hobbes's theory as an archaic form of sovereign power no longer applicable in modernity is that we overstate the discontinuity that power in modernity represents with respect to older forms, but we may also downplay the way in which Hobbes's theory foreshadowed those mechanisms as well.[26] Indeed, a pillar of modern liberal governance is that a collapse of the state means 'anarchy' with frequent references to the 'war of all against all' summoned as justification for the use of force and violence by the state.[27]

Agamben explains the curiously empty city with reference to the distinction between the 'multitude' and the 'people' (2015: 71). He finds in Hobbes the crucial point that the 'people' have no 'distinct body from him or them that have sovereignty over them' (2015: 70).[28] Indeed, upon instituting a sovereign, the 'people, as soon as that act is done, ceaseth to be a *person;* but the *person* vanishing, all obligation to the *person* vanisheth' (Hobbes 1983: 198). This paradoxical formulation of the vanishing people finds expression, Agamben argues, in the empty city. Once the sovereign is instituted the sovereign power of 'the people' is vanished into the sovereign (and hence the figures of the people appear in the body of the king), while the 'dissolved multitude' (Agamben 2015: 73), which appears once the people vanish, cannot be represented. The dissolved multitude, which is a potential cause of the disease of disorder, is represented only indirectly through the figure of the doctor and the guard, the maintainers of security and health of the multitude. By presupposing the people as unrelated (a disunited multitude) Hobbes can offer the solution to this in the figure of sovereignty which produces order. However, the activity of this order is never fulfilled given the existence of the 'dissolved multitude', as we have already seen.

What is striking about Agamben's formulation – that a disunited multitude exists before the creation of the sovereign and the dissolved multitude is what results from its creation – is that the production of order engendered by the Leviathan does not entail the unification of part and whole. That the multitude, though present in the city in its dissolved form, is representable only through the signifiers of 'police' points to one of the crucial points being made here: it is only 'the people' that is one. The dissolved multitude is not unitary and, significantly, this is where the doctor and the guard are found. The *unity* that is produced by – and as – the Leviathan thus precipitates and requires a dissolved multitude found within the city, and thus the only unity to be found is the unity of the essence of sovereignty. While Hobbes is clear that it is 'the *Unity* of the Representer, not the *Unity* of the Represented that maketh the Person *One*' (1996: 114), what is crucial for my argument is that in order to understand the logic of sovereignty at work in Hobbes, and indeed thinkers of sovereignty more generally, we must attend to the way in which power is split even in Hobbes – the thinker of the sovereign 'one' par excellence.

To return to the frontispiece, we see that the guard and the doctor do not appear as part of the body of the Leviathan, but within the empty city that sits below it. This separation of sovereign and guards, between what Hobbes calls the 'right and exercise of sovereign power', is fundamentally connected to the providential paradigm discussed in the introduction to the book, where God is located in a transcendent sphere above the world, but does not interfere directly in the world. It is worth quoting Hobbes at length here:

> we must distinguish between the right and the exercise of sovereign power; for they can be separated. For instance he who has the right but may be unwilling or unable to play a personal role in conducting trials, or deliberating issues. For there are occasions when Kings cannot manage affairs because of their age, or even though they can, they judge it more correct to content themselves with choosing ministers and counsellors, and to exercise their power through them. When right and exercise are separated, the government of the commonwealth is like the ordinary government of the world, in which God the first mover of all things, produces natural effects through the order of secondary causes. (Hobbes 1998: 142)

The doctrine of providence 'presupposes a binary ontology' (Agamben 2011: 126) that delineates two distinct realms: one of transcendence and one of immanence, with the transcendent realm constituting primary causes and the immanent realm corresponding to that of 'effects or immanent secondary causes' (Agamben 2011: 126). Hobbes, in the earlier passage, directly reproduces this doctrine in order to articulate his theory of sovereignty, in which the sovereign reigns but does not interfere directly in the immanent realm of the city. He is explicit that, were the sovereign to intervene directly in the day-to-day affairs of the government, 'in all judgments, consultations and public actions, it is a way of running things comparable to God's attending directly to every thing himself, *contrary to the order of nature*' (emphasis added 1998: 142). It is here that the significance of the dimensions of the frontispiece comes to the fore. Leviathan, who sits outside of the city, is manifestly distinguished from the doctor and guard who dwell within the empty city. While they may be said to exercise sovereign power, they are nevertheless distinguished from the realm of sovereignty which is where the (vanished) people are to be found. Their concern is, rather, with the immanent realm, 'the order of secondary causes'. Indeed, for Hobbes it would be against nature for the sovereign to interfere in all of these matters directly, and thus the doctor and guard become necessary. Residing in the gap that has opened up between what Hobbes calls the 'right and exercise of sovereign power', the doctor and guard represent the link between these two dimensions. Sovereignty thus can stay singular and unitary, while the doctor and the guard (police) represent the *praxis* of government which does not threaten the unity of the essence of sovereignty.

## Conclusion

To recapitulate this chapter has brought to the fore three intersecting claims. First, I have challenged the idea that Hobbes decisively breaks with an Aristotelian conception of 'natural order' and replaces it with one that is 'artificial', though he does attach order to sovereignty. Where Hobbes does break with Aristotle is through an a-teleological conception of motion that underpins his political philosophy. Without an appreciation of this, we remain committed to the view that the *telos* of the state is survival, mere existence, rather than sustained motion and incessant activity that includes common benefit and living well. In identifying moments in Hobbes where this account is contradicted, I presented a different reading, one which emphasizes the slippage between a 'biopolitical' account and a more traditional account which would see Hobbes as portraying an archaic form of sovereignty.

That order becomes the function of sovereignty, however, does not straightforwardly mean that natural disorder *determines* the political form in the sense that 'natural disorder' precedes and requires 'artificial order'. Rather, disorder is a projection from the perspective of the state into a 'previous' time without the state, and in this sense should not be considered 'external' to the state.²⁹ Second, sovereign power is also configured as being unaccountable to the extent that the sovereign may kill an innocent person with no wrong having been committed. The state of fear in the state of nature is transmuted into another type of fear, a fear of the incalculable power of the sovereign.

As shall be recalled from the introduction to the chapter, Neocleous, Derrida and Schmitt all mobilize the concept of police as an explanatory device in their discussions of Leviathan. For Derrida, Hobbes's Leviathan is an 'insurance police [*police d'assurance*] which basically entrusts to sovereignty the very powers of security and protection that will be called "police"' (2009: 42). Hobbes's Leviathan is a dynamic sovereign, one who cannot do wrong as long as there is order and one who can improvise to meet unforeseen threats. The *fear* of anarchy and the investment of a transcendent body with a public will is a potent mix legitimizing an unconstrained power, one not subject to the constraints of law. What Hobbes thus lays the groundwork for is a conception of sovereignty whose function is order and whose power to attain this cannot be constrained. It is no coincidence, then that Leviathan has conjured the figure of police. As I will detail in the penultimate chapter of this book the function of order and investment of a 'public will' is precisely to be found in the figure of police. The authority to improvise to secure public safety and order means that we find anarchy and order divided with the existence of the state (and then police) seen as the only thing that stands between them. If as I've been arguing the 'natural' anarchic violence that is supposedly pushed out in favour of order is to be found in the Leviathan, contemporaneously, it is to be found in the police.

In contrast to the 'artificial person' of Hobbes's state, the state begins to be conceived differently throughout the course of the eighteenth and nineteenth centuries. Indeed, we begin to see the breaking apart of the totalizing identification of state and society and the inauguration of a new sphere – that of civil society.³⁰ This moment finds its most radical expression in the thought of Hegel. The state here is conceived as a 'natural organism'³¹ as opposed to Hobbes's 'artificial man', not to be feared but as what makes possible, and is the highest expression of, human freedom. Hegel wants to posit his own theory of state and participation in the state not as 'external compulsion' but as a mediated unity. However, and as we shall see, civil society stands in need of *ordering* and administering, a task Hegel assigns to *Polizei*.

2

# Hegel and police

## On the relation between universal and particular

Coming at a critical historical juncture, Hegel's *Philosophy of Right* contains a uniquely significant contribution to the concept of police (*Polizei*). Originally published in 1820, its contents betray the highly transitional times in which Hegel found himself. This was a threshold moment, one in which the transition to what has been called modernity was well and truly underway, the old order collapsing, the new not quite born. In this chapter I argue that Hegel's approach to the state in general and police in particular illuminates the inadequacy of simple binary distinctions when discussing sovereign and police power in modernity. Hegel gives us a unique window into the fundamental questions that any consideration of police must confront: What is the relationship between the state and civil society and how do police fit into it? What is the relationship of police to sovereignty, and how, in turn, does this relate to states of emergency?

In contrast to Aristotle, Hobbes and Smith, Hegel's architectonics of the political relies explicitly on mediation. The unity found in Hegel's state is, to be sure, a *mediated* unity. This is the case because, in the Hegelian system, there exists no absolute identification of state and citizens; on the contrary, a gap, or scission, between citizens as autonomous economic individuals and the political sphere opens up as a direct result of the split between state and civil society.[1] Hegel reads this scission as a split between the sphere of the universal, that is the state, and the sphere of the particular, which is comprised of atomistic individuals in civil society. That there is a split here, but simultaneously a desire for wholeness and unity between citizens and state, means that a union between the two poles needs to be effected. It is here that Hegel inserts the idea and institution of police. It is by looking at Hegel's critique of Fichte, however, that the significance of Hegel's police on its own terms becomes clear. Ostensibly, their respective articulations of the concept of police are radically opposed. For Hegel, as argued in his *Philosophy of Right*, *Polizei* is a union of security and welfare, an administration of civil society that raises it from the level of particularity to universality. Hegel's *Polizei* exists to ameliorate the excess of poverty in civil society, an excess that, as will be shown, must be unresolved for Hegel's system of right to work. For Fichte, on the other hand, *Polizei* is a securitarian power designed to prevent the possibility of crime occurring. Hegel vociferously attacks Fichte's system of police,[2] which for him necessarily leads to a state wherein the limitations of freedom must be endless and where everyone must be under constant supervision. The end result of such a system, for Hegel, is not an ethical community of individuals but an unlimited security state. As we will see, however, those elements of Fichte's police state which Hegel denounces appears also in Hegel's own system of right under the significant caveat of the 'emergency' situation.

For many, Hegel's conceptualization of police bears no resemblance to the one we are familiar with today.[3] In general, this difference (and the wider conceptualization of police power) is posited in terms of positive and negative power. That is to say, if the term *Polizei* and Hegel's particular elaboration of it represents a positive, productive power – one in which happiness and security go hand in hand, where the concern is not just order, but 'good order', and where the function of sovereignty is to create the conditions of human flourishing – this is directly contrasted with the contemporary meaning of police, which is dominantly understood in terms of negative power, that is to say, as being concerned only with 'disorder' and its repression. As discussed in the introduction, throughout the course of this book I will show the limitations of this binary and challenge the narrative that sees a radical disjuncture between an old, premodern conception of police and a modern one. However, as I will go on to demonstrate, Hegel's *Polizei* foreshadows modern police power in some critical ways. Most crucially, it is the logic of an unbounded police power that Hegel posits during times of 'emergency' that brings into relief the exceptional character of police power, as well as the originary violence used against the 'uncivilized' that Hegel adumbrates.

In order to understand Hegel's *Polizei* however, something must first be said about his *Philosophy of Right* and the role the state plays within it.

This is necessary in order to grasp Hegel's understanding of universal and particular, and how the police fit into this schema. Following this, there will be an exposition of his conception of *Polizei*. Further, I will look at Fichte's conceptualization of the state and Hegel's critique thereof. Finally, I will attend to Hegel's theorization of sovereignty and violence to demonstrate the point of contact between sovereign and police power. This will frame the discussion that follows of the ever-unmediated particularity Hegel ascribes to Africa and its inhabitants, and what this also reveals about the relationship between violence and freedom in Hegel's thought.

## The Hegelian state

In *Philosophy of Right*, the 'state' is imperative for individual freedom; it is, in Hegel's words, 'the actuality of concrete freedom' (Hegel 1952: 259). However, before any more is said about how Hegel arrives at this conclusion something must be said about what Hegel means by 'state'. For as Friedrich (1954: 44), Pelczynski (1971, 1984), and various others have tried to demonstrate, there are two differing meanings behind Hegel's use of the word 'state':

(1) The 'strictly political state' which is to say, the state as a 'system of public organs, powers, or authorities through which an individual nation, a sovereign community governs itself' (Pelczynski 1984: 55).
(2) The State as an 'ethical community' (Pelczynski 1971: 13), which is much closer to what would in modern parlance be termed a 'nation state'.

Hegel delineates these two aspects in the *Philosophy of Right*, where he distinguishes between 'political sentiment (patriotism)' and the 'substance of the objective world . . . the organism of the state, i.e. it is the strictly political state and its constitution' (1952: 163). However, it would be a mistake to draw too many conclusions from this divide or to think that these two poles can easily be separated. Indeed, it is clear that while the 'political state' is but a part of the 'whole' which is the ethical state, it is an absolutely necessary part. Hegel is clear about this when he writes:

> The state is an organism, i.e., the development of the Idea in its differences. These different aspects are accordingly the various powers with their corresponding tasks and functions, through which the universal continually

produces itself in a necessary way and thereby preserves itself, because it is the presupposition of its own production. This organism is the political constitution; it proceeds perpetually from the state, just as it is the means by which the state preserves itself. If the two diverge and the different aspects break free, the unity which the constitution produces is no longer established.... It is in the nature of an organism that all its parts must perish if they do not achieve identity and if one of them seeks independence. Predicates, principles and the like get us nowhere in assessing the state, which must be apprehended as an organism. (Hegel 2008: 242)

Therefore, for Hegel the state as ethical life exists by and through its political institutions. There cannot be one without the other. Let us return to the question why Hegel conceives of the state as being coterminous with freedom. In order to understand this, it is worth noting the structure of the *Philosophy of Right*. The book itself is divided into three sections: 'Abstract Right', 'Morality' and 'Ethical Life' (Hegel 2008). By starting with 'abstract right' and 'morality', Hegel's aim is to show their inadequacy yet necessity for actualizing freedom in a concrete way. They are incomplete in their form as the 'abstract system of rights cannot itself train agents habitually and intentionally to uphold rather than to violate the system of rights' (Westphal 1993: 249) and further that 'moral reflection is not sufficient of itself, to generate a substantive set of moral norms' (Westphal 1993: 253). This does not mean that abstract right and morality are prior to ethical life, but rather that ethical life is what ultimately grounds the two preceding moments and transcends them. The same three-tiered structure is encountered again in the sub-sections of 'ethical life' itself. These are, in order: 'The Family, Civil Society and The State' (Hegel 2008). These three tiers function in a similar way to the three concepts that make up the entire work: the first two are necessary but incomplete manifestations of freedom and recognition. The third is the transcendent body that represents the overarching totality which conditions and grounds the other two. Differently put, the former two only attain their actuality and truth in the higher third. In this sense 'ethical life' and 'the state' embody 'the realization of the totality of the conditions of freedom' (Williams 1997: 121).

It is not, however, in the state that we find Hegel's *Polizei*, but in civil society. *Polizei* is but one of 'three moments' that are contained within civil society, the other two being 'the system of needs' and the 'administration of justice' (Hegel 1952: 126). The system of needs refers to the needs common to all individuals and the ways in which these are satisfied 'through his work and through the work and satisfaction of the needs of all others' (Hegel 1952: 126). The administration of justice refers to 'the actuality of the universal of freedom therein contained – the protection of property' (Hegel 1952: 126). *Polizei*, the third moment, is paired with the 'corporation' which exists, as *Polizei* does, to guard against the contingencies 'still lurking' (Hegel 1952: 126) in the first two moments and to provide a professional association for individuals which cares for their individual interest as if it were a single, common interest.[4] It is here that Hegel identifies the individual as being able to recognize 'that he belongs to a whole... and that he is interested and actively engaged in promoting the less selfish end of this whole' (2008: 225). Stronger yet, it is essential, for Hegel, that individuals are provided with a 'universal activity over and above their private business' (2008: 227). It is here, then, that the individual transcends individuality and becomes a public person, a member of the state through universal activity, that is 'the active participation in the reproduction of the community' (Honneth 2010: 61).

## Hegel's *Polizei*

In keeping with the tendency to split police temporally and conceptually into 'positive' and 'negative' power, T. M. Knox, the translator of the *Philosophy of Right*, translates police rather vaguely as 'public authority' (1952: 360). This translation has been contested (Neocleous 1998: 43) given that it precludes a fuller understanding of the concept of police in its specificity, that is, it reinforces the idea that Hegel's police has little to do with the institution of police we see today but is rather a form of 'positive' power. Seemingly confirming this position, Hegel lists the things *Polizei* is to provide for, which include among others: street-lighting, bridge-building, regulating the market, providing services for the poor, education and the founding of colonies (1952: 146–52). Thus in Hegel we find that *Polizei* also fulfils a duty to citizens, a positive obligation that consists of providing their subsistence, education, infrastructure, and so on. Police becomes a fundamental concept with regard to the modern state in that it is tasked with ensuring not only the security of the individual but also the social totality.

In the corporations and the police, civil society 'passes over into the political state; they represent the political inside civil society' (Neocleous 1996:

4). It should be noted, however, that *Polizei* represents not merely an organ of administration inside civil society (the political state) but is also a necessary component of the ethical universal (the state as an ethical community). The state, which is the sphere of the universal, must not be confused with civil society. Indeed, the emergence of these two separate realms is regarded as a specifically modern phenomenon (Hegel 2008: 181). The specific end of the state cannot merely be the 'security and protection of property and personal freedom' lest 'the interest of the individuals as such becomes the ultimate end of their association, and it follows that membership of the state is something optional' (Hegel 2008: 228).⁵

Despite his opposition to the individualism that grounds contract theories, individuals in civil society belong, for Hegel, in the realm of particularity, where they exist as 'private persons whose end is their own interest' (2008: 184). However, these self-interested, atomized persons cannot remain as such but must be raised to the level of universality that exists in the state. In other words, 'their particularity' must be 'educated up to subjectivity' (2008: 184). It is this rending apart of civil society and state, the realms of the particular and the universal, that necessitates a *Polizei* 'to actualize and maintain the universal contained within the particularity of civil society' (2008: 224). That Hegel conceives of police in this way has led Riedel to claim that this is classical politics (the Greek concern with morality and ethics) made modern, that is to say, that Hegel proposes a conceptual solution to the split between a de-politicized civil society and the state (Riedel 1984: 152). Riedel points to the Jena lectures, where Hegel 'related the modern "police" to the origin of politics, the *politeia* of classical Greek philosophy: "the *police* here amounts to this – *politeia*, public life and rule, action of the whole itself but now degraded to the whole's action to provide public security of every type"' ( Riedel 1984: 152). Despite having its roots in the classical tradition, however, Riedel maintains that police is a solution to a *modern* problem – that of the split between state and civil society and finds that it is 'the form in which the difference between state and society appears and is permanently mediated' ( Riedel 1984: 152).

In contrast to particular readings of classical liberalism, which sees a 'natural' order to civil society, Hegel regards the latter as constantly on the verge of collapse – the market does not regulate itself, and antagonisms between individuals cannot be left to themselves:

> Particularity by itself [*für sich*], given free rein in every direction to satisfy its needs, contingent caprices and subjective desires, destroys itself and its substantive concept in this process of gratification. . . . In these contrasts and their complexity, civil society affords a spectacle of extravagance and want as well as of the physical and ethical degeneration common to them both. (Hegel 2008: 182)

The existence of poverty in civil society is, for Hegel, unavoidable: 'inequalities in resources and skills' are an 'inevitable consequence' of the functioning of civil society (2008: 192). If poverty cannot be abolished, the dangers of poverty must be, as much as possible, contained. Hegel's concern here is that were the 'masses' to 'decline into poverty' and were there to be 'a consequent loss of the sense of right and wrong, of integrity and of honour in maintaining oneself by one's own activity and work, the result is the creation of a rabble of paupers' (2008: 221). Despite the wealth that civil society creates, poverty remains and with it, the emergence of a 'penurious rabble' is a constant possibility. Yet, although poverty is a necessary condition for the creation of the 'rabble', it is not a sufficient one: 'a rabble is created only when there is joined to poverty a disposition of mind, an inner indignation against the rich, against society, against the government etc.' (2008: 221). Knox adds that 'no single word is available for a mass of rebellious paupers, recognizing no law but their own, and it is this which Hegel means' by rabble (1952: 244). The poor have withdrawn from 'the natural means of acquisition' and are 'more or less deprived of all the advantages of society' (Hegel 2008: 220) and thus become a potential danger to the smooth functioning of that society itself. Consequently, 'the poor fall out of the binding mechanism of civil society and the state because they do not follow the central implicit imperative of the *Philosophy of Right*, namely to be somebody' (Ruda 2011: 32), which, for Hegel, is brought about by being part of an 'estate'. Estates are 'general groups' into which individuals are 'assigned' according to their particular 'systems of needs, means, and types of works relative to these needs' (Hegel 2008: 193).

The estates are for Hegel not only the means by which one becomes recognized by the state but also, and perhaps more importantly, 'they prevent individuals from having the appearance of a mass or an aggregate and so from acquiring an unorganized opinion and volition and from crystallizing into a powerful *bloc* in opposition to the organized state' (2008: 290). It is through labour that an 'individual actualizes himself', by being part of an estate and providing for oneself' (Hegel 2008: 196). This enables a mediation with the universal sphere of the state and the ability to 'gain recognition both in one's own eyes and in the eyes of others' (Hegel 2008: 196). The poor (who do not labour to provide for themselves and thus cannot be part of an estate) are an 'un-estate' and on Frank Ruda's reading mark an internal lack in civil society that it 'cannot overcome' (2011: 33). Civil society inevitably produces an excess, that is, the impoverished mass, which the state is compelled to recognize, but which, by necessity, it *cannot* recognize (2011: 33). As Hegel explains:

> The lowest subsistence level, that of a rabble of paupers, is fixed automatically, but the minimum varies considerably in different countries. In England, even the very poorest believe that they have rights. . . . In this way there is born in the rabble the evil of lacking sufficient honour to secure subsistence by its own labour and yet at the same time of claiming the right to receive subsistence. Against nature a human being can claim no right, but once society is established, poverty immediately takes the form of a wrong done to one class [*Klasse*] by another. The important question of how poverty is to be abolished is one that agitates and torments modern society in particular. (Hegel 2008: 221)

Crucially, it is not only that the rabble cannot provide for their own subsistence but that they also, and as a result, cannot own property and hence they cannot demonstrate 'personality'. Indeed, Hegel's claim is that individuals express their will and 'personality' in the external world, in property. Property, for Hegel, is the '*existence* of personality' (2008: 65).[6] Hegel goes on to add that 'personality essentially involves the capacity for rights and constitutes the concept and the basis (itself abstract) of the system of abstract and therefore formal right' (2008: 55). Personality is thus a capacity for rights that is realized in the external world, the world of things, and of which contractual relations of property are the apex. Personality, which pertains to the individual but takes its universal form through intersubjective recognition and the creation of the 'abstract subject of rights' (Marcuse 1955: 194), is the person as rights bearer. Law, which addresses the abstract subject, defends private property and enforces contracts in civil society, remains an 'external force' (Knox 1952: xi), whereas, in the state, law acquires 'the form proper to its universality, but also its true determinacy' (Hegel 2008: 198).

In light of this we must question the claim that Hegel was challenging the 'abstract formalism' of Roman law, that by 'making personal right depend on the ability to own property, Roman law denied personhood to the propertyless' (Breckman 1999: 40). While it is of course the case that Hegel's account of personality and property is embedded within a system of intersubjective recognition and law, this does not negate Hegel's claim that personality 'gives itself to reality' by claiming 'the external world as its own' (2008: 55). Therefore, if one has no property, the implications are stark; such an individual cannot be a personality.[7] This illuminates the substance of Hegel's bemused declaration that in England even the poorest in society believe they have rights. The poorest, by virtue of not providing for their own subsistence and hence nullifying their ability to own property, have become mere persons, persons without personality and thus without the corresponding rights and duties. The rabble, even more than this, claim their right to subsistence when they have no right and therefore present a threat, since in so doing poverty 'takes the form of a wrong done to one class [*Klasse*] by another' (Hegel 2008: 221). This is not so much a matter of crime, which for Hegel is simply the 'arbitrary willing of evil' (Hegel 2008: 215), but it represents something else. The rabble who have not admitted space for the 'voice that wants to constructively stimulate the universal in him' (Ruda 2011: 70) are excluded from Hegel's system of right, while simultaneously claiming a right.

So far, I have reconstructed Hegel's *Polizei* as it appears in his system of right. Police, for Hegel, is the necessary condition for the functioning of the market and also actualizes the universal contained within the particular realm of civil society. Finally, police must deal with the excess, with those who are unwilling to be subsumed under the imperative of the universal.[8] It is this excess, those who are excluded from his system of right, that the police must try to contain. As we have seen, however, the police will be frustrated in its attempt to do so, given the inevitability of poverty in civil society. However, I want to suggest that there is more at stake in Hegel's conceptualization of police and that this may be unearthed through a reading of Hegel's critique of Fichte. It is by revisiting this debate in different terms, that is, by taking account of the continuities between the two, that Hegel's intervention into the philosophical history of police may be underscored and re-articulated.

## Fichte's police

As already noted, Fichte is a reoccurring foil in Hegel's account of *Polizei*. For Fichte, who originally outlined his concept of police in 1796, 'police' is not, as in Hegel, a concern with the promotion of general well-being and good order but takes on an ostensibly more limited role to detect and prevent crime. While the scope of the former's ideal model of police is thus arguably more limited than Hegel's, on the surface it appears as though the power he would ascribe it is more extensive, culminating in an all-powerful police state. Indeed, in a short statement we are told that '[t]he principal maxim of every well-constituted police power must be the following: *every citizen must be readily identifiable, wherever necessary, as this or that particular person*' (2000: 257). This power of identification leads to a state wherein no subject may commit a crime without a trace being left. For Fichte, the need for the state to ensure no criminal may escape punishment is absolute: 'we have said that the state's coercive power can preserve itself only on the condition that it be continually efficacious; therefore it will be destroyed forever if it is inactive even for a moment; it is a power whose *existence at all* depends on its *existence, or expression, in every single case*' (2000: 138). Were there to be the hope of committing a crime that would go undetected by the state, laws, 'no matter how wise', would not deter the criminal; indeed, for Fichte, this arrangement would mean that we would continue to live in a 'previous condition of nature' (1869: 384).[9] Having thus set out the police's raison d'être, Fichte goes on to set out to prove how the state may achieve the end of ensuring 'that each guilty person, without exception, should be brought to trial' (1869: 384).

Fichte makes a distinction between what he calls 'police laws' and civil laws. Civil laws aim at acts which 'directly interfere with the rights of others, as for instance theft, robbery, assault etc., and hence these laws are not likely to be considered unjust by anyone' (1869: 377). Police laws, on the other hand, aim at prevention, at 'acts which may appear perfectly indifferent, and which in themselves harm no one, but which are circulated to facilitate the wronging of others' (1869: 377). Police laws are also unlimited in scope, given that they aim not at what has been done, but what *might* be done. To be noted here are the seeds of an idea that we have also encountered in Hegel, where it is not crimes or acts of resistance that *have* been committed that are the issue but only their *potential* to occur. In Hegel this appeared in his conception of the rabble, while it seems that, in Fichte, everyone is a priori suspicious. Fichte speaks at some length about, for example, public gatherings and argues that 'if so many people assemble that public security is threatened – and any assembly can pose such a threat if it is strong enough to resist the armed power of local authorities – then the police shall demand an explanation of their intentions, and watch to make sure that they actually do what they claim to be doing' (2000: 258).

What, however, is the role of the police on a more philosophical register? It is through the institution of the police, Fichte tells us, that 'the reciprocal influence between government and citizens first becomes possible' (1869: 374). So, beginning from a similar premise as Hegel, Fichte holds that the police enable mediation to occur between subjects and state. They have a twofold function, that is, to protect the rights of citizens, but also to require 'their obedience to the laws and fulfilment of their duties as citizens' (1869: 374). The prevention of crime emphasized here occurs in two ways: on the one hand through the protection of the rights of citizens, while on the other the police must do their utmost to ensure that crime *cannot* happen by taking measures to ensure identification. As an example, we may cite the idea that all citizens be required to carry a light at night both to ensure they may be recognized by police, and because 'in darkness it is much easier to injure a citizen' (1869: 378). Fichte goes on to argue that 'no one must remain unknown to the police' (1869: 378). Each and every subject must be recognizable to and identifiable by the state. This means that 'no one can leave one place without announcing his next place of residence, which must be marked on the pass and recorded in the books' (1869: 381).[10] In the final analysis, it is thus anonymity, or the possibility of it, that so concerns and disturbs Fichte and which he attempts to theorize out of existence.

## Hegel on Fichte's police

Hegel's critique of Fiche's police operates on a number of different levels. He presents a searing attack on the 'world of galley-slaves' (1995: 212) that he believes Fichte's police must lead to. On Hegel's reading, achieving the end of an omniscient presence wherein the will is constrained to the extent that crime may not occur at all requires and engenders a condition of unfreedom. Under these conditions there is no 'inner majesty', no sphere of inner life that must be left free of interference by the state, and this for Hegel means that 'the people is not the organic body of a common and rich life' but is reduced to 'an atomistic, life-impoverished multitude' (in Smith 1989: 84). The state is reduced to a police state and security of the individual becomes the end of the state.

Given that Fichte wants to ensure no one may escape undetected if they commit a crime, all contingencies must be accounted for in advance by the police. This for Hegel means that the 'bounding of freedom must itself be infinite' (1977: 148), which in turn accounts for why Fichte's police would need to enunciate, down to the finest detail, a system of passports and what can be done to prevent them from being forged. Hegel finds that Fichte's police must deal with 'endless possibility' and thus, in the Fichtean state, 'every citizen will keep at least half a dozen people busy with supervision, accounts etc., each of these supervisors will keep at least another half a dozen busy and so on ad infinitum. Equally the simplest transaction will cause an infinite number of transactions' (1977: 147).[11]

Hegel notes that Fichte describes imperfect states that extend their 'policing authority to just a few types of possible offenses, for the rest they entrust the citizens to themselves' (Hegel 1977: 148). This marks an inconsistency, which for Fichte must be remedied by 'making the police more perfect' (Hegel 1977: 147). Everyone must be policed, and every crime must be foreseen and countered by the all-seeing police. This necessarily leads to an infinite bounding of freedom given that 'there is simply no action at all from which the state could not with abstract consistency calculate some possible damage to others' (Hegel 1977: 146). The police thus do not embody the ethical community but instead represent an external, constraining body.

As Lukács has argued, Hegel's critique of Fichte is not incidental. Rather, it attests to something far more fundamental in the projects of both and the way in which Hegel conceives of his own philosophical system. First, for Hegel, society 'in the course of its development will produce the institutions it requires, and [. . .] these cannot be imposed on it by any external authority, not even that of a deductive philosophy' (Lukács 1975: 293). Second, while a general system of law is necessary in the Hegelian model, 'particular determinations of the law and above all their application to isolated instances must always contain a chance element' (Lukács 1975: 293), which, for Lukács, signifies the fundamental breach between the 'objective idealism of Hegel and the abstract, subjective idealism of Fichte' (Lukács 1975: 293). The content of laws and their application to individual cases can never be deduced from philosophy alone, and since Fichte's exposition of a system of police is an attempt to do just this, what results is an external system of constraint, or a 'rigid and lifeless set of institutions on the one hand, and the empty abstract inwardness of moral man on the other' (Lukács 1975: 294). For Hegel, external authority must not exist in an antithetical relationship to the inner life of man, but, given the organic development of institutions, exist in a constantly shifting, dialectical relation. Hegel sees in Fichte an attempt to deduce, a priori, the content of the law from his philosophical presuppositions, thus creating stasis where there should be movement.

The question animating Hegel's *Philosophy of Right* can be summed up thus: 'how and under what conditions can I view other selves not as impediments to my freedom, from whom I need protection, but rather as the condition of freedom itself?' (Schecter 2000: 147). It is this formulation of the question that highlights Hegel's utter distaste for Fichte's police, indeed why Hegel *must* oppose Fichte's police, which is the necessary corollary to seeing others not as the condition for freedom but only as potential impediments to it. Under these conditions, for Hegel, ethical life is impossible:

> on this presupposition a system is built whereby the concept and the individual subject of ethical life are supposed to be united despite their separation, though the unity is on this account only formal and external, and this relation between them is called "compulsion". In this way . . . the union of universal and individual freedom, and ethical life itself, are made impossible. (Hegel 1975: 84)

Ethical life is made possible through intersubjective recognition in Hegel's system, by seeing other individuals (though not all individuals, as we shall see later in this chapter) as a condition for the subject's own freedom. Hegel is thus compelled to dismantle Fichte's system of police, wherein the union of individuals is not immanent but comes about through compulsion. The universal and particular do not coincide but must be artificially instituted through the medium of constraint. Hence, in the Fichtean model as Hegel sees it 'oneness with the general will thus cannot be posited as inner absolute majesty, but only as something which is to be brought about by an external relation or by compulsion' (Hegel 1975: 85).

Hegel's critique of Fichte is thus centred on the twin notions of externality and compulsion, which may perhaps illuminate why, in the *Philosophy of*

*Right*, the police appears in civil society rather than in the state. Of course, the police is an external institution in one sense, but the notion that it knows where everyone is all of the time is anathema to a state that actualizes freedom for Hegel. It is 'repugnant', Hegel writes, to 'see policemen everywhere' (1995: 212), and it is for this reason that he advocates 'secret police' (1995: 212) which supervise the goings-on in civil society but are not *seen* to be doing so. This is so that public life may be seen to be free and this, for Hegel, justifies the means (1995: 212). Fichte, on the other hand, states that secret police are rendered obsolete in his system, adding that 'secrecy is always petty, base and immoral' (2000: 263). Hegel's advocacy of secret police points towards the issue to be developed in the following section: that Hegel must oppose, but in fact reproduces, some of the core features of Fichte's police. Indeed, the very need for police in Hegel's system of right *itself* attests to the ambivalent nature of his own account of the union of universal and particular that is supposedly organic and non-coercive. Indeed, as we have seen, coercion and surveillance can and must occur in the Hegelian model,[12] as long as it is not visible *everywhere* and *all* of the time for *everyone*. In the final analysis this, then, constitutes the crucial difference between Fichte and Hegel's police.

## *Polizei*, police, police power

Fichte's passport is not only a technique of mediation between the state and individuals but also relations between subjects themselves, 'and this is so precisely in order to assure the security of market exchanges' (Chamayou 2013: 2). Police as understood by both Hegel and Fichte is not merely the penetration of the state into civil society, and is, in that sense, not simply an apparatus that merely constrains, but a condition of possibility for the maintenance of civil society and the market respectively. The police, in other words, is not an additional institution but is fundamental to the workings of the state. In both Hegel and Fichte, then, a conception of *Polizei* arises that pertains to a structural relation of *recognition*, not only in a vertical relation, that is, between state and subject, but also horizontally, between subjects themselves. In Fichte, this recognition should be understood in a very literal sense: the state must be able to recognize the individual. In Hegel, the police not only regulates the market, and ensures security of exchange, but also attempts to bring those who are not recognized by the state (the indigent poor) back into the sphere of recognition.

More important than this disagreement between Hegel and Fichte, however, is the underlying continuity in how they render the problem of police. The problem for both hinges on the tension between the universal and particular (or, more accurately for Fichte, the state and citizen).[13] Hegel criticizes Fichte for forcing his subjects to act in a negative fashion, by means of external constraint. Yet as the earlier discussion of the rabble makes clear, this problem remains present in Hegel's system as well. The poor, given their status as an 'un-estate', must be negatively constrained in order to prevent the emergence of the rabble. This tension, I will argue, is never fully resolved, for, as Avineri has shown, the problem of poverty is never resolved in Hegel; indeed, 'pauperization and the subsequent alienation from society are not incidental to the system but endemic to it' (1972: 148). The state must intervene to ameliorate the effects of pauperization, but since it cannot solve the problem definitively, it must limit its interference to 'external control' only, lest the spheres of civil society and state, which for Hegel are necessarily distinct, collapse into one another (Avineri 1972: 151). The poor in Hegel's state, then, do not contain an 'inner absolute majesty' but must, like the subjects of Fichte's state, be treated with the utmost suspicion and coercion. Indeed, it is not that the poor have done wrong, but that they are constantly on the verge of doing so, which follows from their status (or lack thereof) in civil society: 'the public authority [*Polizei*] takes the place of the family where the poor are concerned in respect not only of their immediate want but also laziness of disposition, malignity, and the other vices which arise out of their plight and their sense of wrong' (Hegel 2008: 220). In Hegel, the tension between, on the one hand, the desire to leave 'citizens to themselves' and designate them as independent and autonomous and, on the other, the existence of the poor is acute.[14]

If Fichte's system leads to endless determinations, down to the finest detail, given its function to constrain the will and prevent crime, Hegel's positive conception of the police also gives rise to a police unlimited in scope and nature. Hegel defines Fichte's police state as a 'world of galley slaves where each is supposed to keep his fellow under constant supervision' (1995: 212). Hegel finds this notion 'repugnant', and yet, in his own system, police supervision must 'go no further than is necessary, though it is for the most part not possible to determine where necessity here begins' (1995: 212). Crucially, then, Hegel himself attests to the radical indeterminacy of the police, which, supposedly by necessity, cannot be delimited either in function or form. It is this moment, the moment of ambiguity with regard to 'where necessity begins', that will be shown to be crucial for the operations of police. Indeed, despite his critique of Fichte, Hegel states that

> there is, therefore, no inherent line of distinction between what is and what is not injurious, even where crime is concerned, or between what is and what is not suspicious, or between what is to be forbidden or subjected to supervision and what is to be exempt from prohibition, from surveillance and from suspicion, from inquiry and the demand to render an account of itself. These details are determined by custom, the spirit of the rest of the constitution, contemporary conditions, the crisis of the hour, and so forth. (1952: 146)

For Hegel, it is the endless possibilities in Fichte, the fact that 'there is simply no action at all from which the state could not with abstract consistency calculate some possible damage to others' (1977: 146) that means 'the bounding of freedom must itself be infinite. This is the antinomy of a boundedness that is unbounded, in which the limitation of freedom and the State have disappeared' (1977: 148). The state, which for Hegel is the actuality of the ethical idea, cannot engage in a bounding of freedom, as it is itself the condition for freedom. Yet, as we have seen, philosophically, Hegel cannot escape the antinomy of a 'boundedness that is unbounded' entirely. While he may take issue with Fichte's technical prescriptions, the philosophy underlying his model of police, whose actions and determinations may not be circumscribed from the outset, is not transcended. Hegel is worth quoting at length here in order to demonstrate his reliance on a philosophy of police power that cannot be constrained:

> here nothing hard and fast can be laid down and no absolute boundaries can be drawn. Everything here is personal; subjective opinion enters in, and the spirit of the constitution and the dangers of the time have to provide precision of detail. In times of war, for instance, many a thing, harmless at other times, has to be regarded as harmful. As a result of this presence of contingency, of personal arbitrariness, the public authority [*Polizei*] acquires a measure of odium. When reflective thinking is very highly developed, the public authority [*Polizei*] may tend to draw into its orbit everything it possibly can, for in everything some aspect may be found which might make it dangerous. In such circumstances, the public authority [*Polizei*] may set to

> work very pedantically and inconvenience the day-to-day life of people. But however great this annoyance, no objective line can be drawn here. (Hegel 2008: 216)

Hegel here outlines the limit-case, the case of the emergency, where police powers come into their own. Everything in this case may be determined as a threat and may legitimately be drawn into the orbit of the police. Thus here we find Fichte's police state, located not outside of Hegel's state but at the centre of an emergency condition which cannot be predetermined.[15] While Fichte prescribes a state in which police power is everywhere unbounded, in Hegel we find the same radical indeterminacy, the moment of emergency ('war for instance') where securitarian police power must be unlimited, where any constraints on that power must be undone.

It is thus no coincidence that police comes to play such a pivotal yet under-theorized[16] role in Hegel's system of right. For Hobbes, for whom there is no separation of state and civil society, the unity of the state is achieved by the unitary nature of the person who holds sovereign power. Hegel's approach, despite his attempts to differentiate it sharply from Hobbes's, ultimately accepts his claims about the state of nature (and, as we shall see, the subsequent claim that sovereign power should be unitary). He regards Hobbes's observation about human nature and the state of nature as substantially correct in that all humans in the state of nature are 'equally susceptible to being killed by the other', adding that

> Equality is therefore based upon universal weakness not as in more recent times upon absolute freedom or autonomy. [Hobbes] says further that in the natural state we all have the will to harm one another. He is right about that. He apprehends the natural state in its authentic sense: there is no idle talk of a naturally good condition, for the natural state is rather the bestial state, the state of desire, of the unsubdued self-will. Hobbes characterizes this natural state more precisely as a *bellum omnium contra omnes*, a war of all against all. That is the quite correct view of the natural state. (Hegel 1995a: 180)

The problem, as Hegel sees it, with Hobbes's notions of natural law – and with contract theory[17] in general – is that it remains limited to a theory of domination; which is to say, limited to a representation in which the opposition between particular and universal, or individual and state, is not transcended but maintained and related only by force (Taminaux 1985: 25). Indeed, rather than transcend the ubiquitous violence in the state of nature, the sovereign only redirects and monopolizes it. The relation that results is one of fear, submission and domination. Hegel sees his own theory as standing in contrast to this presentation and in so doing he invokes the concept of order:

> When we walk the streets at night in safety, it does not strike us that this might be otherwise. This habit of feeling safe has become second nature, and we do not reflect on just how this is due solely to the working of particular institutions. Representational thought [*Vorstellung*] often has the impression that force holds the state together, but in fact its only bond is the fundamental sense of order which everyone possesses. (2008: 241)[18]

That the functioning of institutions has become naturalized to the extent that we no longer reflect on the outcome of that functioning – that is, the 'sense of order' – is for Hegel proof that order is the outcome of 'particular institutions' of the state and not of force. Relations of force must be transcended and negated in the realm of objective spirit, where freedom is made actual. However, and without acknowledging it, Hegel here reproduces Hobbes's notion that 'order' is the proof and outcome of state power. State power, the site where he wants to distance himself from Hobbes, is ostensibly read not in terms of force, violence or domination. Indeed, the violent 'struggle for recognition' that takes place in the *Phenomenology of Spirit* is absent from the *Philosophy of Right* (see Nancy 1982: 495) and the state is constituted as a site of 'peace'. As we shall see, however, once again this exclusionary operation of violence is not as straightforwardly functional as Hegel suggests.

## Violence, nature and Hegel's emergency

Despite his pronouncements on abandoning contract theory's reliance on domination and force, Hegel is aware, even acutely aware, of the violence and force that founds states. In the *Lectures on the Philosophy of History* he speaks of great men, 'heroes'[19] that embody the 'will of world spirit' in their person:

> They may be called Heroes, inasmuch as they have derived their purposes and their vocation, not from the calm, regular course of things, sanctioned by the existing order; but from a concealed fount – one which has not attained to phenomenal, present existence, – from that inner Spirit, still hidden

beneath the surface, which, impinging on the outer world as on a shell, bursts it in pieces, because it is another kernel than that which belonged to the shell in question. (Hegel 1975b, §32)

Rather than adhering to the existing order, these individuals break it by transgressing it. Crucially, however, these heroes cannot exist once a state has been founded; 'they come on the scene only in uncivilized conditions' (Hegel 2008: 98). The use of violence and force, in this sense then, is only a solution to the violence inherent in nature: 'mere goodness' Hegel writes 'can achieve little against the power of nature' (Hegel 2008: 98). It is a barbaric but historic or foreign phenomenon that is contrasted with the 'civilised' state.[20] Indeed, as one author argues: 'this breaking away is a demand and command of reason, though the all-invasive factuality of violence necessitates counter-violence in order to restore a situation of civilized, i.e. rational and reasonable behaviour' (Peperzak 1995: 212), and this leads him to conclude that 'Hegel's hero is more reasonable and more spiritual than Hobbes's tyrant' (Peperzak 1995: 212). Using violence to suppress the 'natural violence' that exists among humans is not absent from Hegel, however, and indeed the claim of 'reasonableness' can only be attributed to these state-founding personalities retrospectively and only if one accepts that their actions were for the sake of a noble political end. Once again, we see violence relegated to the realm of 'nature', while political life is endowed with reason, rationality, spirit – that is, those things which force and violence supposedly are not. For Balibar, 'spirit violently eliminates (ostensibly) its own barbarian roots, its own *primordial violence*, equated with nature and at once contingent and unfree. History is a violent conversion of violence conceived as a process of incessant denaturation' (2015: 47).[21]

The ambivalent status of violence in Hegel's system of right is confirmed by what he says in the *Encyclopaedia*:

the fight for recognition and the submission to a master is the *phenomenon* within which the living-in-common of men was born, as a beginning of States. *Violence*, which, in this phenomenon, is a foundation, is not for all that a foundation of *right*, although it constitutes the *necessary* and *justified* moment in the passage which goes from the *state* of consciousness drowned in desire and in singularity to the state of universal self-consciousness. It is the exterior or *phenomenal beginning* of States, not their *substantial principle*. (in Nancy 1982: 495)

So, while violent struggle lies at the 'beginning' of states, it is not the foundation of right. On the face of it, this is a strange and paradoxical formulation which sees violence as beginning, but not foundation, necessary and justified, yet external to states themselves.[22] Of course, were violence to be the foundation, rather than the beginning, of the state, Hegel would have to admit that violence is not contingent and irrational but is itself rational *and* necessary. Hegel must exclude this violence along temporal and racial lines[23] in order to ascribe 'progress' to history and, indeed, to ensure that the *rechtstaat* is seen not as a *consequence* of violence but rather its negation. Indeed, as Balibar demonstrates, for Hegel there is a 'speculative equivalence of violence and contingency as manifestations of "the irrational"' (2015: 45). Violence can then be characterized as necessary, and justified as a negation of the 'irrational'.

The relationship that Hobbes posits between violence and nature is therefore reaffirmed by Hegel and this has important implications for those Hegel deems in a 'primitive state of nature', which he describes as 'in fact a state of animality' (1975b: 178). Hegel's now infamous characterizations of Africa and African people places the state of nature in a geographical locale while simultaneously excluding it from the trajectory of world spirit. Africa, Hegel remarks, 'has no history in the true sense of the word' (1975b: 190). It is the relationship that people in Africa have to nature that is crucial in Hegel's construction of universality and world spirit as that which Africa is not. This in itself, for Hegel, is a question of order: 'but although these natural forces, as well as sun, moon, trees, and animals are recognised as powers in their own right, they are not seen as having an eternal law or providence behind them, or as forming part of a universal and permanent natural order' (1975b: 179). The recognition of providence and order is what distinguishes European man from the 'savage' and is ultimately what makes *mediation* between universal and particular possible (as was also the case for Christian theologians). This point will be explored more fully in Chapter 5, but for now we should note that in Hegel, universality is the preserve of European minds.

In Balibar's reading of Hegel, 'History is not continuous progress but progress that overcomes the appearance of regression and destruction; in the course of it, the accumulation of violence, suffering and evil is *productively converted* in the forces of emancipation, culture, civilization, and order' (p. 42). In reality, however, a productive conversion can only take place with the right conditions – that is, that those who wield it are acting in the service of universal spirit. If one remains 'particular' as Hegel makes clear in his remarks on civil society, then the only social bond is one of external restriction and constraint. It is perhaps in this light that we should understand his comments on 'the negro' who only 'abides in himself'... and in Africa 'man remains at a standstill' (in Chu 2018: 418). Thus what has been implied as a contradiction in Hegel's thought – his ambivalent endorsement of slavery – might be read more productively as being coherent. For Zakiyyah Iman Jackson, the point is as follows: 'the African is not capable of the rational universality embedded in the concepts of law, ethics and morality... Hegel formulates most systematically a conception of "the African" that is both *of* humanity but not *in* humanity. Thus, humanity is not strictly a biological imperative but a cultural achievement in Hegelian thought' (2020: 30). That both the poor and rabble have at least the *potential* to be raised up to the level of the universal is clear even if this potential is not actualized in those who do not own property or recognize the state. The same cannot be said for Hegel's characterizations of Africans who have no 'consciousness of his freedom' and because of this 'consequently sinks down to a mere Thing – an object of no value' (1975).

What Hegel says about 'coercion' is instructive. *Coercion*, as Hegel has it either by 'a schoolmaster, or coercion directed against savagery and brutishness' is not an initial act of violence but is rather a counterviolence, an act of coercion that follows and responds to an initial act of coercion – 'the merely natural will is *in itself* a force against the intrinsic [*an sich seined*] Idea of freedom which must be protected against such an uncivilized will and be made to prevail within it' (2008: 97). 'Coercion' for Hegel in the sense above is always already legitimate because it is a response to an initial 'force' against freedom. Thus we see the existence of the state of nature and the 'merely natural will' not simply as antithetical to ethical life but as a force that is pitted *against* freedom, in other words as something that threatens freedom and against which freedom must be protected. The implications of this will be explored further in Chapter 5, but for now it is worth noting that Hegel sees in Africa, and in the people that reside there, not a latent potentiality for their particularity to mediated with universality, but a necessarily violent vacuum where not only is there not freedom but from which freedom must be guarded against. Coercive violence against 'savagery' will therefore always already be 'necessary' and 'justified'. This violence that is marked by necessity is thus distinguished from violence that is *contingent*. If police power can be characterized by the violence of contingency and contingent violence as we've seen, then this violence is expressed by necessity – outside of the scene of universality and ethical life – but nevertheless constitutive of it by producing that scene and its 'outside'.

The idea, furthermore, that the Idea of freedom must be made to 'prevail' in the uncivilized also attests to a constantly frustrated logic: given the status of the African in Hegel as being 'at a standstill'. The 'indignant' disposition that Hegel assigns to the rabble and that stands as testament to their potential capacity for the universal – even as they might refuse it – is not present in Hegel's remarks on Africa. This brings to the fore the importance of not subsuming the experience of Black people in the global space as an experience of the proletariat or to make an equivalence between the experience of 'the worker' whose demands can cohere around issues of work and exploitation. For the Black person's position is, as Wilderson argues, incoherent through, and disarticulating of, 'Gramscian categories: work, progress, production, exploitation, and historical self-awareness' (2003a: 21). Even more, for Wilderson, Black people 'live in the world, but exist outside of civil society' (2003: 237), and this is why, he argues that for Black people, it is the case that 'civil society *itself* – rather than its abuses or shortcomings – is a state of emergency' (2003a: 19). What Wilderson here points to, and I will go on to discuss, is the notion that police power does not become excessive or 'brutal' in the face of emergency but that the emergency/normal situation divide is rendered indifferent through the nature/violence nexus that is not *within* civil society but constitutive of it, through anti-Black police violence.

Unsurprisingly, however, Hegel provides us with an account which distinguishes between times of peace and 'situations of exigency' (2008: 266). Times of peace are constituted by the individual pursuit of one's own ends which is 'brought back to the aim of the whole' through 'direct influence of higher authority' (2008: 266). In situations of exigency, however, the various powers within the state '[fuse] into the simple concept of sovereignty' (2008: 266). It is only at this point, 'that ideality comes into its proper actuality' (2008: 267). For Marx, Hegel has presented a stark reality: 'A proper reality, accrues to this ideality only in "war or a situation of exigency" so that the essence of the real existing state is seen to be a situation of war or exigency, while its peaceful "condition" consists precisely of the war and exigency of self-seeking'. (1992: 79) What I will go on to show, however, is that it is precisely in the figure of police that the distinction between 'peace' and exigency cannot be maintained.

Furthermore and while these themes will be examined in more detail in Chapter 4, for now we must note the idea that Marx has underlined that not only does state sovereignty attain its actuality in times of 'emergency' but also sovereignty, for Hegel, becomes 'blind unconscious substance' (1992: 79) that ultimately must terminate in an individual: the monarch (1992: 81). That Hegel's sovereign is necessarily an individual is made clear when he writes that 'sovereignty, at first simply the universal *thought* of this ideality, comes into *existence* only as subjectivity certain of itself, as the will's abstract and to that extent ungrounded self-determination in which finality of decision is rooted' (2008: 267). This conceptualization of sovereignty leads Marx to claim that it is 'nothing but the Idea of *caprice,* of the *decision* of the *will*' (1992: 81). This is illuminated when we turn to the issue of pardoning criminals which, by necessity, is a 'groundless decision' (Hegel 2008: 275)[24] that only the sovereign can take. It is groundless precisely in the sense it does not stem from any metaphysical principle or law – it is merely the contingent decision and will of the sovereign that can enact a pardon. Curious, then, that Hegel describes this right as 'one of the highest acknowledgements of spirit' (Hegel 2008: 275). This elevates what one might assume is an exceptional and relatively unimportant power to the status of something much larger and more fundamental in Hegel's thought. That sovereign power must be invested in an individual[25] has been read by some as contradicting the spirit of his philosophy.[26] As I have shown, however, contingency and arbitrary decisions are not incidental to Hegel's philosophy of right but exist by *necessity* in lawmaking, policing and indeed in sovereign power itself.

In this light, it is also worth considering Hegel's treatment of crime and punishment. Punishment and coercion are not, for Hegel, an unfortunate evil to be meted out in order to exact revenge[27] but rather 'crime, as the will which is null in itself, *eo ipso* contains its negation and this negation as manifested as punishment' (2008: 104) and further 'members of a court of law are, indeed, also persons, but their will is the universal will of the law and they aim to import into the punishment nothing except what is implied in the nature of the thing' (2008: 106). Lawmakers, like the state-founding heroes that preceded them, are not carrying out actions that are the implementation of their own subjective will, rather they embody in their person a universal will. However,

Hegel does not leave it there but rather insists that in the gap between the law and its application[28] – an inevitable consequence of the fact that the law is not applied mechanically (2008: 200) – or indeed, in the universal being applied to the singular case; 'the concept merely lays down a general limit, within which vacillation is still possible' (2008: 202). Crucially, however, he adds 'this vacillation must be terminated, however, in the interest of getting something done, and for this reason there is a place within that limit for contingent and arbitrary decisions' (2008: 202). Thus we see that the elimination of contingency in history (Hegel 1975: 28), indeed the regulation of all people 'in accordance with a rational norm' (Balibar 2015: 44), presupposes that which it supposedly sets out to eliminate. In short, if the goal is the 'self-elimination of chance' (Balibar 2015: 45) this requires agents who are authorized to act in arbitrary and contingent ways.

What the preceding discussion has uncovered, then, is though Hegel wants to distance himself from a Hobbesian state of fear, he nevertheless creates one himself. As Andrew Benjamin has highlighted, given that the sovereign must act outside of the sphere of right – the groundless decisions that are made and the contingency this brings to light – means that there is an 'always already present sense of threat' (2015: 152). This threat, the threat of contingent violence and the violence of contingency, is not, however, the same as violence characterized as a necessity – the violence that is foundational and constitutive – but construed as external to – states. In order to understand this further and how what Denise Ferriera da Silva calls 'the subjects of necessitas... where the state deploys its forces of self-preservation' (p. 378), a deeper consideration of the nexus of violence and nature as an anti-Black paradigm will need to be undertaken, a task that I attempt in Chapter 5.

Seemingly sublating the positions that have gone before him, Hegel has been seen as both continuing and breaking with Aristotle and the Greeks (Ilting 1971: 97), Hobbes (Taminaux 1985 and Peperzak 1995) and of course Adam Smith (Avineri 1972: 147). Forging a midway between the Greek emphasis of the collective over the individual and the liberal emphasis on the individual over the collective, Hegel sees his own organic, mediated unity as existing in and through non-natural institutions that exist after and aside and against barbaric natural 'disorder'. The assumed 'gap' or point of non-correspondence between universal and particular and also between the monarch's decisions and their application are given as distinct but linked reasons for the existence of police. But if there was any doubt as to whether the particular individual has any claim against the state in Hegel, this is quashed when Hegel remarks that 'this substantial unity is an absolute unmoved end in itself, in which freedom comes into its supreme right. On the other hand, this final end has supreme right against the individual, whose supreme duty is to be a member of the state' (2008: 228).

Theorizations of sovereignty run into many aporias and contradictions not only on their own terms – due to the lawless character of sovereign decisions – made clear in 'emergency situations', but also, and more importantly here, as a consequence of the critical place of the police not being considered. The preceding chapter has brought to light the key issues in this regard: Hegel ascribes a function to police – the mediation of universal and particular – that not only must be continually frustrated but also and perhaps more importantly underlines how Hegel conceives of freedom against nature and natural violence – the state of nature – that he sees as existing in the continent of Africa. Second, both police and sovereign power are shown, despite his critique of Fichte, to be unconstrained and unbounded in times of emergency. This contingency and arbitrariness means that Hegel, though wanting to distance his state from a state of domination and force, does not succeed due to the character of sovereign and police power outlined earlier. It is precisely the unbounding of police power and its relationship to the exception that is the concern of the second part of this book.

Part II

# Police order

# 3

# Law, sovereignty and the exception
## Benjamin and modern police

In thinking through the relation of law and police, one is commonly confronted with the idea that police are the enforcement or embodiment of law. Liberal jurisprudence has conceived them as a functional institution tasked with detecting and punishing any infraction of the law. This presumes a temporal dynamic where law comes first and then the institution of the police enforces this already existing law. I claim, however, that this common perception of the police fails to capture the nature of law, the character of the police or the connection between the two. It therefore actively misconstrues the complex and overlapping relations between law, violence and the police.

In the prologue I indicated that arguments which see police power as subsumed under law with the advent of the liberal state were insufficient to explain police power. If liberal treatments of police tend to see police power as enforcing or upholding the law there are also critical studies of police which also fail to grasp the locus of police power. As I discussed in relation to Foucault, there is a process in which sovereign power is seen as transformed (from sovereign power to biopolitics) or subsumed into something other – and police becomes *either* a limited institution enforcing the law or a catch-all concept pertaining to the regulation of society which takes many forms. These views fail to grasp the relationship of police to order, itself based on the relationship between universal and particular – the philosophical bedrock upon which police has been thought.

What, then, is the character of police power in modernity – after the decline of the 'police state'? What happens to sovereign power once it is no longer in a position to act immediately and directly on its subjects as was the case under absolutism? How are we to understand arguments that transform the 'rule of police' into the 'rule of law' in modern states?[1] And what relationship do the police have to law and its application? To answer these questions, I turn to a different constellation of thinkers whose thought on police, I argue, enable us to grasp the nature of police power in modernity and its relationship to order: Carl Schmitt and Walter Benjamin. It is in their writings that the ambiguous transformations of sovereign power in modernity are illuminated. This prepares the theoretical terrain for a different understanding of police power – one that treats it neither as merely enforcing the law nor as a synonym of social control. Rather, police power travels along the same vectors as sovereign power, yet acts in dislocation from it. Indeed, through a consideration of the exception we can begin to see police power as a groundless force-of-law, one which suspends the law while claiming to apply it.

Before turning to Benjamin, I will briefly outline Schmitt's conceptualization of sovereignty and the exception. Schmitt's theorization of the exception is useful for thinking through police power. However, his diagnosis of modern sovereignty, which he aligns with the increasing excision of transcendence falls short precisely because he does not consider the figure of police. Benjamin, on the other hand, does consider the police but leaves open the question of how police relate to sovereign power. Bringing together Benjamin's critique of Schmitt's notion of sovereignty in the *Origin of German Tragic Drama* with his comments on police power in the *Critique of Violence*, I attend to the particular character of modern police power and its relationship to sovereignty and law. This prepares the groundwork for properly analysing modern police power, neither as an execution of a sovereign will nor as the implementation of law, but as a *force-of-law* or a being-in-force without law.

## Schmitt's sovereign

For Schmitt, political concepts are analogically structured by, and are secularized forms of, theological concepts:

> all significant concepts of the modern theory of the state are secularized theological concepts – in which they were transferred from theology to the theory of the state, whereby for example, the omnipotent God became the omnipotent lawgiver – but also because of their systematic structure, the

recognition of which is necessary for a sociological consideration of these concepts. The exception in jurisprudence is analogous to the miracle in theology. Only by being aware of this analogy can we appreciate the manner in which the philosophical ideas of the state developed in the last centuries. (2005: 36)

Schmitt sees sovereignty as structurally identical to a theological notion of God as author and creator.[2] He identifies a 'continuous thread' that 'runs through the metaphysical, political and sociological conceptions that postulate the sovereign as a personal unity and primeval creator' (2005: 47). Schmitt does not merely propose that political concepts are analogous to theological concepts; rather, there exists a structural identity between them that goes beyond mere analogy.[3] Schmitt attempts to prove that political concepts have a corresponding 'real' and metaphysical form. Thus, for Schmitt, every epoch has its own conception of sovereignty that corresponds to a 'metaphysical image' (2005: 46).[4] As discussed previously, Schmitt identifies Hobbes as a key figure for this political theology.[5] For Schmitt, the modern concept of sovereignty emerged from a need to produce order in the absence of a 'metaphysical image' of a natural order produced by an interventionist deity. No longer was political philosophy the contemplative exercise of observing a predictable, rhythmic, cosmic order; it was now faced with the exigency of upheaval, civil war, and the demand to produce order out of chaos.

Schmitt answers the question of who produces order in the absence of God with the twin cardinal concepts of the exception and the decision. Schmitt's famous dictum 'sovereign is he who decides on the exception' (2005: 5) conjoins the two terms into a singular substance, sovereignty. The phrase implies two moments in the sovereign decision: (a) to decide and declare an exception exists and (b) to decide what is to be done in the face of said exception. Indeed, the problem of the 'decision', and, relatedly, who decides only becomes salient once order is no longer conceived of as natural or predictable. Here, the question of contingency is inscribed into the concept of sovereignty through the thought of the exception. The exception (arising from contingent conditions itself) necessitates a decision that cannot be given in advance, or, in other words, a decision that is groundless: 'looked at normatively', Schmitt writes, 'the decision emanates from nothingness' (2005: 31).

Occurring *ex nihilo*, the Schmittian exception cannot be decided upon in advance, nor can its constitutive content be identified before the fact.[6] The actions necessary to eliminate the threat cannot be foretold and therefore the legal order absolutely cannot account for the exception. The decision that an exception exists cannot be derived from a norm, and so cannot be 'codified in the existing legal order' (Schmitt 2005: 6). Schmitt characterizes the exception as 'a case of extreme peril, a danger to the existence of the state or the like' (Schmitt 2005: 6). Yet, and Schmitt is emphatic on this point, it is not the case that any emergency constitutes an exception; rather, the exception 'is to be understood to refer to a general concept in the theory of the state' (Schmitt 2005: 5). The decision is a pure originary act, not mediated by any legal norm. If the exception is the product of a decision by an unmediated sovereign will, it gives sovereignty life by providing closure against a chaotic, irrational outside and making distinct an orderly inside.

In order to grasp exactly what Schmitt means by the exception and order he is worth quoting at length:

> such a jurisprudence confronts the extreme case disconcertedly, for not every extraordinary measure, not every police emergency measure or emergency decree is necessarily an exception. What characterizes an exception is principally unlimited authority, which means the suspension of the entire existing order. In such a situation it is clear that the state remains, whereas law recedes. Because the exception is different from anarchy and chaos, order in the juristic sense still prevails even if it is not of the ordinary kind. (Schmitt 2005: 12)

For Schmitt the exception necessarily entails the suspension of the *entire* legal order. This feature distinguishes it from a 'police emergency'. The exception cannot exist in part but must constitute a whole, suspending a totality of legal relations and replacing them with the force-of-law.[7] Schmitt, however, emphasizes that the exception is not simply chaos and that order 'in the juristic sense' remains even if this 'order' is different than the one that normally prevails. Under the state of exception, while the order that prevails may count as 'juristic', it is manifestly distinct from law: law has retreated, yet (extraordinary) order reigns. We thus find in *Political Theology* a tripartite distinction between juristic chaos or anarchy (2005: 14), the exception or extraordinary order (2005: 12), and the legal system that exists in a 'normal situation' (2005: 13). Order is thus not reducible to legality given that it exists in the exception as well. Schmitt therefore claims that the exception is distinct from anarchy and in so doing annexes anomic violence to the law through the exception.[8]

By placing what cannot be deduced from legal norms simultaneously at the centre and at the most extreme point of his theory of sovereignty, Schmitt's political topology renders the normal situation marginal in any contemplation of the state: 'the rule proves nothing; the exception proves everything: it confirms not only the rule, but also its existence, which derives only from the exception' (2005: 15).[9] If sovereignty is a secular substitute for God in the world, then the exception is the manner in which the sovereign manifestly intervenes in that world, just as God intervened through miracles (Schmitt 2005: 36). Schmitt laments and attempts to reinvigorate the loss of this intervention via miracle, or in political terms, the sovereign's intervention into the 'normal' legal situation via the exception. We thus come back to the idea, that I challenged in reference to Smith, that the pivot on which sovereignty turns is intervention. Without intervention, sovereign power remains invisible and thus devoid of real power. Schmitt reads liberalism and legal positivism as disavowing this form of intervention.[10] He rails against 'the idea of the modern constitutional state triumphed together with deism, a theology and metaphysics that banished the miracle from the world' (2005: 36). For Schmitt, liberalism's ascent means increasingly that the transcendent pole of sovereignty is pushed aside in favour of immanence.

Schmitt charges liberalism with an 'offensive thrust against feudalism, reaction and the police state' which was 'judged essentially peaceful, in contrast to warlike force and repression' (2007: 75). *The Concept of the Political* thus (and in slight contradistinction to *Political Theology*) seems to reiterate a common trope I identified in the prologue, whereby Schmitt casts political economy and liberalism as the negation of the police state: a peaceful, self-regulating order that overcomes absolutism's violently interventionist order. Together with his comments on the excision of the exception, Schmitt presents a highly interventionist 'police state' increasingly replaced by a highly technocratic non-interventionist (non-police) state. He goes on to describe a historical development towards the 'total state' where there was a trend towards the 'democratic identity of state and society' which '[put] an end to the principle that an apolitical economy is independent of the state and that the state is apart from the economy' (2007: 25). The idea that the state (or sovereign) could then 'intervene' thus becomes absurd under these conditions. This is the reason, for Schmitt, that as liberalism and positive jurisprudence advance, the transcendent is increasingly made immanent because state and society become increasingly indistinguishable. Moreover, conceptions of transcendence will no longer be credible to most educated people, who will settle for either a more or less clear immanence-pantheism or a positive indifference toward any metaphysics. Insofar as it retains the concept of God, the immanence philosophy which found its greatest systematic architect in Hegel, draws God into the world and permits law and the state to emanate from the immanence of the objective. (2005: 50)

Yet there is a tension in Schmitt's work on this point. He charges positive jurisprudence with disavowing state intervention while simultaneously relying on state intervention for its very functioning; 'the state' Schmitt writes, 'intervenes everywhere' (2005: 38). It is thus not simply the case that liberalism or positive jurisprudence expels the state and banishes intervention, rather, it disguises or disavows that which it still ultimately rests on: the decision. In Schmitt's own words:

> But sovereignty (and thus the state itself) resides in deciding this controversy, that is, in determining definitively what constitutes public order and security, in determining when they are disturbed, and so on . . . After all, every legal order is based on a decision, and also the concept of the legal order, which is applied as something self-evident, contains within it the contrast of the two distinct elements of the juristic – norm and decision. *Like every other order, the legal order rests on a decision and not on a norm*. (emphasis added, Schmitt 2005: 9–10)[11]

Given that there is 'no norm that applies to chaos' the decision on whether a 'normal' situation obtains is prior to the law. The decision, however, affects and modifies the legal order. Every decision, Schmitt writes, necessarily contains a 'constitutive element' (2005: 26). This constitutive element gives the law its form and makes it more akin to a living thing than a mechanically applied static element. The problem of the decision arises, in Schmitt's terms, because the law cannot translate itself into reality and a gap opens between law and its application: 'because the legal idea cannot realize itself, it needs a particular organization and form before it can be translated into reality' (2005: 28). Schmitt argues that legal positivism simply cannot account for this problem. The idea of the rule of law contains a transcendental deficiency – it has no concept of the specificity of legal form. There is, then, no concept of law or the state as an evolving thing that changes with each decision, and with this comes a gradual 'technologization' that reduces the state to a 'machine' (Schmitt 1996: 42). Indeed, it is this, Schmitt argues that constitutes a 'negation of state and the political, its neutralizations, depoliticalizations ... are polemically directed against a specific state and its political power'. In so doing, liberalism, he goes on, 'has attempted only to tie the political to the ethical and subjugate it to economics' (2007: 61).

Schmitt thus touches on an ambiguity at the heart of liberalism and legal positivism: its self-presentation of the state as value-neutral and resting on an autopoietic system of law is deceptive. However, Schmitt misses how and why this is the case: simply charting a process of technologization increasingly governed by immanence says little about the character of sovereign power in modernity, or indeed the increasingly complex relation between transcendence and immanence. As an engagement with Benjamin will show, the changing character of sovereign power in modernity cannot be reduced, neither to the simple proposition that transcendence is disavowed while still being secretly operative under the liberal state nor that transcendence has been simply excised. The transcendent is rather *emptied* and this, Benjamin argues, endows modern sovereign power with catastrophic force.

## The transcendent made immanent: Benjamin's response

That Walter Benjamin's *Origin of German Tragic Drama* was in part written as a response to Schmitt's *Political Theology* is now well known.[12] Moreover, as Agamben has tried to reconstruct, there appears to be an 'exoteric dossier' in the form of a debate between them that 'took place in various forms and at differing levels of intensity between 1925 and 1956' (2005: 52). What is important here, however, is that the question of sovereignty forms the crux of this debate and the way in which they conceive it in modernity following a process of secularization.[13] As Beatrice Hannsen argues Benjamin's analysis of the German *Trauerspiel* and the baroque era can be read 'predominantly as a study on the literary, aesthetic and philosophical foundations of the modern era' (2000: 50). It must be noted, however, that while Benjamin and Schmitt both agree in different ways that the concepts of modernity result from secularization, they have very different notions of secularization. For Benjamin, secularization entails a transformation of the way in which space and time are conceived, and, in particular, a foregrounding of space over time.[14]

Benjamin argues that the baroque period saw a radical transformation in the conceptualization of time. Previously thought of as linear, developmental and ultimately progressing towards an eschatological climax, time loses this sense of religious fulfilment and redemption (1977: 79). A preoccupation with space then filled the void, and 'history merges into the setting' (1977: 92). What is the consequence of this shift for the conception of sovereignty? While both Benjamin and Schmitt identify political-theological upheavals that result in a loss of transcendence, they disagree on when they took place. For Schmitt, the seventeenth and eighteenth centuries were still very much in thrall to the idea of transcendence, through the figure of the decisive personalistic sovereign. For Benjamin, however, the baroque period is devoid of transcendence that previous eras had known, and in particular, 'knows no eschatology' (1977: 66).[15] This loss of eschatology entails a sovereign far removed from Schmitt's: 'the level of the state of creation, the terrain on which the *Trauerspiel* is enacted, also unmistakably exercises a determining influence on the sovereign. However highly he is enthroned over subject and state, his status is confined to the world of creation; he is the lord of creatures but he remains a creature' (1977: 85).

For both Benjamin and Schmitt, then, the question of contingency comes to the fore with these secularization processes, albeit in different ways. For Benjamin, losing an eschatological understanding of time means that where once events could be found to have meaning as a consequence of the end, or eschaton, its absence leads to a view of disparate events with no essential meaning. Simultaneously, the figure of the sovereign, reduced to its creaturely characteristics as the 'hopelessness of the earthly condition' (1977: 81) means that what might have been a transcendent, redemptive figure is subsumed under what Benjamin sees as the 'rash flight into a nature deprived of grace' (1977: 81.). In this way, earthly power does not mirror transcendent, divine power but is part of the world. However, this transformation does not deprive the ruler of power; on the contrary, 'the ruler, the supreme creature, the beast, can re-emerge with unsuspected power' (1977: 86). On the other hand, for Schmitt, secularization inscribes contingency into the very foundation of sovereignty. Without divine order, contingency becomes the main concern and well-spring of the production of order. That is to say, the sovereign function must be God-like, producing order in the face of the exception. Benjamin alludes to this conception when he writes that 'the function of the tyrant is the restoration of order in the state of emergency: a dictatorship whose utopian goal will always be to replace the unpredictability of historical accident with the iron constitution of the law of nature' (1977: 74). However, and in contrast to Schmitt, Benjamin's reading of the baroque sovereign does not replace unpredictability with order but is plagued by indecision (1977: 71). If Schmitt aims to identify the ways in which the sovereign is like a God on earth, Benjamin's wants to demonstrate that sovereignty, at its foundational moment in the modern era, was manifestly un-Godlike. The sovereign no longer transcends the world, but as the loss of a sense of historical time (in particular a Christian sense of time) and eschatology proceeds, the sovereign must become part of the world.

For Benjamin, it is not so much that losing transcendence defangs sovereign power. As Samuel Weber argues 'the function assigned to sovereignty by the baroque, according to Benjamin, is that of transcending transcendence by making it immanent, an internal part of the state and of the world, of the state of the world' (1992: 12). That the sovereign is no longer 'God-like' does not mean that it becomes less powerful or more benign, but rather, its violence becomes catastrophic (Benjamin 1977: 66).[16] Indeed, it is precisely that 'an antithesis to the historical ideal of restoration [the baroque] is haunted by the idea of catastrophe. And it is in response to this antithesis that the theory of the state of emergency is devised' (Benjamin 1977: 66.). The state of emergency appears not as a constitutive ordering element but a desperate, ineffective response to an absence of an overarching narrative of redemption and the inescapable feeling of a lurking catastrophe. It is not that the transcendent disappears with modernity but that it becomes 'emptied of everything which contains the slightest breath of this world' (1977: 66) and so is only evacuated of all 'possible representable content' (Weber 1992: 12). Rather than 'doing away with transcendence, however, such emptying only endows it with a force that is all the more powerful: that of the vacuum, of the absolute and unbounded other, which, since it is no longer representable, is also no longer localizable as "out there" or a "beyond"' (Weber 1992: 12).

Benjamin and Schmitt do agree that modernity inaugurates a new era of disorder.[17] Both describe how this legitimates untrammelled sovereign power. If, as Koepnick writes, 'absolute monarchy originates from the tumultuous void of the sixteenth and early seventeenth century, and its explicit function is to exclude the possibility that history once more falls into the abyss of chaos' (1996: 287) then Benjamin shows how sovereign power catastrophically fails to do so. Benjamin charts a contradictory process whereby the increasing demand for order only finds a further malfunctioning of power and, in the concomitant view of nature as decaying and degenerating, the deepening of the crisis of authority.[18] This is, however, not something unique to baroque sovereigns, and, as Koepnick argues, Benjamin's text 'overtly alludes to the cultural conditions and political predicaments of the 1920s; the *trauerspiel* book simultaneously reads the baroque through the lenses of Weimar and mirrors Weimar in the baroque' (1996: 280). Crucially, then, we see a logic of sovereign power in which its named function – to produce order out of disorder – not only legitimizes its violent power but also fails to do any such thing. Not merely a feature of seventeenth-century sovereignty, baroque sovereignty, for Benjamin and in contrast to Schmitt, 'triggers a pathogenesis of modern politics' (1996: 290).[19]

Schmitt sees in liberalism, then, a mythological, fantastical vulnerability of sovereignty. Benjamin masterfully subverts this conception, showing that where Schmitt sees sovereignty and sovereign power at its zenith – the sixteenth and seventeenth centuries (which is the time of Hobbes too) – is paradoxically where it malfunctions and radically *differs* from a transcendent God. Conversely, we might say, then, that where Schmitt sees sovereignty at its weakest (under the liberal state): all is not what it seems. The malfunctioning of sovereign power is not the same as weakness, and indeed the *indifferentiation* of exception and rule that Benjamin outlines in the eighth thesis on the philosophy of history, does not entail sovereignty's excision:

> The tradition of the oppressed teaches us that the 'emergency situation' in which we live is the rule. We must arrive at a concept of history that corresponds to this. Then it will become clear that the task before us is the introduction of a real state of emergency; and our position in the struggle against fascism will thereby improve. (Benjamin 2005a)

As I began to argue at the end of Chapter 2, in Marx's reading of Hegel, sovereignty attains actuality only in conditions of emergency. Hegel also thought these conditions actualized police power and set its infinite unbounding in motion. Where Hegel described an 'emergency situation' in which no objective line could delimit police action and the police may 'draw into its orbit everything it possibly can' (Hegel 2008: 216), Benjamin shows the distinction between emergency and norm no longer holds. Refusing Schmitt's characterization of the exception as an existential threat to the state, Zartaloudis (following Agamben) remarks:

> The state of exception is constitutive of the juridical order rather than some mere unusual instance or crisis. The law of the exception, if posed as a limit concept, always separates itself into a virtual duality or bipolarity: an *anomic* realm, a space and time devoid of law and a *nomic* realm, a space and time of juridical rule; in other words into a constituent or constitutive and a constituted power whose relation is paradoxically assumed as juridical in itself. The pseudo-dialectical economic functionality between its two posited realms instead shows that the law is grounded on an undecidable void, a *kenomatic* state and as such on a particular fiction of *anomie* as the outside of law. The functional relation between the fiction of an anomic state and a nomic state presupposes the state of exception as a virtual *kenomatic* (void) state that now covers the space of the *polis* in its entirety. (Zartaloudis 2010: 133)

I will attend to this in further detail in the following chapter; however, for now it is worth noting that the fictitious state of anomie posited as being outside of the law paradoxically sustains the law itself (as we saw with Hobbes). While here Zartaloudis focuses on the exception, I suggest that the figure of police ties together the fictitious anomic state and nomic state. To grasp this, however, requires looking more closely at Benjamin's *Critique of Violence*, where his analysis of police illuminates the exceptional character of police power.

## Violence and critique

Benjamin's *Critique of Violence* outlines his desire for a critique that enables a view of the 'outside' of law, and, crucially, how this 'outside' can be considered only with a philosophical-historical view of law. As Andrew Benjamin has noted this 'entails constituting the appearance of law's law-like quality as an object of knowledge' (2013: 106). Law, which must necessarily present itself as general and universal, that is, 'law-like', cannot tolerate, yet is fundamentally dependent on and presupposes, an 'outside'. Critique, in Benjamin's sense of the word, realizes this claim. Benjamin is worth quoting at length:

> The critique of violence is the philosophy of its history. 'Philosophy' of that history because only the idea of its outcome makes possible a critical, discriminating, decisive approach to its temporal data. A gaze directed only at what is close to hand can at most perceive a dialectical rising and falling in the lawmaking and law-preserving formations of violence. The law governing their oscillation rests on the circumstance that all law-preserving violence, in its duration, indirectly weakens the law-making violence represented by it, through the suppression of hostile counter-violence . . . this lasts until either new forces or those earlier suppressed triumph over the hitherto law-making violence and thus found a new law, destined in its turn to decay. (1978: 299)

The *Trauserspiel* also presents this rhythmic, dialectical rising and falling, where Benjamin writes that 'the constantly repeated spectacle of princely rise and fall. . . stood before the poets' eyes not so much as a morality play but by virtue of its persistence as the natural side of the historical process' (1977: 88). This 'confusion' (Weber 2008: 181) of history with nature characterizes the baroque play and indeed sees only an inevitable rising and falling of princes 'identified with the nature of a fallen creation lacking any discernible, representable possibility of either grace or salvation. It is the loss of a redemptive perspective that marks the baroque conception of history and renders it inauthentic and akin to a fallen state of nature' (Weber 2008: 181). It is this, then, that the sovereign and law have in common; both are made to appear as destined to rise up and decay before a new one rises up again. Benjamin's critique aims to expose the radical contingency of this oscillation.

Benjamin's critique is not strictly normative,[20] but rather a sustained attempt to understand violence; to analyse and judge it without recourse to a juridical framework or moral criteria.[21] Counter-posing positive and natural law, Benjamin demonstrates that neither tradition allows for a critique of violence as such, only an assessment of means or ends. In Benjamin's words, 'if natural law can judge all existing law only in criticizing its ends, so positive law can judge all law only in criticizing its means' (1978: 278). However, Benjamin tells us that positive law is somewhat more acceptable as a starting point 'because it undertakes a fundamental distinction between kinds of violence independently of cases of their application' (1978: 279). Indeed, positive law distinguishes between sanctioned and unsanctioned violence, because positive law demands of 'all violence a proof of its historical origin, which under certain conditions is declared legal, sanctioned' (1978: 280). Nevertheless, a critique of violence cannot satisfactorily occur within the sphere of positive law, given that both natural and positive law share the same assumption that 'just ends may be attained by justified means, justified means employed for just ends' (1978: 278). This, for Benjamin, does not enable a critique of violence but rather remains trapped in the legal order of representation, in which violence is considered just or unjust depending on its relationship to the juridical framework. If the ends are just, the means used are legitimate, and thus the 'criteriology would then concern only the application of violence, not violence itself' (Derrida 2002: 265). A 'critique' of violence is thus not an assessment of its legitimacy according to pre-established criteria based on the means used or the ends sought, but seeks to unravel the object of critique, in this case *gewalt*, in order to situate it historically, philosophically and ground it in experience.[22]

The question remains, however: How to critique police power? For Benjamin, 'unlike law, which acknowledges in the "decision" determined by place and time a metaphysical category that gives it a claim to critical evaluation, a consideration of the police institution encounters nothing essential at all' (1978: 287). This raises the question as to whether a critique of the police is possible at all given there is no metaphysical category that can give rise to critical evaluation. My purpose here is to show that while Benjamin correctly identifies the absence of a metaphysical category with regard to police power, this does not mean that no critique is possible. Indeed, Benjamin outlines tools in the *Critique of Violence* which can help us to do just this. As I will go on to argue, there is a tension at the centre of the police concept with regard to law. They are intimately connected with the legal order but as such must necessarily operate outside law. As with violence, more generally, for a critique to be possible, a standpoint must be found outside of legal thought to examine the police. From a legal perspective, the police enforce, or apply the law, and through concepts such as 'discretion' police activity is tied to the sphere of the juridical.[23] In this sense they are secondary – first there is the law, and then there is the institution concerned with its application: the police. As I've argued we cannot be content with this formulation, but neither can we say police have no relation to the law either. How then, to conceive of this relation?

## Benjamin's police

Benjamin describes both the institution of police and its violence as 'eerie', 'spectral', 'ghostly' and 'spirit' (1978: 286–7). They are a presence without presence, a formless manifestation 'nowhere tangible, all-pervasive' (1978: 286–7). As previously discussed, Benjamin argues that in law there is at least a 'decision' that 'acknowledges a metaphysical category through which it lays claim to criticism', something absent in the police.[24] This gives rise to the claim that there is no substance in the institution of the police to grasp; it is 'formless' (Benjamin 1978: 287). 'A decision in law' is 'determined by place and time' (Benjamin 1978: 287): it is, as such, inherently contestable. It is marked and refers to a metaphysical category, a substance that one can grasp. The absence of such a decision when it comes to police means that violence 'degenerates' (Benjamin 1978: 287). Not marked by a specific time or place, not referring to anything outside of itself, police violence cannot be grasped and thus contested in the way that (at least hypothetically) a legal decision can.[25]

Given these pronouncements, one would be forgiven for thinking that Benjamin falls precisely into the trap I had previously identified in positing such a deconstructed notion of police that it is merely a synonym for some form of social control. Derrida's analysis of, and disagreement with Benjamin's *Critique of Violence*, however, shows us that this is not the case:

> By definition the police are present or represented everywhere there is force of law [*loi*]. They are present, sometimes invisible but always effective, *wherever there is preservation of the social order*. The police are not only the police (today more or less than ever), they are there [*elle est là*], the figure without face or figure of a *Dasein* coextensive with the *Dasein* of the *polis*. (Derrida 2002: 278, emphasis in original)

Here, Derrida cites the police as 'preserving' social order, and in this way as coextensive with the *Dasein* of the polis. The police are framed not as an institution enforcing the law but as a spectral presence preserving order. Derrida is here referring, however, not to *the* police ('in uniform, occasionally helmeted, armed and organized in a civil structure on a military model to whom the right to strike is refused and so forth') (Derrida 2002: 278). Indeed, Derrida argues that while 'Benjamin would still want for it [police] to remain a determinable and proper figure to the civilized states' (Derrida 2002: 278), his notion of police does not take such a determinable form. Derrida here pushes Benjamin beyond Benjamin, taking what Benjamin says about the ghost-like presence of police to what he sees as its logical conclusion: police is anywhere and everywhere that the preservation of the social order is found. This argument I propose not only fails to grasp the specificity of police power in modernity, given that the institution becomes subsumed under a more general logic of social ordering, but also renders police all but impossible to critique given this all-pervasive, amorphous character.

Benjamin distinguishes between two different types of violence: law-preserving and law-founding (1978: 284), but it quickly becomes clear that this distinction cannot be so readily maintained in the figure of police. However, although Benjamin touches on this central ambiguity he holds on to the distinction. Law-preserving violence occurs in order for the 'subordination of citizens to legislation' (1978: 284) to take place. Law-founding violence, on the other hand, is a violence in which there is a 'victory', the inauguration of a condition of 'peace' establishing new conditions 'being acknowledged as a new "law"' (1978: 8). The legal order becomes constituted as a state of 'peace' in which legal subjects may not use violence, where violence is at one and the same time excluded and included within the legal order itself. This is why 'after the ceremony of war, the ceremony of peace signifies that the victory establishes a new law' (Derrida 2002: 273). This condition of 'peace', however, is in reality not a peace constituted by an absence of violence or an absence of war. Rather, it is a peace that can be understood only as a 'postponement of war' (Caygill 2001: 76).[26] This constitutes one of the ways in which the legal order can present itself as peaceful, against a violent, chaotic pre-legal or post-legal state. That is to say, violence is 'excluded' in that legal subjects may no longer use violence for their own ends (Benjamin 1978: 280), yet is simultaneously included as the very core of the 'non-violent' legal order. In order to continue as law, law must preserve itself through violence.[27] Therefore at stake in this analytic distinction between law-founding and law-preserving violence is the oscillation between the two types of violence. Indeed the legal order is 'destined' (1978: 300) to decay through the repetition of the violence of its preservation. This is so, Benjamin claims, due to the ways in which law suppresses any 'counter-violence' (1978: 300). Once it falls into ruin, a new law, established through violence, is instituted and the cycle begins again.

Despite making an analytical distinction between law-founding and law-preserving violence, Benjamin describes the way in which police violence is 'emancipated' from the conditions that characterize both types of violence. While law-founding violence is described as necessarily revealing 'itself in victory', law-preserving violence is 'subject to the restriction that it abstain from setting itself new ends' (1978: 286). Police violence, however, conforms to neither of these given that its function 'is each and every decree that it enacts with legal entitlement' (1978: 286). It is in the institution of the police, then, that the distinction between lawmaking and law-preserving violence collapses, and in so doing problematizing the very basis of that distinction in itself. Derrida has put it thus:

> In the *Aufhebung* that the police signifies in itself, the police invent law; they make themselves 'rechtsetzend', legislative. The police arrogate the right, arrogate the law . . . each time the law is indeterminate enough to open a possibility for them. Even if they do not make the law [loi], the police behave like a lawmaker in modern times, if not the lawmaker of modern times. Where there are police, which is to say everywhere and even here, one can no longer discern between two types of violence – preserving and founding – and that is the ignoble, ignominious, revolting ambiguity. (2002: 277)

Derrida's conceptualization of the future anterior helps elucidate this law-making power of the police. It is not so much that all police actions *are* legal but rather that they *will have become* legitimate.[28] Law-positing violence is not legitimated by what has gone before but operates by appealing to a future anterior, a coming legal order that will retroactively legitimate that violence. It is a mistake, however, to only see the police as law-positing and law-preserving. As Benjamin argues the idea that the *ends* of all police violence are connected to law is false.[17] In reality, police (re)produce the legal order by acting outside law. Thus, police, in this sense, are not only preserving the law as it stands or founding law. Though there are of course moments when police violence intersects with the law-preserving and law-founding dynamic, what Benjamin highlights is the potential police have to exceed this dynamic. Note that in the institution of the police the distinction between law-preserving and law-founding violence is 'suspended' [*Aufgehoben*] (Benjamin 2013: 118), and thus we find here the law itself also suspended.

## Force-of-law

The problem that we have pointed towards yet not explicitly discussed is the gap between the law and its application:

> In the case of law, the application of a norm is in no way contained within the norm and cannot be derived from it . . . Just as between language and the world, so between the norm and its application there is no internal nexus that allows one to be derived immediately from the other'. (Agamben 2005: 40)[29]

It is in this gap that the idea of the 'force of law' comes to the fore. Derrida states that while there are unenforced laws, there is no law without its applicability, an applicability that must necessarily inhere in force, 'whether this force be direct or indirect, physical or symbolic, exterior or interior brutal or subtly discursive – even hermeneutic – coercive or regulative, and so forth' (2002: 233). In other words, force-of-law refers to the law's potentiality to be applied through force. Force-of-law, in this sense, is not just enforcement but rather refers to the force within the law that 'remind us that law is always an authorised force, a force that justifies itself or is justified in applying itself' (2002: 233). Thus, Derrida's idea of the force-of-law is characterized by the relationship between the law and its application. He finds this force-of-law in, first, the decisions of judges, and second, the police. With regard to judges, Derrida describes an act of judgment, and what it would take for it to come close to something like justice:

> for a decision to be just and responsible, it must [*il faut*], in its proper moment, if there is one, be both regulated and without regulation, it must preserve the law [*loi*] and also destroy it or suspend it enough to have [*pour devoir*] to reinvent it in each case, rejustify it, reinvent it at least in the reaffirmation and the new and free confirmation of its principle. Each case is other, each decision is different and requires an absolutely unique interpretation, which no existing, coded rule can or ought to guarantee absolutely'. (Derrida 2002: 251)

Derrida's language echoes Benjamin's text in which he describes the suspension or collapse of the distinction between law-upholding and law-founding violence. In the judge's action the law must preserve the law, but also destroy it or, if you will, found it, 'reinvent' it in order to come to a just decision. Simply applying a codified rule without the above cannot be a just decision for Derrida, 'simply because there was, in this case, no decision' (2002: 251).

In a judge's decision, there is a temporal dynamic at work that enables us to delineate distinct stages. In Derrida's formulation, the judge's decision must pass through a moment of undecidability in order to be rendered just and responsible. The judge considers the case, interprets the law and makes a decision which in turn alters the law itself. It is precisely in the gap between the law and its application that the moment of justice might arise – in considering a case a judge must reckon with its uniqueness. Thus, Derrida finds in the moment of application a way that the law might be used against itself, a way that 'incorporates its ethical other' (Thurschwell 2005: 189).

What to make, then of the fact that Derrida also locates this force-of-law in the figure of police: 'the police are the force of law [*loi*], they have force of law, the power of the law' (2002: 277). Indeed, as we've seen, the police, given the gap between the law and its application, cannot apply codified rules either. The police must also deal with cases in their absolute singularity. If the power to apply and thus reinvent the law poses an opportunity for something approximating justice to come in, it is striking how, not only is the force-of-law found in police but also how it is precisely this force-of-law which reveals the rotten nature of police power. Paraphrasing Benjamin, Derrida writes that it is in the police we find an 'ignoble, ignominious, revolting ambiguity' (2002: 277) that subtends this mixing of 'founding and preserving' of the law and that, as a result, becomes 'all the more violent for this' (2002: 278). The gap between the law and its application it seems, for Derrida at least, presents an opening not only for justice but also for tyranny.

At stake is not only a question about whether one believes law to be redeemable through the law itself[30] but also how one conceives of this force-of-law that characterizes police power. While Derrida would emphasize the legal effects (i.e. reinvention through interpretation and application) that force-of-law has, Agamben's perspective presents a challenge to this view when he writes that force-of-law

> refers in the technical sense not to the law but to those decrees (which, as we indeed say, have the force of law) that the executive power can be authorized to issue in some situations, particularly in the state of exception. That is to say, the concept of 'force of law' as a technical legal term, defines a separation of the norm's *vis obligandi*, or applicability, from its formal essence, whereby decrees, provisions, and measures that are not formally laws nevertheless acquire their 'force'. (2005: 38)

Thus, for Agamben, the concept of force-of-law itself reveals the gap between the law and its application; the 'essence' of law and the activity which bears its force in the world. However, Agamben finds that there is a distinction between the 'efficacy of the law – which rests absolutely with every valid legislative act and consists in the production of legal effects – and the *force-of-law*, which is instead a relative concept that expresses the position of the law or acts comparable to it' (2005: 37–8) which he locates in entities like the constitution (seen as superior to the law) and executive decrees (seen as inferior). Thus, while Derrida points to the legal effects that the police produce by applying and thus reinventing the law – they 'invent the law, publish ordinances' (2002: 277) – Agamben shows that the force-of-law does not so much produce legal effects but, rather, expresses a force *without* law. In this way, 'acts performed during the suspension of the law escape legal definition since they are neither executions, legislations nor transgressions of the law' (Zartaloudis 2010: 138).

Crucially then, the moments of enforcement or application do not exhaust the relationship between law and violence, however important they might be for understanding this relation. A focus only on these two moments fails to capture those moments in which there is authorized force without law. In short, those moments where police action makes no reference to law but simply is or acts as force. *Polizeigewalt* is not exhausted in law. Indeed there is another modality of violence explained neither by its law-preserving or law-founding qualities, but only in its dis-connection to law. That is to say, to give an example used by Benjamin, those endless 'security situations' that are enacted, in an immediate fashion, by police, but more importantly, anti-Black police violence that cannot be categorized as founding or preserving the law but must be seen as constitutive of the realm of civil society and ethical life and its 'outside'. I will expand on this in the final chapter.

By bringing together Agamben on force-of-law and Benjamin on the excess to the law-preserving and law-founding dialectic found in the police, the idea that the police are 'applying' the law, even if this notion of application contains the critical sense of reinvention that Derrida stipulates, is insufficient to account for the nature of police power. In their 'emancipation' from the conditions that characterize law-positing and law-preserving violence, in their enactment of decrees and the positing of new ends to which they are the means, their violence cannot be read only as an application or invention of the law through force. Rather, it is a force that exceeds law. Therefore, just as with the exception, where the law is not applied but suspended: so too with police power. Through spectacular rationales like security and order, the function of police lies in a threshold of indistinction between violence, law and sovereignty.

As I demonstrated in the first half of this book, the Western political philosophy canon has obsessed over the question of sovereignty while doing very little to notice the critical place of police within it. In being a force-of-law – a being-in-force without decision – the figure of police lay bare the contradictions of the law. Indeed, it is precisely in the figure of police that the gap that exists between the law and its application is shown for what it is: an unbridgeable divide that presupposes the suspension of law to be rendered operative. This is why, however, it is so difficult, nay impossible, for police activity to be held to account by the law. Once it is understood that police are not executing, legislating or transgressing the law it becomes clearer why, even when there is footage of unspeakable violence against an unarmed person, for example, the law so often does not find police officers guilty of any crime. To speak in terms of the illegality of police actions is of course to press on the very contradiction that I have been outlining here. To say a police action is 'illegal' renders visible and jams the machinery of the legal form; in naming themselves as the law acting in the world – yet paradoxically acting in dislocation from it – police suspend the law while bearing its force. Indeed, it is the power to *not apply* the law, yet still wield violence constructed as legitimate, regardless of the circumstances, that ensures the exceptional character of police power in modernity.

Benjamin claims that under absolutism the spirit of police was 'less devastating', given their representation of the fusion of legislative and executive supremacy, while in 'democracies where their existence, elevated by no such relation, bears witness to the greatest conceivable degeneration of violence' (1978: 287). This chapter has argued that this degeneration is in turn linked to the indifferentiation of exception and rule in tandem with the collapsing of, and excess to, the cycle of law-positing and law-preserving violence found in the police. Under absolutism police was the name given to the execution of a sovereign will in the name of order. Under liberal democracies, with the separation of powers, and indeed, state and civil society, the form of the relation between sovereignty and government shifts. There is no decision to be made on the exception which can return liberalism to a fusion of powers (which is precisely what Schmitt desires),[31] rather as the rule and the exception are made indifferent, it is sovereign indecision that characterizes the modern condition. Together with the exceptional character of police power which, in individual cases can suspend the law, we are presented with a groundless force-of-law which nevertheless claims to be applying the law. Together with the ability to project law, order and sovereign power as that from which their power derives, police power is fundamentally *an-archic*, and it is this notion that the next chapter will delineate.

4

# The *an-archy* of order

## Agamben and the police

One of the themes of this book has been outlining the centrality of relationality and order analysis of police. Indeed, to go back to Hegel's claim that I discussed in Chapter 2 – that police mediate the universal and particular – we can see that there is already an underlying matter of a *relation* that is the grounds upon which police has been thought. That is to say, with the separation of state and civil society, and with order no longer the expression of a divine plan as such, police become the answer to a metaphysical problem turned political: How can universal and particular be mediated in the absence of God? Or, to put it slightly differently, how can a *relation* between a universal sphere and a particular sphere be constituted that does not construe them as either radically separate or collapse them into each other?[1]

Through the work of Agamben, I argue, the full implications of police as a concern with relation can be grasped. Not only this, but Agamben's theoretical tools enable a different view of how philosophy has thought (and not thought) police that I have so far discussed. I have so far foregrounded the notion of order as the domain of police, and the unbounded character of police power that this entails. The purpose of this chapter is to bring together these elements and argue that police are in fact the metaphysical condition of possibility for sovereignty and law. With a focus on what Agamben sees as the divided character of power, this chapter argues that the function of police is to make a specific economy of power operative, a shuttling back and forth between a transcendent order and an immanent one, a process captured by the term *order*.

Central to this endeavour so far have been questions regarding the relationship of police to sovereignty and to law. While police are clearly differentiated from the law, they also have an intrinsic relation to it which, as I argued in Chapter 4, cannot be subsumed to enforcement or implementation, given police actions' law-founding and law-suspending properties. Furthermore, the relationship of police to sovereignty is similarly vexed and cannot be described simply by recourse to the idea of implementation. Yet, it is also not simply the case that police have no relationship to sovereignty. As I discussed in the previous chapter, the contiguity between police power and sovereign power can be illuminated by the idea of force-of-law. Therefore, the question that now comes to the fore is how to grasp and articulate this relationship? In a short essay entitled 'Sovereign Police' Agamben provides an alluringly simple answer to this question. It is here that he identifies the (first) Gulf War as a turning point, or threshold moment, in which, 'sovereignty has finally been introduced into the figure of police' (2000: 114). He goes on to claim that police are always 'operating in a similar state of exception' (2000: 114) to that of sovereignty citing 'public order' and 'security' as the rationales which come to characterize this decisionistic mode of police.

I want to suggest that this thesis, in which police operate in a state of exception that belies their sovereign function, is, in fact, mistaken. While Agamben is right to highlight the decisionistic, exceptional character of police action, the claim that sovereignty has finally been introduced into the figure of police is one that I argue goes against the gesture of his wider *Homo Sacer* project. While a full exposition of this project lies outside of the bounds of this chapter, I would like to dwell on some crucial interventions he makes in order to underscore the centrality of police to Western politics. I argue that when Agamben states that sovereignty is 'introduced into the figure of police' I argue he makes a mistake, one that is, in fact, counter to many of the claims made elsewhere in his work. Indeed, if police are posited as an empty cipher, one that at a certain point in the 1990s was filled with sovereign power, we miss the crucial point being made here, that police cannot be considered one power among others, but is the pivot on which what Agamben calls the 'governmental machine' turns. My thesis will ultimately be that police are not *invested* with sovereign power but are in fact the *an-archic*[2] condition of possibility for sovereign power.

Agamben comes extremely close to formulating this point in *The Kingdom and the Glory* where he writes that 'the central mystery of politics is not sovereignty, but government, it is not God, but the angel; it is not the king, but ministry; it is not the law, but the police – that is to say, the governmental machine that they form and support' (2011: 276). Two things are striking here; first, police are placed in a relationship to law that is at least analogous to that of sovereignty and government. Second, the police are placed in a secondary-axis Agamben outlines, conceived as 'forming' and 'supporting' what he calls the governmental machine. I will turn to *The Kingdom and the Glory* to analyse Agamben's methodological strategy, which is, I argue, key to his understanding of relationality and therefore will prepare the groundwork from which to understand the notion of police order being developed here.

First I will analyse Agamben's characterization of the division of power that takes place as a result of the problem of a split between God's being and action, which gives rise to the idea of *oikonomia* as a form of government as praxis. I shall then examine his treatment of the question of contingency as it takes the form of 'collateral effect'. I will then use this as the groundwork from which to use Agamben's work on 'order' to develop the idea of 'police order' being developed in this book. Finally, I will attend to the 'an-archic' character of police power that follows from police as charged with the maintenance or production of 'order'.

## Divided power and *Oikonomia*

As briefly discussed in the introduction, Agamben's *The Kingdom and the Glory* carries out the genealogy of power that takes the form of *oikonomia*. Agamben sets out the wider, more general aim of the *Homo Sacer* project as a whole, claiming that his aim was always to articulate 'the double structure of the governmental machine, which in *State of Exception* (2005) appeared in the correlation between *auctoritas* and *potestas*, here takes the form of the articulation between Kingdom and Government' (2011: xi).[3] The main gesture of this text arises in response to the question, 'why is power originally divided?' (2011: 100). The answer lies, for Agamben, in the division between 'auctoritas (that is, a power without actual execution) and the *potestas* (that is, a power that can be exercised): the Kingdom and the Government' (2011: 103).

Agamben's strategy is to expose two 'antinomical but functionally related' paradigms that derive from Christian theology: 'political theology, which founds the transcendence of sovereign power on the single God, and economic theology, which replaces this transcendence with the idea of an *oikonomia*, conceived as an immanent ordering – domestic not political in a strict sense – of both divine and human life' (2011: 1). In the previous chapter I discussed the former paradigm as conceptualized by Schmitt in order to further specify the relationship of police to political theology. As I argued, Schmitt's thesis – that with liberalism came the disavowal of transcendence (or personalistic decisionism) – was mistaken for precisely the reason that he does not consider the police. And yet, it is not simply the case that police can be characterized merely as taking the place of a transcendent sovereign (in itself based on the power of the single God). Rather, it is this divided character of power[4] to which our attention must be turned in order to grasp police. Here my aim is to understand *oikonomia* as part of the way in which power is divided and to then expose how this divided character of power is produced and ultimately rendered operative.

In his genealogy of economy and government, Agamben traces the idea of *oikonomia* in its displacement from Aristotle to the Church Fathers for whom *oikonomia* (order) becomes a way to solve the problem of the Trinity. The issue of conceptualizing the condition for the government of the world becomes salient because of the split between God's being and action, ontology and praxis. God, as unitary, singular and sovereign, cannot act 'according to particular wills, infinitely multiplying his miraculous interventions' as this would mean that there would be 'neither government nor order, but only chaos and what one might call a pandemonium of miracles. For this reason, as sovereign, he must reign and not govern' (2011: 269). This splitting of power is evident throughout modern conceptions of government[5] wherein a divide between those who make law and those who interpret or apply it takes the form of separate but related institutions.

The government of the world thus takes the form of an *oikonomia*, that is, a form of governing that supposedly does not adhere to transcendental principles but is rather concerned with ad hoc reactive measures to create and maintain *order*. *Oikonomia*, then, refers to the way in which the activity and praxis of government become possible while not threatening the unitary nature of sovereign power. If sovereign power itself is seen to be divided its very existence would be threatened,[6] and hence a scission between sovereign power and its exercise in the world becomes necessary. This enables a view of sovereign power as unitary, singular, undivided and a second axis of power as secondary and derivative. As I discussed in the introduction, this scission takes the form of two different orders – transcendent and immanent – where the transcendent supposedly is the primary founding and legitimating power, and the immanent is the exercise and application of that power in the world, or, in other words, the power that the founding power founds. Here 'one appears as the execution of the other's *ordinatio*. As such, immanent order is not that different from transcendence since it is always understood through the imagination or reflection of a transcendental order, even if it is now a transcendence that orders silently in its withdrawal' (Zartaloudis 2010: 82).

We find here a common presumption, in which there are two orders – transcendent and immanent – whereby the immanent comes to be seen as either a reflection of the transcendent order or directly derived from it. This view comes to predominate modern politics: there is a founding, or legitimating sovereign/legislative power, and a secondary implementing power which is subordinate or derivative. Or, in terms that interest us here: there is law and secondarily, there is police which is there to administer that law. Indeed, those invested with sovereign power, or those who make law, are not those charged with attending to the way those laws work 'in the world' as it were, and this leads to two heterogeneous, yet related, elements of power. Crucially, however, this relationship also means, for Agamben, that with the split between ontology and praxis, praxis is fundamentally groundless (Agamben 2011: 55). This realm of action is contingent, and so cannot simply be the implementation of a sovereign will or higher law. It is a 'managerial and non-epistemic' paradigm, which, as the name *oikonomia* suggests, takes its cue from the household management that Aristotle opposes to the polis. For Agamben, this legacy of bifurcating sovereignty and government, transmitted from Christian theology, is decisive for modern politics:

> Through these distinctions, the entire economic-providential apparatus (with its polarities ordinatio/executio, providence/fate, Kingdom/Government) is passed on as an unquestioned inheritance to modern politics. What was needed to assure the unity of being and divine action, reconciling the unity of substance with the trinity of persons and the government of particulars with the universality of providence, has here the strategic function of reconciling the sovereignty and generality of the law with the public economy and the effective government of individuals. (2011: 276)

With the split between being and acting, the second element, praxis, is not, and cannot be simply derived from being. Were this to be the case the whole apparatus and problem of government would not arise: being would be identical with itself and government would remain passive and a mere technical instrument for the execution of sovereign power. It has been my contention that when we consider the police, the latter proposition cannot be maintained. In other terms, the law is not mechanically applied to particular cases, and thus a gap appears between the being of law and its application. Crucially this gap is the condition for police action to appear as a problem in and of itself. Indeed, were police action reducible to the mechanistic application of the law or simply the execution of a sovereign command, issues such as discretion, the de facto/de jure distinction and *sub rosa* police practices would all be non-existent. As Agamben argues, this poses a problem not only for sovereignty and law but for language as such:

> In the relation between the general and particular (and all the more so in the case of the application of a juridical norm), it is not only a logical subsumption that is at issue, but first and foremost the passage from a generic proposition endowed with a merely virtual reference to a concrete reference to a segment of reality (that is, nothing less than the question of the actual relation between language. This passage from *langue* to *parole*, or from the semiotic to the semantic, is not a logical operation at all; rather it always entails a practical activity. (2005: 39)

There is then a gap between norm and fact, general and particular, in which the particular cannot be mechanically subsumed under the general.[7] However, it is also not the case that police action should be seen as having no reproductive function in terms of social order. Indeed, police activity is not arbitrary which raises the question: If police activity is not purely contingent, what is its relationship to necessity?

## Fate, government and collateral effects

Agamben traces the development of the idea of first and secondary causes as 'collateral effects' through the concept of fate. In doing this, he turns to a commentator on Aristotle, Alexander of Aphrodisias, who argued against the Stoic idea of providence. For the Stoics, providence meant that God attended to each and every happening in the world, whereas for Alexander this would mean that God would be of 'a lower rank than the things he provides for' (Agamben 2011: 115). Alexander thus formulates providential action that is neither simply 'voluntary activity' nor the 'unwitting accident' (Agamben 2011: 117) but a third term: the 'collateral effect that is calculated' (Agamben 2011: 118). This third term is crucial for the conceptualization of the government of the world that is split from a transcendent order of first causes. In this sense, in the oscillation between first causes and secondary, or collateral, effects (that are nonetheless calculated), government appears to aim not at 'the general or the particular, the primary or the consequent, the end or the means, but their functional correlation' (Agamben 2011: 122). Government as collateral effect then is the result of a 'zone of undecidability between law and general economy that it regulates or correlates' (Watkin 2014: 222) and yet, the idea that this means government acts are 'merely tactical' (Watkin 2014: 222) is called into question.

This leads to a conceptualization of the government of the world which is not general or particular, and not a singular will governing all, nor a set of accidental occurrences, but rather the 'knowing anticipation of the collateral effects that arise from the very nature of things and remain absolutely contingent in their singularity' (Agamben 2011: 118–19). Though of course this was not Alexander's aim, this positing of collateral effects unwittingly produces a governmental paradigm. Christian theologians took up this reformulation via the concept of fate. Fate and providence are 'strictly entwined' (Agamben 2011: 120), and Agamben finds in Plutarch a conception of providence, which again is divided. There is, as previously discussed, a need to solve the paradox of God's existence and how the world is governed in its particularity. Providence, in Plutarch, refers to the universal condition, while fate 'establishes the general conditions according to which connections between particular facts will then take place' (in Agamben 2011: 120). The providence-fate machine that results is the correlation of two distinct but connected planes:

> The activity of government is, at the same time, providence which thinks and orders the good of everybody, and destiny, which distributes the good to individuals, constraining them to the chain of causes and effects. In this way, what on one level – that of fate and individuals – appears as incomprehensible and unjust, receives on another level its intelligibility and justification. In other words, the governmental machine functions like an

incessant theodicy, in which the Kingdom of providence legitimates and founds the Government of fate, and the latter guarantees the order that the former has established and renders it operative. (Agamben 2011: 129)

Fate is thus distinct from, but related to, general providence. Fate is the administration of things, the immanent effects of happenings in their activity and motion, with fate being characterized as a 'subordinated, yet autonomous, power' (Agamben 2011: 128), whereas providence is at the general, universal level. The providential machine is for Agamben that which joins together the two planes and thus renders the government of the world possible. However, what is crucial for my argument is that the acts carried out through fate are posited as having a 'discretionary character' (Agamben 2011: 128). Indeed, for Plutarch, while fate 'corresponds to the level of particular effects' that derive from general providence, the way this manifests in the world is not a predetermined chain of events but rather 'nothing is more ambiguous than the relation of 'collaterality' or of 'effectuality' (Agamben 2011: 122).[8] A transformation thus takes place that enables contingency to be inscribed into a logic of 'collateral effects'. Through the prism of collateral effects, then, we can begin to see the activity of government not as the result or creation of a singular event or general law. The contingent operations of government are related to a wider, transcendent (though empty) order through the operations of the collateral effect:

> in this sense it is not surprising that the collateral effect presents itself more often as consubstantial with every act of government. What the government aims at can be obtained, due to its very nature, only as a collateral effect, in an area in which general and particular, positive and negative, calculation and unexpected events tend to overlap. Governing means allowing the particular concomitant effects of a general 'economy' to arise, an economy that would remain in itself wholly ineffective, but without which no government is possible. It is not so much that the effects (the Government) depend on being (the Kingdom), but rather that being consists of its effects: such is the vicarious and effectual ontology that defines the acts of government. (Agamben 2011: 142)

The collateral effect then is the manner in which transcendent and immanent, general and particular, providential plans and unforeseen events collide in a zone of indistinction. As we can see there are two poles of the governmental machine – be that sovereignty and government, law and police, transcendent and immanent order – and these express two elements: a founding power and a founded power. The founding power is presumed to be the condition for, and that which gives rise to, the founded power. Or, in the terms that interest here sovereignty founds government. Yet what Agamben's analysis offers is an understanding of government and collateral effects which projects sovereign power as its founding ground, but where the relationship is in fact the reverse: that sovereign power in fact consists of nothing but its effects.[9] Indeed, as Zartaloudis argues the immanent order of *oikonomic* power necessitates a transcendent power for its own legitimization but, in truth, does not derive from the transcendent sphere (Zartaloudis 2010: 185).

What is supposedly a power of administration is, in actuality a founding power itself. The founded power, however, needs something outside of itself to justify its exercise. While this originary, founding power can take different forms, they share the common mythological projection of a founding, legitimating power that in reality presupposes a founded element that this power itself is supposed to found and justify (Zartaloudis 2010: 185). For Zartaloudis, this manifests, in modernity, in the 'spectacularization of terms like "humanity", "democracy", "progress", security and so forth that are used without any other attempt at a definitional precision than their supposed self-referentiality' (Zartaloudis 2010: 187). In this way, older 'mystical foundations of authority and power' (Zartaloudis 2010: 187) such as the state of nature or God are superseded by different 'mythologemes', but the architectonics remain intact. In fact, I would argue that Zartaloudis's list of terms that justify the exercise of founded power misses a crucial term: order.

Order, I argue, is the self-referential, legitimizing term par excellence.[10] As I will clarify, the meaning of order comes not from the semantic definitional content of the word itself but rather from how it 'allows things to be said or understood' (Watkin 2014: 22). Order, seen in this way, is fundamentally relational. It has no substance as such: no essence of order can be defined. This absence of substance is why, I argue, attempts to define order tend towards banal statements concerning what it is not (i.e. disorder). It is also why it is so crucial for police. The lack of content means that the meaning of order can shift[11] depending on what the power invoking it says it is in a given situation. In this way it is similar to the operation of the (Schmittian) exception as discussed in Chapter 3, whereby the exception is not defined by a certain set of circumstances but is rather contingent on the decision which in itself brings it into being. The presence or absence of order is thus not defined by certain events taking place but rather depends on a decisionistic process by which police can declare whether or not they believe 'public order' is being transgressed.

Order is crucial for addressing a fundamental problem of modern government, and police in particular: how can its power can be legitimated so as to undermine the sense that it is being exercised despotically, arbitrarily or as a form of domination. Order, as we have seen, is construed as presupposing government, enabling it to presuppose, in modern democracies, the 'freedom of all as its very condition of possibility' (Zartaloudis 2010: 83). In this way, order can appear not as imposition but a condition that individual freedom necessitates. More concretely, and I will go into more detail later in this chapter, in appearing as deriving from law, the will of the public, and as upholding order, police activity appears not as *violating* liberty but as its condition of possibility.

As I argued in the first half of this book, Aristotle, Christian theologians and theorists of sovereignty variously considered order as essential to political life. Order in its displacements across all of these fields is seen to be the outcome of an antecedent point, be that the first mover, God or the sovereign. This relationship is then posited as necessary, rather than contingent; order being the proof that the antecedent point exists and actively structures the world. When this dynamic gets displaced into the political realm, order becomes the proof and outcome of sovereign power, without which order is not possible. A further displacement occurs, I argue, when order becomes the responsibility of police.

## The signature of order

Before discussing this, however, it will be helpful to clarify what Agamben's methodological strategy towards order, which I only briefly touched on in the introduction. Order, for Agamben, is a 'signature', which is crucial in demonstrating what Agamben is *not* claiming, namely, that there is a secret theological foundation to all of contemporary politics. In his critique of his archaeology, Alberto Toscano argues against what he perceives as Agamben's search for theological *origins*:

> behind this reference lies not only Agamben's sympathy towards the Schmittian notion of secularisation but the conviction, mediated by a pervasive Heideggarianism, of a historical-ontological *continuity* which allows one to argue that our political horizon is still determined – and worse, *unconcsciously* determined – by semantic and ideational structures forged within a Christian theological discourse. (2011: 128)

It is a mistake, however, to see Agamben's method as a search for origins in this sense. While there is not scope here to fully elaborate Agamben's method, reliant as it is on (among other things) a Benjaminian notion of *now-time*, the category of the signature allows Agamben to posit a notion of origin that does not designate a historical moment which founds and determines what comes after it.[12] It is not that politics has been determined and captured by a theological *origin* in Toscano's sense. Rather, it recalls Benjamin's category of origin which, although a 'historical category',

> has, nevertheless, nothing to do with genesis [*Entstehung*]. The term origin is not intended to describe the process by which the existent came into being, but rather to describe that which emerges from the process of becoming and disappearance. Origin is an eddy in the stream of becoming, and in its current it swallows the material involved in the process of genesis. That which is original is never revealed in the naked and manifest existence of the factual; its rhythm is apparent only to a dual insight. On the one hand it needs to be recognized as a process of restoration and re-establishment, but, on the other hand, and precisely because of this, as something imperfect and incomplete. (1977: 45)

Thus, the origin is not the 'beginning' or emergence of a thing that comes into existence, and, as Weber has it, is 'thus not merely distinguished from becoming or from coming-to-be: it is directed simultaneously toward the future and toward the past'. Its effort is not simply to bring something radically new and different into being but rather to 'restore', to 'reproduce' (2008: 135–6). While not identical, this comes extremely close to Agamben's conceptualization of the *arché* in *The Sacrament of Language*: the *arché* that archaeology moves towards is not understood as being placed in either a temporal register such as 'prehistoric' or in an atemporal metahistorical structure', and in this way 'the *arché* is not a given, a substance, or an event but a field of historical currents stretched between anthropogenesis and the present, ultrahistory and history' (2010: 10–11). We can now better make sense of the ways that, as Watkin writes, 'every *arché* is constructed by our contemporary discourse as the found origin' and how in this sense 'the present founds the past through its attempts to access it as a legitimating origin' (2015: 139).

The idea that Agamben proposes a theological origin that determines contemporary politics is also fundamentally challenged by his insistence, first, that we cannot separate the theological and political and/or legal spheres into discrete temporal stages, such that one forms the basis of the other. Taking the example of the oath, Agamben refutes the idea that it is a religious rite that later becomes a juridical institution as 'arbitrary' (2015: 17) and that, 'we have no reason for postulating a prejuridical phase in which the oath belonged solely to the religious sphere, but perhaps our entire habitual way of representing to ourselves the chronological and conceptual relationship between law and religion must be revised' (2015: 19). Second, Agamben rejects the notion that we can take these discrete spheres and then track back to a time prior to their distinction:

> Taking the sphere of law as an example, it may be the distinction between the religious sphere and the profane sphere, whose distinctive characteristics appear to us, at least in the historical epoch, to be in some measure defined. If he reaches in this area a more archaic stage, the scholar has the impression that the boundaries become blurred, so he is led to hypothesize a preceding stage, in which the religious sphere and the profane (and often also the magical) are not yet distinct. (2010: 16)

Agamben's strategy in *The Kingdom and the Glory* does not use a sense of chronological progression or displacement, because his archaeology calls into question the very binary distinction between sacred and profane. The category of the signature illuminates this paradoxical and aporetic process: 'signs do not speak unless signatures make them speak' (Agamben 2009a: 61). Thus, something like 'order' is a signature that can be displaced between different fields (politics and theology) without losing intelligibility. As Watkin makes clear, Agamben is not arguing that a signature is infinitely elastic, it is, rather 'held to specific meaning possibilities' (Watkin 2014: 24). It controls the intelligibility of certain propositions across different disciplines and epochs and in this way enables communicability.

Order's displacement from theology to politics (and vice versa) does not entail a theological underpinning for all politics. Rather, political power is intelligibly conceived and made operative through the signature 'order', which refers to a split between ontology and praxis and the attempt to hold them together in the form of a relation. Agamben traces order as relation to Aristotle's *Metaphysics* and *Politics* where he points out Aristotle's difficulty in the problem of splitting 'the object of metaphysics', (2011: 83) to which order becomes the solution. Aristotle cannot 'tackle the problem directly' and instead must rely on the paradigm of the army and the house to illustrate his point. Analogous to an army, the relation between soldiers 'must be in relation with the command of the strategist' but each must 'follow their own nature while actually conforming to a single principle' (2011: 83). In this way 'order is replaced by its strategic displacement at the junction between ontology and politics, which makes of it a fundamental *terminus technicus* of Western politics and metaphysics' (2011: 82).

Therefore, Agamben finds in order a critical concept, central to politics and metaphysics, ontology and theology. In order to grasp order's significance, Agamben is worth quoting at length:

> Order is an empty concept, or, more precisely, it is not a concept, but a signature, that is, as we have seen, something that, in a sign or a concept, exceeds it to refer it back to a specific interpretation or move it to another context, yet without exiting the field of the semiotic to construct a new meaning. The concepts that order has the function of signing are genuinely ontological. That is, the signature 'order' produces a displacement of the privileged place of ontology from the category of substance to the categories of relations and praxis; this displacement is perhaps medieval thought's most important contribution to ontology. For this reason, when in his study on ontology in the Middle Ages, Krings reminds us that, 'being is ordo and the ordo is being, the ordo does not presuppose any being, but has the ordo as its condition of possibility', this does not mean that being receives a new definition through the predicate of order, but that, thanks to the signature 'order', substance and relation, ontology and praxis enter into a constellation that represents the specific legacy that medieval theology leaves to modern philosophy. (Agamben 2011: 87–8)

Crucially not only does order refer to relationality as such, but it also displaces the focus on substance in ontology to praxis. This displacement, I argue, enables Agamben to claim that the crux of politics lies not in (mythological) sovereign power but the activity that constitutes the work of government and which I argue is actually the activity of police. Through the signature of order, relationality (between sovereignty and government, and being and praxis) is rendered legible and enables a view of what would otherwise be obscure: the divided character of power. The obfuscation of this division can tend towards differing conceptions of the political with stark results. On the one hand, there are those that would emphasize the transcendent sovereign pole at the expense of everything else (à la Schmitt) or conversely, the immanent governmental pole at the expense of the sovereign sphere (à la certain readings of Smith). Focussing on order provides the sense that both are articulated in a bipolar machine, rendered operative by the incessant operation of (police) power. If one loses sight of the transcendent pole, the transcendent legitimizing power (even if mythological) is obscure and one is left with an analysis of the practices of government without a sense of the sovereign power which they project as their foundation. Conversely, if one's emphasis lies with this sovereign power, the practices of police seem only to derive from this transcendent order, losing any sense of the groundlessness of their acts.

A relation, Agamben argues, can be defined 'as what constitutes its elements by presupposing them, together, as unrelated' (2015: 272). Order is thus what constitutes its elements (Kingdom/government, transcendent/immanent, being/praxis) in a bipolar machine and is that which constitutes the split between sovereignty and government and also tries to heal the fracture between them. Order, for Christian theology, both expresses the split between a transcendent and immanent order and the way these two elements relate. In exposing this, Agamben turns to Thomas Aquinas, whom he charges with trying to make order 'the fundamental ontological concept, which determines and conditions the very idea of being' (2015: 85). Agamben finds in Thomas's very Aristotelian conception of order a fundamental duality between the relations creatures have with God and the relations creatures have among themselves (2015: 85). This division formulates relations that occur in the world (immanent order) and the relation between the world and a transcendent, divine end (transcendent order) as co-constitutive, but consequently an aporia emerges:

> Things are ordered insofar as they have a specific relation among themselves, but this relation is nothing other than the expression of their relation to the

> divine end . . . the only content of the transcendent order is the immanent order, but the meaning of the immanent order is nothing other than the relation to the transcendent end. (2015: 87)

This aporetic relation forms one of the characteristics of the signature of order, that is, order makes communicable the way that power becomes operative through shuttling back and forth between an empty transcendent end and an immanent order ostensibly necessary for that end. This aporia also points to another of Agamben's central theses: the 'throne' of power is empty; sovereign power has no substance and the 'collateral effects' that government consists of cover over this emptiness. In modernity as the question of how the 'chaos' of the world can be ordered comes to the fore with the loss of a redemptive horizon, this *oikonomic* form of governing acquires its *katechontic* force.[13] Indeed, that government and sovereignty constantly refer back to each other in an infinite dialectic, and with an empty foundation, modern government can appear as an ordering force in a disorderly world while in fact producing what it claims to combat: an-archic, lawless violence.

It is in this light that we can see that the displacement of order does not refer to a process of secularization where police order represents a secularized transcendent power analogous to that of God or a Leviathan. Rather, as order becomes displaced from divine/natural to sovereign to police, the visibility of this displacement renders legible the relationship of modern forms of government to older forms, yet the specificity of the present is also made clear. If sovereign order was the pre-eminence of the transcendent pole, whereby acting in an unmediated fashion on its subjects articulated this relationality in a particular way: police was the name given to the order constructed by a sovereign will.[14] In this sense both police and order are imbricated, politically and philosophically, from the outset. However, when order becomes the responsibility of police, the articulation and operation of this relation shifts. Order neither expresses a divine plan nor applies an unmediated sovereign will. Rather, it articulates a transcendent and immanent order where a general will has some relation to the particularity and contingency that constitutes the sphere of human activity. If both divine and sovereign order, then, express an order seen as constituted by a plan, police order refers to the *an-archic* operation of police, neither derived from law nor a general 'plan' but which nevertheless must be seen to relate to law, sovereignty, 'the people' and so on.

Indeed, when police are charged with creating or maintaining 'order' they then project the founding mythological, mystical power of the legislative power or law as their legitimizing justification. In reality, however, this mythological projection is just that: a projection of a founding power which legitimizes its own action without actually deriving from it. Thus police can claim to act in the name of 'the *public*'[15] for the sake of 'order', which has no content other than a projected legitimacy which, it can claim, founds its own power. If order was the aporetic relation between beings and a divine end, and among beings themselves, then the loss of *telos* does not entail the malfunctioning of the governmental machine that Agamben identifies. Rather, order becomes visible as the *sine qua non* of sovereignty and government. Order (as relation) is both condition of possibility for government and its end, and thus becomes immanent to itself.

In short, police order refers to a specific conjuncture which represents a particular configuration of the relation between transcendent and immanent, being and action, and sovereignty and government. If divine and sovereign order represented, in some ways, an unmediated relation between transcendent and immanent, then police order does not constitute an epistemic break with these forms, but rather displaces the signature of order such that the relation's configuration changes. Order transforms from what is seen to be the product of a sovereign will or plan to that of an an-archic and groundless yet nevertheless calculated and violent operation of power located in the figure of police.

What concerns me is the way police makes state violence operative through their articulation of what Agamben would call an 'effective economy' of the state via order. Police order is not only the form that *oikonomia* managerial government takes (and thus not solely reducible to 'government' as such) but also perpetuates the vicarious economy between the transcendent and immanent orders: police makes order operative and effective. Police order is thus the apex of the process that Agamben charts in the *Kingdom and the Glory*. Having 'the public' and the law as the mythological legitimizing (transcendental-metaphysical) foundation of its power, police power becomes unconstrained and dislocated from the law, while at the same time appearing as intrinsically linked to it.[16] Central to this operation is order, which simultaneously acts as another mythological legitimizing founding element, but is also that which expresses the articulation between the transcendent and immanent order. Once we grasp that it is police that are charged with the function of order then we must conclude that police are not one institution among others. This is why, against thinkers who would see police as a concept interchangeable with 'social control', I argue that the specificity of police as a concept and as an institution is absolutely critical to any understanding of sovereignty and government.[17] We must see police in its proper locus, which is to say not as some elusive, amorphous 'social control' or method of discipline but as the an-archic condition of possibility for sovereignty itself.

## The *an-archic* character of police power

The legacy of the idea that anarchy is the absence of order is a powerful one, particularly evident in theories of sovereignty and government that depart from older conceptions of order as natural or God-given. In Chapter 1, I argued by way of Hobbes that sovereignty in fact comes to be seen as defined by the production of order. In what follows, I will describe the fundamentally an-archic character of police power and violence. In so doing, it follows that an-archy and order, law and anomie, are not mutually exclusive, but, following Agamben, an inclusive exclusion, where what seems external (an-archy, anomie) in fact makes state power operative. Not only this but an-archic power intrinsically connects to the groundless *oikonomic* government of the world.

Anarchy is contemporaneously defined as both a condition without government and a 'state of disorder' (OED 2006: 47). Anarchy has thus been conceived as the pre-political or post-political condition without government and, crucially, without order. For Agamben, however, 'power is constituted through the inclusive exclusion (ex-ceptio) of anarchy' (2015: 275). That this anarchic element is closely linked to the exception is clear, given that it is that which is excluded by power (or sovereignty) only to be included by its very exclusion.[18] The task then is to expose this anarchic element that constitutes power, without falling into the metaphysical machine that would constantly posit it as something external to sovereign power, or indeed as that which sovereign power necessarily precludes by its very existence. If the anarchy internal to power is highlighted it is only then 'that the possibility of thinking a true anarchy' can arise (2015: 275).¹⁹

Indeed, if order has been seen as the outcome and proof of an antecedent power, and, conversely, anarchy has been construed as proof of the non-existence or dissolution of this power then it remains to be seen how, far from excluding anarchy, order in fact presupposes it through its prohibition. For Agamben, the state is not founded on a substantive relation, or bond, but only on the negative foundation that is the prohibition of the dissolution of this 'relation':

> It is in this sense that one is to read the gesture in 4.6 of Homo Sacer 1 toward the necessity of no longer thinking the political-social factum in the form of a relationship. From the same perspective, developing the idea that the State does not found itself on a social link but on the prohibition of its dissolution, 4.3 suggested that the dissolution is not to be understood as the dissolution of an existent bond because the bond itself does not have any other consistency than the purely negative one that it derives from the prohibition of dissolution. Since there is originally neither bond nor relation, this absence of relation is captured in state power in the form of the ban and of prohibition. (2015: 237)

Indeed, in the terms that interest us here, it is anarchy that is prohibited and sovereignly banned; it has been constructed as the dissolving of the relation of the state. Anarchy, then, is a political construction projected (much like the Hobbesian state of nature) back into an imaginary past and into a hypothetical future without the state but lies, in fact, at the centre of state power. The full significance of linking anarchy and *disorder* now appears: anarchy is posited as the dissolution of *relationality* (that is to say, order) that the state produces. The relation consists, however, in reality, of the perpetual oscillation between a produced universal that has as its content nothing but the praxis of immanent government. Thus anarchy can be linked to the prohibited dissolution of *order*, which in reality covers over the an-archy that is precisely captured in and through the figure of police.

However, while police power is, I argue, an-archic in form it is not the case that it is purely arbitrary or consisting in purely ad-hoc reactionary measures. Indeed, to say that police power does not have a foundation in a transcendent will is not to say that it has no relation to a wider order. Through the related ideas of collateral effects, vicariousness of power and the projected foundation discussed earlier, the aporetic relation between law and police can be seen more clearly. That is to say it is not the case that police are simply acting 'outside' of the law but neither are they implementing it. Rather, as the next chapter will more clearly highlight, it is in the relationship to nature and necessity in which the locus of police power can be more clearly delineated.

Thus, when Benjamin writes that there is nothing more anarchic than the bourgeois order' (in Agamben 2015: 275) we can further specify this with regard to the idea of police order being developed here. The unbounded character of police power found when police are charged with creating or maintaining 'order' – that as we have seen has become an overarching (mythological) legitimizing foundation for the exercise of police power itself – characterizes the exceedingly an-archic bourgeois order. The groundlessness of police power – that cannot be traced back to an originary command but is also not absolutely arbitrary – shows that police activities can be both an-archic and ordered. Or, in other words, that an-archy is presupposed wherever order is invoked.

## Potentiality, exceptionality, police

Agamben finds in the Aristotelian category of potential one key to articulating the composition of sovereign power, law and the state of exception. There are two forms of potentiality – the potentiality to be, which crosses over into actuality, and the potentiality not to be, which is impotentiality:

> In the potential/act apparatus, Aristotle holds together two irreconcilable elements: the contingent – what can be or not be – and the necessary – what cannot not be. According to the mechanism of the relation that we have defined, he thinks potential as existing in itself, in the form of a potential-not-to or impotential and act as ontologically superior and prior to potential. (2015: 276)

In contingency and potentiality we find the components that are captured in the state of exception that Agamben outlines in the earlier writings of the *Homo Sacer* project. While sovereignty is traditionally considered in its affirmative 'dimension of potentiality (I can) to be worthy of the name this potentiality must be accompanied by its negative counterpart (I can not) which refers precisely to the possibility for the sovereign to suspend the law that it itself gives, to treat the commonwealth *tanquam dissoluta*' (Prozorov 2014: 117). It is precisely the structure of the exception and 'sovereign ban' by which the law applies to life in its suspension that sovereign power captures potentiality or impotentiality in the governmental machine.[20] Indeed, for Agamben 'the law presupposes the nonjuridical (for example, mere violence in the form of the state of nature) as that which maintains itself in a *potential* relation in the state of exception' (emphasis added 1998: 20). Indeed, that this nonjuridical, exceptional violence is precisely that which I have been outlining as characteristic of police power.

A focus on police order lays bare the oscillation between sovereignty and government that characterizes the modern state without being wholly reducible to either. The activities of police are irreducible to the general and particular, the transcendent and immanent. The power of police to declare whether order exists or not is, I have argued, *the* exceptional power that relates contingency to necessity in the form of acts neither reducible nor simply exterior to the law. In this way police are also not solely reducible to the 'governmental' pole of administration. Therefore, using Agamben's thought as a heuristic device but going beyond him by focussing on police, I have attended to the specificity of relationality as crucial for thinking through the locus of police in political thought, and in so doing highlighted the metaphysical grounds on which police has been thought.

In summary, this chapter has endeavoured to demonstrate that the anomie/an-archy that is (fictively) supposed as existing outside of (or indeed before or after) the law is actually the very thing presupposed by the law, that the law must capture in order to be operative. While the state of exception represents, for Agamben, the vital configuration of this relation of the law and its suspension – its *impotentiality* – our gaze cannot solely be trained on this paradigm. Indeed, if, as I have argued, that police make order operative, we must rethink some of the political categories surrounding the state of exception. What has become clear in the course of this discussion is that the concept of the 'state of exception' as put forward by both Schmitt and Agamben is deficient because of the ways in which both thinkers try to delimit and delineate it. As discussed previously, for Schmitt, the state of exception must be totalizing and cannot exist in part, which is what distinguishes it from a 'police emergency'. For Agamben, it is the concentration camp that is the concrete manifestation of the exception in modernity. As Agamben puts it:

> When our age tried to grant the unlocalizable a permanent and visible localization, the result was the concentration camp. The camp – and not the prison – is the space that corresponds to this originary structure of the nomos. This is shown, among other things, by the fact that while prison law only constitutes a particular sphere of penal law and is not outside the normal order, the juridical constellation that guides the camp is (as we shall see) martial law and the state of siege. (1998: 20)

What is striking about this passage is the way in which Agamben resorts to legal categories themselves to differentiate prison law which he locates in the 'normal order' of law and the camp which lies outside of this order. The problem, as I see it, is that in making this distinction, Agamben simultaneously presupposes and denies the separation of legal normality and the exception. It is the camp that appears for Agamben in modernity and which constitutes the concrete manifestation of the indifferentiation of norm and exception that he takes from Benjamin's *Theses on the Philosophy of History*. Yet crucially prisons are excluded from this typology due to their location within the 'normal order'. Contrary to this work which has sought to demonstrate that police power is an-archic in character, which is to say, if police are the institutional manifestation of the an-archic 'outside' of the law which the law must nevertheless retain a relation to, it becomes difficult to maintain that the 'normal legal order' (of which police are surely the archetypal manifestation), can be so clearly distinguished from the exception in the way that Agamben describes earlier. Similarly to Schmitt for whom police measures were not exceptional and who sought to circumscribe the exception, Agamben seeks to show that the legal character of the exception (martial law) is distinct from criminal law, thus denying the constitutive character of the indifferentiation (or, for Benjamin, the suspension of the law-founding, law-preserving distinction) that the figure of police attests to.

This problem emerges I argue because of the racial lacuna at the centre of this theorization of the state of exception. Without attending to the racialized scaffolding of the state of nature that Agamben argues appears internally in states as the state of exception, then what counts as a state or space of exception will be *exceptionalized* – given over to and embracing of its own mythology as a discrete temporal and spatial configuration that conforms to legal categorization. As Weheliye has noted, however, the racialized nature of state violence in the form of the criminal justice system means that for Black people and some other racialized groups, the state of exception is indeed an ordinary affair (2014: 86–7).[21] A closer look at how nature, necessity and violence – the metaphysical grounds of the exception – coalesce in the figure of police through anti-Black violence shall be the focus of the next chapter.

5

# da Silva

## Nature, necessity and violence

This chapter is an examination and troubling of narratives of police power that see police power as being split along spatial and temporal lines. On the one hand, there are narratives that police power, as it existed in premodernity, was 'unbounded', unconstrained by the rule of law and the enactment of a sovereign will on its subjects. On the other, we find narratives about police power centred on the idea that an 'excessive' police power was used in Europe's colonies, which at some point rebounded or 'boomeranged' back into the heartlands of empire, with brutal police violence finding its way back onto European territory. In this chapter I want to question these narratives about the origins and locations of police power, which sees an unbounded police power – one unconstrained from legal limits – located in an 'elsewhere'. In troubling these narratives my point is not so much that colonial histories of policing are irrelevant to understanding police power today, or that police power is identical to its premodern forms, but it is rather to understand what happens to our account of police power when it is structured by an originary bifurcation between premodern and modern, and colony and metropole.

This chapter therefore begins by repeating a question, asked by Denise Ferreira da Silva, in the context of police violence and killings: Where is that place where what should not 'happen to nobody' happens every day? Why is it that, in so many places found in every corner of the global space, so many human beings face that which 'no one deserves'? (2009: 120). Not content with the responses to this question that come in the form of what she calls the 'expulsion thesis', da Silva describes a number of theorists that have 'explored how the racial delimits the reach of law and humanity' but are 'yet to ask how it produces the principles – universality and self-determination – these notions comprehend. How precisely does the racial (re)produce the universality of the law?' (2007: 11) While not wrong per se, da Silva questions the notions of exteriority that such theorizing necessarily invokes in trying to explain why the state can kill Black people in particular, and it not precipitate any legal ramifications or an ethical crisis. That is, by positing police violence as something *external* to the universality of law and ethics, the immanent coherence of these terms is maintained with some people simply 'excluded' from their reach and application.

By uncovering those moments internal to modern political, juridical and ethical thought where what she calls the 'analytics of raciality' precipitates a process that sees police killings as necessary for the self-preservation of the state, da Silva's work offers a way out of the impasse that is formed when police violence is argued to be 'unlawful'. Her thought therefore offers us a way to think about the relationship between violence, law and police without succumbing to simplistic analyses that forego a thorough reckoning with the notions of 'universality' and 'progress' that usually unthinkingly structure explanations of police violence and impunity.

Challenging liberal historiographies of the police that present its origin in nineteenth-century London and the creation of the Met has given rise to a number of counter-histories that would recentre the colonial history of policing. One of the aims of this chapter is to demonstrate why even these 'critical histories' that point to the colonial origins of police to explain the racialized violence which police engage in today are not sufficient to account for that which they seek to explain. This is not to say that these histories bear no significance when thinking or critiquing police power today. But we also must go further than a simple repetition of the myth of the *origin* that repeats the liberal idea of time as an arrow. Indeed, moving beyond what da Silva sees as a positioning of the racist violence of policing as an unfortunate remnant of bygone times, a 'hangover', and the exhibition of a 'non-modern' consciousness, entails an approach that does not rely solely on an idea of 'origin' to make sense of the present.

This engagement with da Silva emerges, then, not only because she engages with those thinkers I also see as being crucial for thinking through these questions but because her analysis offers a path beyond what has frequently been argued in the pages of literature on police, even those that are deemed 'critical'. Not only this but her work forces a thinking through of the narratives of periodization (premodern/modern) as well as spatialization that sees whiteness and Blackness coming to signify different temporal and spatial registers. Thinking with da Silva, as well as returning to the forefathers of the *an-archic* police power I analyse in this book – Hegel and Hobbes – I argue that anti-Black police violence should not be considered an unfortunate remnant of a bygone history, nor the result of contact between different countries and different 'cultures' across global space but is rather a repetitive and productive violence that cannot be disentangled from some of the oppositional relations under examination in this book: *physis/nomos,* state/civil society, universal/particular.

## The racial and the modern

The 'analytics of raciality' that da Silva names encompasses a construction of 'man' and 'modernity' that uses 'the racial' and 'race difference' as a way to signify 'which kinds of modern space, and which kinds of human beings, lie within the domain of Universal Justice' (2001: 423). Ultimately race difference, for da Silva, provided the modern episteme with a 'grid of intelligibility': one that connected people and places to forms of consciousness and thereby political, legal and social categories such as equality, freedom, the Just and the Good (2001: 423). This process saw whiteness constituted and imbricated with universality, justice and so on, while Blackness represented a 'departure from modernity' (2001: 423). Important here is the work of Cuvier who stood at the forefront of a burgeoning 'scientific racism' that sees race difference biologized and also spatialized:

> Cuvier introduces race difference as a scientific category, a signifier, which connects certain bodily traits, place (continent) of 'origin' and 'mental functions'. In this process whiteness was produced to indicate the form of consciousness able to conceive of universal principles that emerged in the European space – the only raced consciousness able to fulfil the material and moral projects of modernity. (2001: 431)

We see then a complex relationship between periodization, geography and the production of race difference which functioned to tie the temporal (modern/

premodern) and spatial together by delineating when and where (and with whom) one can find the domain of universality, freedom, justice and ethical life.

Important here, then, is that the analytics of raciality is essential for understanding the machinations of police power and, more specifically, how police violence functions not as deviation or aberration from modern philosophical concepts and constructs tied to liberal thought and the enlightenment. This is in opposition not only to liberal conceptions of race injustice which see 'police brutality' as contravening the tenets of modern liberal values and principles, for example by citing these acts as 'unjust', but also to those theories which adopt a more critical stance. On the latter, theorists that da Silva groups together under 'critical legal scholarship' (2001: 424) take to task previous conceptions of race injustice that saw racism as extraneous to modern law. This stance, by contrast, sees racism as part of law and considers how '"racial power" informs legal discourse and strategies' (2001: 424) but analyses this power mainly as it emerges in 'discriminatory (segregationist) acts and policies' (2001: 425). Ultimately, for da Silva this means that critical race theory in some ways suffers the same shortcomings as 'the liberal legal construction of racism, the view that if one's *race difference* is not explicitly found to determine unfavourable social thoughts or actions, exclusionary ideas and behaviour, it cannot be proven to be the ultimate cause of the ensuing harm to that person's rights' (2001: 426, emphasis in original). This line of thinking thus leaves untouched the problem of the constitutive relationship of the law and the racial by presupposing a category of racism and racial domination that is part of legal power but sees its effects as exclusionary and discriminatory rather than productive of legal universality itself.

In a similar vein, and in a critique of Foucault's treatment of racism and biopolitics, Alexander Weheliye notes that Foucault also presupposes a category of race and racism that leaves untouched questions of the construction of race and racism *through* an apparatus of biopolitics. Although Foucault does engage with the issue of race and racism in *Society Must Be Defended* and locates its birth in colonialism, Foucault's interest is not so much in the 'external' racism that pre-exists the birth of biopolitics, but rather the 'internal racism' that finds its way into modern European states. We see this at work through Foucault's identification of two different categories of racism, one between 'alien races' of Europe and its others and one that becomes internal to Europe and is intimately connected with biopolitics. Foucault also distinguishes different racisms in terms of their temporality. The nineteenth-century transformations of power see the inauguration of biopolitics and a category of 'the racial' that is distinct from its seventeenth- and eighteenth-century predecessors. For Foucault, in the latter centuries race manifested as a 'race war', a clash between races that finds expression in national histories about invasion and struggle. As Foucault has it:

> the war that is going on beneath order and peace, the war that undermines our society and divides it in a binary mode is, basically, a race war. At a very early stage, we find the basic elements that make the war possible and then ensure its continuation, pursuit and development: ethnic differences, differences between languages, different degrees of force, vigor, energy and violence; the differences between savagery and barbarism; the conquest and subjugation of one race by another. (Foucault 2004: 59–60)

It is in the nineteenth century, however, that 'the racial' becomes transformed and the discourse shifts predominantly to one that fabricates a single race that is construed as necessitating biological protection from internal threats to its 'purity' (Foucault 2004: 59–60). It is at this point, for Foucault, that 'state sovereignty thus becomes the imperative to protect the race' (Foucault 2004: 81). It is, once again, the nineteenth century which is the site of historical rupture, where racism and a discourse of biology are knitted together; an altogether different kind of racism than that which had been seen in the seventeenth and eighteenth centuries. Here, 'the racial' is not a race 'that came from elsewhere' (Foucault 2004: 61) but is, rather, internal to state and society, one that is 'infiltrating the social body' (Foucault 2004: 61). He goes on: 'what we see as a polarity, as a binary rift within society, is not a clash between two distinct races. It is the splitting of a single race into a superrace and a subrace ... it is the reappearance, within a single race, of the *past* of that race' (emphasis added, Foucault 2004: 61.).

Similarly, and as Weheliye notes from a text that Foucault draws on but does not cite, Hannah Arendt's *The Origins of Totalitarianism* draws divisions between 'continental' and 'overseas imperialism' (Arendt 2017: 291) that also rests on a distinction between the imperial projects of Europeans realized abroad and those imperial projects of 'Pan-Germanism and Pan-Slavism' (Arendt 2017: 290) that were internal to Europe. For the latter, Arendt sees the concept of race as being 'completely ideological in basis and developed much more quickly into a convenient political weapon than similar theories expressed by overseas imperialists which could always claim a certain basis in authentic experience' (Arendt 2017: 292). On da Silva's reading, this statement – though not the same as what Foucault wants to claim – sees the foundation for such arguments that draw lines between colonial power and a racism exercised 'elsewhere' as distinguished from techniques of power and racism exercised internally to Europe. These bifurcations are then used as an analytical device when considering how power is exercised, how the racial functions and how violence is used 'at home' and 'abroad'. The racism internal to Europe is distinguished from the racism of Europe towards its 'others'.

There is therefore a long line of critical theorizing that, though it might agree that race is a construction, tends unwittingly to take for granted or reproduce a notion of *race difference* by treating racism as an *effect* of racial discrimination that stems from an unexamined clash of 'cultures' or racist attitudes that grow from a distinction between racial groups that is presupposed rather than interrogated as to its production. In Weheliye's analysis of Foucault's treatment of race, the critique is formulated thus: 'This line of reasoning rests on the assumption that such a thing as alien races exist, that the confrontation between them (ethnic racism) need not be explained, and that Europe . . . was internally cohesive because racism dwelled elsewhere prior to the ascent of biopolitics in the late 18th and early 19th centuries' (2014: 61).

For both da Silva and Weheliye, then, a problem emerges because 'the racial' does not figure as prominently as a product of power/knowledge in the sense that only one side of the nexus is fully considered when 'the racial' is discussed: that of power. In neglecting the other side of the coin, that of knowledge, the racial begins to emerge as something pre-discursive or as da Silva puts it in her analysis of why Foucault's writings on biopolitics don't fully explore race and racism: 'the racial belongs to another mode of power, the "symbolics of blood," one that does not operate via the production of minds' (da Silva 2007: 24). We can see that there are overlapping temporal and geographical splits when race and racial power are considered – there is an idea of racism which sees it as spatially differentiated – the racism between Europe and non-Europeans and a racism *internal* to Europe which itself is a product of a temporal rupture in power relations in the nineteenth century. In what follows, I argue that these conceptions of race and racism have had a significant part to play in shaping historic and contemporary understandings of police power with regard to 'excess'.

## Police power and colonial boomerangs

In trying to account for the racialized nature of police brutality and killings and indeed how these are largely carried out with impunity, there have been many texts that trace a 'brutal' or 'excessive' police power to a 'prehistory' of policing as it existed in European colonies. The argument that there existed a bifurcation of power between colonies and metropole and, indeed, that the power exercised in colonies was more transparently barbaric than the power exercised 'at home' is one we can find scattered in different variations throughout critical scholarship, not least the works of Karl Marx, who writes, 'The profound hypocrisy and inherent barbarism of bourgeois civilization lies unveiled before our eyes, turning from its home, where it assumes respectable forms, to the colonies, where it goes naked' (1942: 192). In Foucault a similar though distinct gesture is repeated in *Society Must Be Defended*, where he argues that while 'European models' of juridical and political power and weapons were exported to other continents, 'it also had a considerable boomerang effect on the mechanisms of power in the West, and on the apparatuses, institutions and techniques of power' (2004: 103). Colonial power, in many ways, is then read as the frontier of new technologies of subjugation that eventually find their way back into the metropole.[1] Police power has been read as being a significant element of this process.

In order to understand this more fully, it's worth looking at the way that states of emergency and outbursts of state violence were being conceived of and theorized by jurists in colonies. Writing of the use of martial law in Jamaica in the nineteenth century, Nasser Hussain discusses a protest in October 1865 which turned violent and in which protestors were killed. Martial law was afterwards declared, and according to the official account, by January 1866, '439 people were put to death, either by being shot on the spot or hanged after court martial, 600 men and women were publicly flogged, and over 1,000 cottages were burnt down' (2019: 110). This event garnered unusual attention and debate in England not least because of the execution of George William Gordon. Gordon, a 'prominent mulatto', had become a landowner, married a white woman and worked as a magistrate and politician (2019: 110). Shock was expressed and the legality of Gordon's execution was questioned because it emerged that he was not involved in any of the violence that immediately preceded the declaration of martial law nor even in the location at the time the protest took place.[2] A royal commission was instigated to look into these events and decide whether there were grounds to prosecute the person responsible – the British Governor Edward John Eyre. The commission decided not to prosecute on the grounds that 'there had been a genuine danger' and that Eyre had been right to react vigorously. They also argued, however, that marital law had been maintained for too long and that the punishment meted out had been 'excessive and barbarous, the burning of houses wanton and cruel' (Hall 1989: 183). For Hussain, the fact that the commission found that Eyre was in the right to react as he did, despite claims of excessiveness, created a 'split between the legal identity of the metropole and of the colony' (2019: 111) because Gordon could not be considered an immediate threat to the British state. Given that Gordon was not 'an insurgent, not imminently involved in violence against the state at the moment of his execution' (2019: 111) meant that the necessity of his execution could not necessarily be sustained by reference to the English 'doctrine of necessity' (2019: 111). This resulted in a back and forth between parliamentarians, jurists and others who sought to question or defend this execution on grounds of legality. The question of race, however, became central to the defence of Eyre and the violence he enacted in Jamaica. As Hussain notes, a jurist named Finlason decried those who wanted to prosecute Eyre for 'missing the crucial racial dimension of the situation' (2019: 112). He goes on to say that

> The fact that the ratio of the black population to the whites was 450,000 to 13,000, and that the whites feared a planned conspiracy to expel or kill them, meant for Finlason that the response to the rebellion had to look beyond the imminent violence. The Lord Chief Justice had, according to Finlason, made the mistake 'that he looked only to the outbreak, and forgot the rebellion of which it was the outbreak. In other words, he was thinking of a riot or a casual revolt'. (2019: 112)[3]

Crucially, to the extent that English common law did apply in the Jamaican colony, Finlason argued that it was meant for the English and their offspring, 'not for Africans' (2019: 113). For Hussain, this use of martial law and its legal justification then inevitably had 'ideological consequences' that returned 'to

Britain itself' (2019: 114): an expanded martial law that sees both the powers permissible and how long it may be in place for enlarged as a consequence of its use in the colonies. However, what I wish to underscore here is that we cannot neatly use the colony/metropole distinction to understand this use of 'excessive' and 'barbarous' violence precisely because both the colony and the metropole are *internally* differentiated along racial lines. In other words, the subjection to pre-emptive state violence on the grounds of self-defence and necessity does not occur because the colonies were subject to different law(s) (indeed, as we saw, English common law was thought to be operative in Jamaica but only for white people) but because whiteness was being constructed *through* anti-Blackness[4] – a process that was not bifurcated strictly along geographical and territorial lines.

The argument that an unbounded police power emerges elsewhere to rebound back to 'the West' is not an argument that has disappeared but can be found in many contemporary analyses of security, policing and state violence. Along with specific institutional arrangements found in prisons, it is thought that technologies like 'the fingerprint, the checkpoint' (Abourhame 2018: 107) first emerged in colonial governance to then be exported back to European heartlands. This theorization is also found in contemporary literature discussing security, warfare and police practices, where it is stated that 'interrogation procedures, urban assault and crowd control' as well as 'shoot to kill policies' (Denman 2020: 1144) are all part of contemporary 'colonial boomerangs'. For Stephen Graham, there is a 'new military urbanism' that is experimented with and tested on people in 'colonial warzones such as Gaza or Baghdad' where colonial strategies are subsequently 'imitated' and 'diffused through the securitisation of Western urban life' (2010: xvi–xvii). In *Empire's Endgame* the 'militarisation of everyday life' is considered to be a 'colonial aftershock, making its belated appearance on the shores of the mother country' (Bhattacharyya et al. 2021: 153). What this highlights is that there is an underlying current of theory and scholarship that sees state violence, states of exception, 'militarisation of the police' and so forth as techniques of power exercised on 'other' populations before being used on domestic territory. Or, in the terms of my argument, there is an unbounding of police power that occurs elsewhere before it rebounds back 'home'.

Turning back to Agamben for a moment, his idea that it is the first Gulf War that sees sovereignty 'finally introduced into the figure of police' (2000: 114) can now be seen in another light. The fact that it is the Gulf War that for Agamben constitutes this 'threshold moment' is not incidental but rather speaks to a spatial configuration that sees the unbounding of police power in an 'elsewhere' – that is, not within the geographical borders of the 'West' – that is enacting this sovereign/police power abroad. The date of these arguments Agamben makes about police and sovereign power is striking: 1991 was also the year that saw the release of the footage showing the beating of Rodney King, the subsequent acquittal of all the police officers involved the year after and the Los Angeles uprising that followed. Given that it was the United States at the forefront of the Gulf War, to speak of a newly 'sovereign' US police power being exercised *internationally* with no mention of how it was being exercised *domestically* speaks to the problems posed by the construction of temporal and spatial splits to comprehend the functioning of police power being analysed here.[5]

To see an unbounding of police power occurring in an-other time or space means that, as per da Silva, a thoroughly 'modern' West emerges in bounded territoriality that can disavow the origins of an 'uncivilised' police power as either being 'back then' or 'over there' but nevertheless may also have unfortunate reverberations in the here and now. The 'boomerang' thesis also holds on to this configuration in that it doesn't question the split between domestic and international but rather reproduces it in order to explain how police power becomes unconstrained and displays its brutality in European lands. This idea or variations of it has been reproduced by some in seeking to explain the 'excessiveness' of US policing. And it is precisely this that is challenged by Stuart Schrader, who examines American policing both internally and abroad and argues that

> such an account of how the violence of empire reverberates domestically relies on two implicit claims that can reassert the nationalism of the liberal creedal narrative of providential transcendence of the history of US racism. First it suggests that techniques of rule in imperial peripheries are inherently more violent than actions elsewhere and thus corrode otherwise liberal, democratic polities at home when they return. This claim however risks colluding in isolationist, nationalistic arguments against US empire that raise the specter of the degradation of US character through sexual, violent, and /or cultural encounters. (2019: 232–3)

For Schrader, far from a clear distinction between police powers used abroad and on American soil, there was a 'unified field of vision that did not distinguish security practices used overseas from those used at home' (2019: 258).

Contemporary accounts of British police power have also seen a plethora of arguments that see it as 'excessive' to then rebound back to the mainland to be meted out on 'formerly colonised populations' (Bhattacharyya et al. 2021: 153). The difficulty in understanding how and why certain people are subjected to police power over and above others is indicated by the term 'formerly colonised populations': a term that is here bearing a weight that I argue it cannot withstand. Once again an excessive and racialized police violence is turned onto a certain demographic of people that is explained by reference to a previous colonial era. Much like the previous critiques of the racial studied in this chapter, this doesn't actually constitute an explanation because those who are subject to police violence are described as 'previously colonised' and thus their racialization is presupposed and explained by reference to a historic and foreign elsewhere that appears in the metropole. This then gets folded into an idea of race difference, thus circumventing an analysis of the *production* of race difference. Indeed, if we take for granted the notion of 'formerly colonized' when analysing who is subject to a 'militarised' form of governance then our understanding of the machinations of state and police violence is limited to an idea of racism which tends to repeat that 'excessive' police violence is the result of (an unexamined) race difference and that this police violence can then be understood by its historicization.

The case of Northern Ireland is particularly illustrative in this regard and holds a significant place in narratives about police power and colonial violence in Britain. It is Northern Ireland that is seen to provide the 'material infrastructure for militarised policing on the British mainland, while the ever increasing presence of racialised immigration provided the discursive justification' (Bhattacharyya et al. 2021: 153). The oft-cited fact that rubber bullets were used to quell unrest and resistance in Northern Ireland but not used on the British mainland provides contemporary critiques of police power with grounds for the claim that it is colonial policing that is exercised in more violent and more despotic ways which then reverberates back to the mainland later.[6] However, it is worth asking the question: What does the rubber bullet symbolize for narratives about colonial versus domestic policing that actual bullets do not? The answer might lie, I would argue, in the category of the racial being analysed here. That is to say, if rubber bullets have been used to quell 'public order' situations and uprisings against British rule, then it is worth thinking about the actual bullets that have been used on 'individuals' not necessarily part of a wider protest or 'public order' event. Chris Kaba, Mark Duggan, John Charles de Menezes and Azelle Rodney were all shot and killed by police officers in England. While not totally irrelevant, I wonder what is lost or obscured when these killings are framed as a process of police 'militarization' or indeed as the result of colonial 'boomerangs' or 'aftershocks' because this is to make external something immanent and internally productive. That is, if we are to understand racialized police violence we cannot resort to pregiven racialized terms (such as formerly colonized) because this is to see racial subjection as a consequence of racial difference and not as productive of it.

We also should not necessarily see this violence as a consequence of a (post) colonial power because this is to see police power as *becoming excessive* in the colonial encounter which does not account for how the racial already operates internally and immanently to justify state violence on the grounds of necessity. To cite the colonial origins of police is not to critique police power, precisely because it does not answer the question of why acts of police violence are repeated in the present, something that cannot be grasped by attending simply to a historical 'origin'. Without attending to the truly global ramifications of 'the racial' that da Silva tracks, we are left with an analysis of police violence that sees people subject to police violence and indeed the unbounded character of that violence as (post)colonial. Therefore, as much as this book is challenging the *periodization* of police power that posits unbounded police power as 'premodern', I would also like to insist that the spatial split that sees unconstrained police violence finding its origin and zenith 'elsewhere' as needing to be troubled.

For da Silva, sociological theorizing after the Second World War propagates the idea that racism is a consequence of the interactions between different racial groups, posited as 'cultural' difference – and therefore represents a departure from earlier nineteenth-century theorizations of scientific racism. Nevertheless racism and its effects are frequently posited as being a hangover from a previous time, a non-modern presence in the present that has failed to modernize. These sociologies posit that race difference results in the exclusion of racial groups within 'an otherwise modern (egalitarian) social space' (2001: 433). The notion that racism is something external to modernity even if frequently found within it is problematized, and this becomes visible in her study of sociological theories of race relations where she finds that 'a crucial effect of the historical re-signification of race relations was to suggest that people of colour and *racist* whites both exhibit signs of non-modern consciousness, both effects of the former's *race difference*' (2001: 434, emphasis in original). Hangovers of a bygone era, racism and its effects are posited as being something that originated 'elsewhere' in another time – a 'signifier of outsidedness, entailing the emergence of "mental contents" foreign to modern minds' (2001: 434). When trying to account for racialized police violence, therefore, it is important to understand wider epistemic transformations that does not take for granted an idea of race difference, nor posit police violence as something 'external' that then appears 'inside'. This is to say that without attending to the epistemological shifts that occur, and the political ontology of concern here, indeed how the racial produces subjects and spaces that are divided along a bifurcation between 'law' and 'nature', one cannot grasp the machinations of police power as it exists today.

## Revisiting the state of nature

What has become clear in this investigation is that nature and violence have been constructed as inextricably linked – a double process whereby nature is conceived as the site of violence but also where violence is naturalized in the sense that it is coupled with *necessity*. This nature/violence nexus is seen as the external beginning of the state and of law which must be excluded from ethical life and the state. In Hegel, this takes the form of a violent beginning (but not foundation) where 'heroes' violently transgress 'uncivilized' conditions in order to found a new, civilized order. With the coupling of nature and violence, where the right to use violence as a form of self-defence is conceived as a 'right of nature' (Hobbes 1996: 91) we can begin to see how nature, necessity and violence coalesce in police power. It is precisely through the invocation of necessity, self-defence and indeed order that police power is hinged to sovereignty. If (the state of) nature functions as a principle internal to sovereign power then what is the relation between this and *an-archic* police power and anti-Black violence?

The linking of Blackness to a 'state of nature' is a point that can be perceived in enlightenment thought as well as in the critiques of enlightenment thought that point to the racialized contents of concepts used by thinkers such as Kant, Hegel and Locke. For Charles Mills, Black people are conceived in this Western tradition of political thought 'as carrying the state of nature around with them, incarnating wildness and wilderness in their person' (1999: 87). For Hegel, 'the negro is an example of animal man in all his savagery and lawlessness' (1975: 177) and, furthermore, this 'sensuous barbarism can only be restrained by despotic power' (1975: 186). The violence of the state of nature is thus constituted as necessitating a despotism – the suppression of natural violence through sovereign violence. For Hegel this takes the form of 'the "great man" or "great individual" . . . who unites consciousness and unconsciousness, morality and crime in his person, setting himself apart from the multitude at the risk of being violently reintegrated into it by being punished for his audacity' (Balibar 2015: 39). Hegel's 'heroes', however, act only in 'uncivilised conditions' (Hegel 2008: 98), and it is precisely these 'uncivilised conditions' that constitute the state of nature seen as a historic and foreign phenomenon that is external to the state and ethical life.

It is this movement – the movement that seeks to justify a previous violence through an inclusive exclusion – that is under consideration here. The desire to position this violence as necessary and justified – and indeed, foundational for – but simultaneously excluded from ethical life. This is precisely what da Silva tracks in her 'scene of nature' whereby the 'natural' violence of necessity coupled with the analytics of raciality are *productive* and not merely exclusionary. Once we dispense with ideas that see anti-Black police violence as remnants or hangovers from a brutal past, but rather as having a productive function that is inseparable from 'ethical life' and law we can begin to dispense with notions that see anti-Black police violence as a non-modern, unethical event in an otherwise modern, ethical world.[7]

The question of temporality is also raised by the thought that the state of nature exists *prior* to, or *after* the state, but as we have seen via Agamben we would do well to consider it as immanent to sovereign power. da Silva makes sense of this by deploying the concept of 'scene of nature' (2017), distinguishing her own concept from the Hobbesian 'state of nature'. She explains:

> needing neither expression nor actualization, belonging neither to time nor to space, being neither possible nor potential, the *scene of nature* is virtual, whatever takes place there is *known*. *What-is-known* does belong in signification, it presumes signifiers, but the closure, signification, takes place in justification, as it provides an explanation for that which is a privilege of the living (sovereign) thing, namely, the decision. (da Silva 2017: 287)

Yet, returning to Hobbes's *De Cive* we can see that the idea that the state of nature exists in a time *prior* to the state is complicated by his formulation of state of nature as something where the state is thought of "*as if* it were dissolved" (emphasis added, in Agamben 1998: 36). The *as if* here functions to suspend the temporal dimension of the state of nature and indeed its placement *outside* of the state, making it much closer to da Silva's scene of nature described earlier.[8] For Agamben as well, 'the state of nature is therefore not truly external to *nomos* but rather contains its virtuality. The state of nature (certainly in the modern era, but probably also in that of the Sophists) is the being-in-potentiality of the law, the law's self-presupposition as "natural law"' (Agamben 1998: 36). It is da Silva's concept of the racial, however, that constitutes the substance of this state of nature that forms the virtual terrain on which *an-archic* police power operates. Indeed it is this concept of the racial that '(trans) forms acts otherwise conceived as contingent into expressions of universal determinants, the "laws of nature" as apprehended in scientific signification, which always already define how certain modern subjects appear before the law' (da Silva 2017: 277).

In this regard, James Trafford's discussion of Kant's concept of the state of nature is particularly illuminating:

> As state of nature, Black people are positioned not simply as antithesis to the lawful subject whose freedom would be guaranteed under social order produced through lawfulness. Since for Kant anybody existing outside of a (European) nation-state embodies the state of nature, they represent a threat to order. As he writes, '[somebody] in the state of nature deprives me of this security; even if he doesn't do anything to me – by the mere fact that he isn't subject to any law and is therefore a constant threat to me'. In other words Black and Indigenous people – slaves and colonized – were a perpetual threat. The threat is not limited to political sovereignty, but as disordering alterity that could open-out thought and law – destabilising both – undoing property and so also undoing freedom. (2022)

As such, regardless of whether they engage in criminal *acts* the Black person is positioned outside of the law, not as a criminal, but in a condition that precedes the distinction between criminal and non-criminal. This means that those that are subject to police violence do not need to have engaged in any criminal acts for the violence to be justified by police by the invocation of necessity and *what-is-known*. Conversely, those acts of police violence are not considered to be criminal because of the logic of police power being outlined here. This logic is epitomized by the case of the Jamaican revolt discussed earlier in this chapter, and how the extreme violence and martial law that ensued was conceived of and justified; that is, that the extreme violence and deaths at the hands of the English and declaration of martial law in Jamaica in 1865 were *justifiable* because there was a fear of violence and that fear was based on *what-is-known*, that is, that the Black people in Jamaica represented an ever-present threat that could not be reduced to a singular event or moment of violence. This is why even the execution of someone who was not an 'immanent threat' could be described as an act of 'defence' by those wishing to cast the violence as falling within the doctrine of necessity. In this reasoning, then, riots or uprisings do not need to break out to justify the pre-emptive violence of the state. Those that recoil from said violence as 'excessive' are then pointed to the wider 'atmosphere' of violence that justifies police violence that is positioned as (self)defence.

This logic is also confirmed in accounts by the police themselves of the places that they police, describing entering 'hostile zones' replete with references to war, and with the streets of those places being considered by police 'like foreign territory' (Schrader 2019: 2). Former Met police sergeant Simon Willmott speaking about the 2011 London Riots with BBC news said that 'being in such an area as this [Tottenham, North London] with the link to the firearms that it has, there's that risk of threat as well' (BBC 2016). Didier Fassin documents accounts of police officers entering the banlieues in Paris, where police officers on the beat described the banlieues as a 'jungle' and as a 'war zone' and where officers felt they faced constant threats of being attacked (2013: 52). The mainly Black residents of the banlieues were discussed by the police officers intervening in those areas as being 'savages' (2013: 52), mirroring the language of the violence/nature nexus found in the construction of the state of nature under consideration here. The effects of this construction of these areas are not hard to predict: 'Both internal administrative investigation by disciplinary committees and external judicial investigation by examining judges ended in a no further action 9/10 cases' (p.115). Police violence in these areas rarely appears 'in front of the law' but when it does, in nine out of ten cases it is considered so straightforwardly justifiable that no further investigation is needed.

A particularly stark case in point is the case of Amadou Diallo, which da Silva discusses at length. Diallo was a Guinean student who was shot *forty-one times* by police in the Bronx; this was not considered to be a crime by a jury, which acquitted all the police involved. The court case testimony is saturated with 'references to danger, fear and crime' that the South Bronx epitomized, a place so dangerous and fearful and violent 'that the state itself trembles at the core of its authorized violent apparatuses' (2017: 288). She writes: 'the killing of Amadou Diallo, in the South Bronx on February 4 1999 was not considered an "act punishable by law" nor "injurious to the public welfare": the four officers were acquitted of two charges of second-degree murder and one charge of reckless endangerment' (2017: 275). No crime was said to have been committed because of the invocation of necessity and objectivity: this killing was not, da Silva writes, a criminal act but a legal-rational one. She continues: 'Before and after the legal decisions – the *shooting* and the *acquittal* – the killing of Amadou Diallo would not constitute a crime because the *scene of nature* always already resolves it as a racial event, that is, as "urban violence"' (2017: 277).

Irreducible to either category of law-founding or law-preserving violence, we cannot make sense of this event solely by reference to the concepts of foundation or preservation because it exceeds both. Crucial to this suspension of the distinction and indeed the concept of force-of-law discussed earlier in the book, however, is the construction of Blackness as signifying 'a domain outside the terrain of the legal' (da Silva 2001: 426) while whiteness was produced to 'indicate the form of consciousness able to conceive of universal principles that emerged in the modern European space – the only raced consciousness able to fulfil the material and *moral* projects of modernity' (da Silva 2001: 431). For da Silva, 'The most crucial effect of this socio-logical construction has been to produce blackness, and the place of residence of black people as *natural* (pre-conceptual and pre-historical) signs of social pathology' (2001: 426). Here, the racial and the figure of (state of) nature is productive of the terrain of the legal in a similar way to how the state of exception has been defined. In Agamben's recapitulation of the state of exception, acts which are neither legislations nor transgressions of the law, but rather acts of nonjuridical violence or force-of-law find expression in places such as the 'camp'. Here, however, we can see that without attending to the racial, the state of exception remains a discrete temporal/geographical space of sovereign power which later becomes 'normalized' or expanded to include more and more geographical space and over longer periods of time.

The violent suppression and negation of nature and natural violence and a violent elimination of the state's own 'primordial violence equated with nature'

(Balibar 2015: 47) is met with the 'natural law' of self-defence here construed as *an-archic* police violence – a principle *internal* to modernity and the machinations of Western legal powers. Police power, then, not only as mediating universal and particular but as a constant violent suppression, engagement and production of 'nature'. By resisting the narratives that posit the unbounding or unboundedness of police power in either a temporal or spatial 'elsewhere' but rather locating it in the heart of the modern liberal state via the concept of nature, we can begin to dispense with the idea that the brutality of police power is 'revealed' or uncovered in Western states in times of crisis and/or war. Precisely what is at stake here is an *an-archic* police power that confounds the distinction between contingency and necessity by invoking necessity (self-defence) in order to suture acts that could be considered 'irrational', 'particular' or 'immediate' to the sphere of legality and universality, the realm that, for Hegel, is the realm of 'ethical life'.

Much like we must question any periodization of the state of nature which would posit it as a time *preceding* the time of the state, we should also question the idea that an association of Blackness with the state of nature is to construct Blackness as representing a temporal structure outside of modernity.[9] That is, Black people are not *excluded* from the categories associated with modernity, progress, justice law and so on by virtue of supposedly existing in a temporal plane that precedes these concepts. Indeed, it would be simple enough at this point to see police violence as the result of placing Black people outside of history, outside of reason, in a distant 'past' that they have yet to escape. In other words, the association of Blackness with a previous condition that Europeans feel themselves to have left behind with the advent of modernity – a condition that over and again in Western political thought necessitates a violent response, one where the condition can only be surpassed through a law-founding violence. Yet the complexity of the temporality of anti-Black violence is elided in this formulation as will become clear when we further consider the relationship between past and present regarding the analysis of police power.

## Time and anti-Black violence

One of the key points about police power under consideration here is how the split between a premodern and modern police power functions as a consequence of the modern construction of that split. It is the present construction of a past that is then conceived in contradistinction to it that is at the centre of the work of Kathleen Davis who tracks the *'becoming-feudal'* (2008: 7) of the Middle Ages. The argument Davis presents is that a modern European 'present' was distinguished from a feudal European 'past' that was to be fashioned as an epoch of subjugation and slavery. Connecting this to theories of secularization and sovereignty, Davis attends to the manner in which feudalism was constructed in terms of a retroactive split:

> the redefined humanity so crucial to colonial rule and to the logic of empire *also* depended upon a reworked, embattled identification of and with a European 'past', which was articulated in minute detail yet superseded by a historiographical idealism that ultimately bonded – in the breach, so to speak – the 'Middle Ages' and the colonial subject (2008: 34).

Ostensibly paradoxically, it is the apex of European empire building and slavery that sees authoritarian subjugation under forms of absolute sovereignty relegated to a past and also an elsewhere. The 'feudal past' of Europe is constructed, Davis argues, through juridical and political commentaries on sovereignty, which grounded 'arguments regarding the "free" political subject and a social contract and facilitated the transference of the problem of the contemporary slave trade to a brutal past' (2008: 8). This construction is perfectly exemplified in the work of Jean Bodin, for whom slavery is a danger to the unity and liberty of the commonwealth in the sense of a 'divided household', and therefore slavery means, for Bodin, civil war (2008: 47–8). Slavery is also, however, necessarily in Europe's past, something he sees as being threatened by the activities of the Portuguese and Spanish bringing slavery to Europe:

> Bodin finds that the recent encroachment of slavery within Europe through the actions and example of the Portuguese threatens to erase this territorial distinction by undoing time... the renewal of slavery would unbury the past, and reverse the process of forgetting that is necessary... "for the creation of a nation". Unity is only possible if the violence of past difference is forgotten (Davis 2008: 48).

We see here, once again, the stakes of conceptualization of time and slavery – whereby modern European states are constructed on the basis that slavery in modern Europe is an impossibility because (modern) sovereignty is predicated on a relationship between free political subjects and sovereign that the existence of slavery would undermine. For thinkers like Bodin, slavery could only exist in the present, then, if it was elsewhere. The significance of slavery and violence for conceptions of time is here illuminated in startling detail. Violence in this tradition acquired a temporal index – violence is natural-past or present-elsewhere. But wherever it resides, it will always be justified by the legal order in its relationship to nature and law. It might not be strictly part of the legal order but it is legitimate. It might be excessive, but it is necessary, and this is known because of the temporal register it indexes. However, what is important here is that this temporal index becomes complicated when one considers anti-Black police violence.

The relationship between past and present weighs heavy on anyone that tries to make sense of police power. Scholars wishing to make sense of police violence have tended to do so by constructing narratives that see the present as following on in linear progression from the past. It is like that *now* because of how it was *then*. People are brutalized by the state because they are 'formerly colonized'. Police violence is excessive because it was made to be so in the colonies. In these formulations, police violence is made sense of only inasmuch as it references another time or another place. A circular argument forms in the place of analysis. Yet scholars of Black study challenge theorizations of the temporal that sees anti-Black violence in terms of linear sequentiality. Christina Sharpe's 'Wake' (2016), Saidiya Hartman's 'afterlives' of slavery (2021) and da Silva's 'racial event' (2017b)[10] all point to the necessity of seeing history and time *otherwise*. Hartman's 'afterlives' do not posit that anti-Black violence lies unchanged since slavery; this is *not* a temporal grammar that signals either continuity or rupture, but rather their indistinction. Hartman conceives of these afterlives in *Lose Your Mother* where she writes the following:

> Slavery had established a measure of man and a ranking of life and worth that has yet to be undone. If slavery persists as an issue in the political life of black America, it is not because of an antiquarian obsession with bygone days or the burden of a too-long memory, but because black lives are still imperiled and devalued by a racial calculus and a political arithmetic that were entrenched centuries ago. This is the afterlife of slavery – skewed life chances, limited access to health and education, premature death, incarceration and impoverishment. (2021: 6)

Once again this is not to claim that anti-Black violence lies unchanged, nor to posit slavery as a temporal *origin* of all that comes after. Rather a temporal register is inaugurated that cannot be categorized as 'past' or 'future' but rather as Biko Mandela Gray articulates it 'the always':

> The 'always' remains. It is not properly phenomenological, but it is a structure of experience, a structure of *existence*. It is temporal, and it is engendered by the hold, but the hold is not a *genesis* (when did slavery begin? When did it end? 1619 is certainly not a proper time stamp for slavery.) The hold engenders and maintains a stunted temporality, one that disallows the marking of time. In the hold, the always persists. Interminably. (2022: 5)

If law is suspended in the state of exception, a happening that allows for an unalloyed violence or force-of-law to take hold, we might think of time as being suspended here in a similar manner: linear, progressive time is suspended and a violent interminable 'now' appears so that linear time can be produced as something stable for those whose existence is not marked by such suspended time. For Calvin Warren, we need a new category of time altogether to understand the afterlives of slavery – one that he calls 'black time' – which is 'without duration, it is a horizon of time that eludes objectification, foreclosing such idioms as "getting over", "getting through" or "getting beneath"' (2016: 56). This is to say that linear sequential time cannot be applied to slavery and its afterlives but, rather, throws 'the past, present and future into virtual crisis' (Warren 2016: 62). For Warren the attempt to periodize slavery in itself is a form of metaphysical violence, an attempt to dominate and transform something that was not a singular event, but rather throws the notion of time and event into question. By trying to force anti-Black violence into an 'object-event' that can be gotten over, gotten through and left behind, there is an attempt to transform slavery and its afterlives into something that can be made knowable and calculable in and through time – as brutal 'past' or an unfortunate remnant of that past in the present. As Warren argues, 'Metaphysics seeks to dominate and to transform the event-horizon into an object-event' (Warren 2016: 57) and these 'Object-events are fraudulent for they present an impossible and orderly world that is fully knowable, transparent and calculable within metaphysical logic' (Warren 2016: 57).

How might we understand the construction of the 'event' of police violence as an object-event with a beginning and an end, a cause and effect? In attempting to conceive of the 'event' in this way we posit that we can 'know' it through its passage through time. And this is precisely what scholars such as Warren are challenging through their work on time. This is why we cannot speak of origins because this would be to assume that the police violence we witness today has its 'origins' in colonial violence which have continued into the present rather than a repetition of the 'always now', which is to say, gratuitous violence that does not have an immediate cause in the past. It is also not the case, however, that we should idealize the relationship between past and present as one of *rupture*, where time is split into a before and after. Following Agamben, we can see that to conceive of political institutions in this way falls prey to the idea that one has 'found' a temporal split, and that one can gain access to the 'before' as distinguished from the present, rather than the before being in fact founded in and by the 'after'.

The split between 'premodern' and 'modern' policing should not then be seen as the outcome of an actual historical bifurcation, with premodern police power located in Europe that is coterminous with absolutism, and therefore, by extension, unfreedom that is separated temporally from modern policing that is refashioned and tamed in line with doctrines of liberty, liberal government and democracy. In questioning this periodization as well as the assumed functional split between domestic and international, we can begin to unravel the ways in which the past and the elsewhere are indeed *present* in both senses of the word: that is, not somewhere else or in another time but are operative *in the here and now*. For thinkers such as da Silva, in the eyes of the state, this past (that is not past) and the elsewhere (that is not elsewhere) are visible through the anti-Black violence and murder of Black people by police that is made to be – and constitutive of – the legal-rational through the invocation of necessity and self-defence. Taking seriously da Silva's intervention thus means that a repetition of the colonial *origins* of policing cannot grasp anti-Black police violence today, in the sense that this violence is not a *remnant* but rather what Martinot and Sexton call 'the avant-garde of white supremacy' (2003). Indeed, by seeking an *origin* of racist police violence, therefore, some may be unwittingly contributing to the narrative that the excessiveness of police violence and white supremacy can be made legible (and therefore unravelled) through its historicization. For Martinot and Sexton this would be mistaken because

> white supremacy is nothing more than what we perceive of it; there is nothing beyond it to give it legitimacy, nothing beneath or outside of it to give it justification. The structure of its banality is the surface on which it

operates. . . . There is no dark corner that, once brought to the light of reason, will unravel its system . . . it is in fact nothing but its very practices. (2003)

Much like the *an-archic* character of police power I am theorizing in this book, Sexton and Martinot theorize white supremacy, and thus we should think about the relationship between the two as we might think about the relationship between a hand and a glove.

# Concluding remarks

### 'No drugs were found'

This refrain that reverberates and echoes so much in reportage on instances of police violence often deemed egregious, excessive and brutal are addressed to someone, but whom? The repetition of the statement of the absent drugs serves as a ghostly presence that indicates the *potential* for drugs to have been there. This ruse that the law is able to conjure operates to produce the terrain on which 'universal' law can operate by marking those for whom the distinction between a transgression of the law and the non-transgression of a law matters and those for whom it doesn't.[1] Two cases on opposite sides of the Atlantic: Child Q and Breonna Taylor. One, a traumatizing strip search of a child on her period and the other, the killing of a 26-year-old woman – prompted the following declarations:

> Two officers later arrived at the school, Child Q, was escorted out of an exam, and they initiated a strip search of her, but no drugs were found. (House of Commons Library 2022)

> police had alleged in their warrant that Glover was receiving drug packages at Taylor's home, but no drugs or cash were found. (Yahoo, Associated Press 2021)

The retrospective, post-facto statements that simply and coolly announce an absence of drugs serve to conceal the *an-archē* of the machinations of police power that operate, as this work has shown, without an origin or foundation outside of its exercise. Which is to say the stated 'search' for drugs functions to retroactively alloy police violence – which has already occurred and for which there is no redress – to an account or a narrative which renders that violence not situated in, but constitutive of, the domains of the legible, the sensible, the 'rational' and the legal. The universality of the law is thus produced by acts of racial, metaphysical violence which situate certain people as eliding the distinction between guilt and innocence, criminal and non-criminal. The repetition of the refrain, 'no drugs were found', is thus a ritual of myth-making, a reference to an antecedent origin or foundation for the ensuing action that veils their gaping absence.

For Jackie Wang, 'a liberal politics of recognition can only reproduce a guilt-innocence schematization that fails to grapple with the fact that there is an *a priori* association of Blackness with guilt (criminality)' (2018: 263) The problem with this formulation is that it is assumed that the distinction between guilt and innocence is functional with regard to anti-Black violence. One issue to be found in many critical texts that grapple with this issue is that the problem becomes the conflation of Blackness with guilt and criminality, what Paul Gilroy has termed a concern with the 'alien predisposition to crime' that 'contaminates' 'any black, all blacks' (1982: 52). However, a critique of the 'myth of black criminality' (1982: 52) is also not a critique of police power. For if we agree that the problem is the presupposed 'guilt' then this is to presume that police violence is a consequence of a presumed 'guilt'. Once again the police are placed in a secondary position to the law, their violence a response to a perceived *transgression* of the law (whether or not this is actually the case) that is signified by the race of the target of the police violence in question. The question of race once again is rebounded back onto the race of the individual victim of the violence: that is, that the racism they experience is a *consequence* of a racial difference that, as I have shown via da Silva, does not explain that which it sets out to. To be clear, the myth of Black criminality cannot explain anti-Black police violence because this is to assume that the police violence in question is a response to 'criminality'. Once we take into account the previous discussion of the state of nature, where there is no 'crime' or criminality, but only the natural state of violence and self-defence, then the idea that anti-Black police violence can be explained by the liberal idea of law and its categories becomes untenable. In other words, the distinction between criminal and non-criminal is a distinction *internal* to civil society itself, a distinction that is incoherent in the domain that is constitutive of, but rendered as external to civil society and the state: the state of nature.

To recapitulate, this book has argued that police power is *an-archic* in character. Police power should not be seen as the implementation of a sovereign will, nor as the enforcement of law. It should not be seen as upholding an order the content of which is known in advance, nor simply as the repression of disorder. By becoming responsible for order itself police power becomes unbounded and dislocated from sovereignty and law while simultaneously being linked to them, in the form of a mythological projection of a legitimizing, transcendent power from which its own power derives. It is this economy of power, or vicarious ontology, an incessant shuttling back and forth between immanence and transcendence, that I have attended to, arguing that police are the an-archic groundless ground of sovereignty itself.

As I discussed in the beginning of this book, the commonplace understanding of the history of police is structured around a series of breaks. One such break supposedly occurs between the Aristotelian conception of order, which casts order as a *natural* phenomenon, and the Hobbesian paradigm, which sees order as *artificial*. This in turn is followed by a liberal paradigm, which once again sees order as natural or spontaneous and as, for that reason, requiring limited government. At each break, it is supposed that the underlying metaphysics of order determines the predominant political form that sovereignty and government take.

This binary between natural and artificial order is not restricted to interpretative accounts of the canon of Western political thought; it is, in fact, also operative in this canon itself. Indeed, in the Hobbesian model, natural disorder and violence are thought to necessitate an artificial order administered by a strong all-powerful state; in its liberal counterpart, the natural order to things is thought to require a limited state which should interfere only to repress disorder (which is seen as the function of police). Whether it is conceptualized as a divine hand, a sovereign plan or providential touch, order has been seen as the proof of a transcendent will structuring the world. In a separate but related strand of argumentation, anarchy and order are commonly linked together in an oppositional relation, casting these two concepts as mutually exclusive, and positing the very existence of the state as the dividing line between the two. Here, anarchy is conceived as a pre- or post-political condition without government and, crucially, without order.

What I endeavoured to demonstrate is that these conceptual binaries – between artificial and natural order, metaphysics and political form, anarchy and order – do more to obscure than illuminate the shifting relationships between transcendence and immanence, sovereignty and government, in and around which police power takes shape. Once we dismantle the presupposition that the metaphysics of order unidirectionally determines politics we can begin to see how it works in the other direction, that is, how the political form in fact determines the metaphysics of order that it has to presume as prior. In the terms that interest us here, it is not that the police function is limited and circumscribed by the 'nature' of order but rather that what order is, is determined in itself by the (police) power invoking it.

By noting the signatorial operations of order across a range of thinkers – in other words, by showing that order cannot be placed in an 'originary' position as either natural or artificial, divine or sovereign, but that it must be seen as always already relational – the stakes of police power in modernity can be rendered visible.[2] Following Agamben, who writes that 'the historical object is never given neutrally; rather it is always accompanied by an index or signature that constitutes it as image and temporally determines and conditions its legibility' (Agamben 2009: 73), I argue that the historical object of police should not be taken for granted but should be interrogated for how it has been constituted and conditioned by certain presuppositions and crucially its relationship to the signature of order.

As discussed in relation to Hobbes, the configuration of sovereign power as unconstrained from the law, decisionistic and improvisational has its roots both in the demand for 'order' and the suppression of anarchy, and in the manner in which the sovereign is seen as representative of a public will. The projection of the people as a transcendental legitimizing force dislocates sovereign power from the law; it is for this reason that the sovereign can justifiably kill an innocent person, since the will of the sovereign is by definition the will of each of its subjects. As I argued, far from disappearing after the decline of the police state and absolutism, this logic is to be found elsewhere, namely in the figure of police.

For Hegel, *Polizei* is that which mediates between the universal and particular, suturing the divide between a chaotic civil society in which individuals pursue their own self-interest and the realm of universality and freedom found in the transcendent state. What Hegel thus provides is the sense that police exist for the purpose of *relationality*, forming a bond that is not external and coercive but immanent and organic. I challenged Hegel's presentation of the state and of police through a reading that highlights, first, the existence of the 'rabble' and the poor who are the target of police power but also those who have only an 'arbitrary will' in Africa and with whom there can only be a relationship of coercion and 'despotism'. Far from a bounded power that Hegel wishes to present, police power becomes, in crucial moments in Hegel's system, necessarily unbounded.

In the second part of the book I examined in more detail the connection between police and law and police and sovereignty. In doing so I drew on critical theory, Benjamin and Agamben in particular, to demonstrate that Benjamin's diagnosis of modernity and sovereign power can illuminate the complex and shifting relationship between transcendence and immanence. The commonplace account of modernity as engendering the triumph of 'immanence' and the gradual excision of transcendence was shown, via Benjamin, to fall short for precisely the reason that the figure of police is not usually considered. Emblematic in this regard is Schmitt, who tussles with the problem of sovereign intervention in modernity, decrying its gradual excision with the ascent of liberalism. Without considering police, however, Schmitt ultimately cannot reckon with the *relation* between transcendence and immanence, and the economy of power that is precipitated in modernity, which is why the turn to Benjamin is necessary. It is in Benjamin that we find the notion that the transcendent is not excised, but rather that transcendence is 'transcended', making it immanent. The stakes of this subtle but significant difference with Schmitt's thesis is that sovereign power can re-emerge with catastrophic force, without being *representable* as such. Indeed, the God-like Leviathan sitting over and above the city that we find in Hobbes's frontispiece is no longer representable but neither does it disappear. In order to come to terms with this, I argue, a consideration of police power is crucial, for it is in the figure of police that this force is found.

It is also when considering police power via Benjamin and Agamben that we can understand that the gap between the law and its 'application' is not – and cannot be – resolved through recourse to concepts such as police discretion. Rather, it is in the figure of police that the distinction between 'law-founding' and law-preserving violence is suspended. Indeed, it is here I argue that while police are named as the law acting in the world, in reality they act in dislocation from it. Police are, I argued, a 'force-of-law', that is, they suspend the law while bearing its force, and it is here that the contiguity between the state of exception and police power reveals itself.

By attending to and reworking Agamben's account of the governmental machine, I argued that police are not simply reducible to an immanent governmental pole but, rather, exist in a complicated relation with sovereignty via the collateral effect, becoming the critical axis on which the governmental machine turns. That is, it is through a consideration of police power as projecting that from which it supposedly derives – sovereignty, the public, law and order – police power cannot be considered as auxiliary to the modern state.

This force-of-law is finally shown, via da Silva, as neither an exceptional event, nor a colonial remnant, but intrinsically linked to the production of 'race difference' that means Black people face disproportionate levels of police violence across different times and spaces. In so doing, I track the temporal index that violence has acquired as being natural-past or present-elsewhere that sees an *an-archic* and anti-Black police violence justified on the grounds of necessity and self-defence, a violence that was conceived of as (state of) nature. Revisiting the state of nature with da Silva we saw how this violence is not only rendered necessary but is productive of the operations of the machinations of legal-rationality.

Once we see that what has been presented as a remedy to the 'natural' anarchy that would reign without the state and without the police is, in actuality, a characteristic of police power itself, the notion that they uphold order, implement law or protect the common good can be firmly extinguished. In doing this, perhaps the work of imagining a world, where the always already justified state violence of necessity and self-defence is overcome, where the suspension of law/force-of-law continuum itself is rendered impossible and where police and sovereignty meet their end, can begin.

# Notes

## Introduction

1 In this regard see Campesi (2016), Dean (2006), Gordon (1991), Johnson (2014), Pasquino (1991).
2 See Burchell et al. (1991).
3 The British charity Inquest monitors and gathers data on deaths during or following police contact. Since 1990 there have been 1,691 deaths with no officer ever prosecuted for any of these deaths (2019).
4 In this way, I find my own project distinct from Dubber's (2005, 2006) for whom 'a comprehensive theory of the police would have to find room for the police department and its members, but one cannot hope to come to grips with the concept of police by focusing exclusively on the duties and skills of the cop on the beat' (2006: 108). My starting point, by contrast, was exactly the way in which the 'cop on the beat' could exercise what has been generally considered sovereign power.
5 See Mbembe (2003). For Foucault 'in the classical theory of sovereignty, the right of life and death was one of sovereignty's basic attributes' (2004: 240). Agamben, on the other hand, writes 'the sovereign sphere is the sphere in which it is permitted to kill without committing homicide and without celebrating a sacrifice' (1998: 83). As we will see, this power to take life is made particularly explicit by Hobbes, for whom the sovereign can kill an innocent person and this not be considered unjust (Hobbes 1996: 148).
6 Here we could also look to Jean Bodin for whom sovereign power is necessarily unconstrained by law. As Quentin Skinner writes, 'Bodin argues instead that the concept of positive law must be defined "without any other additions" as "the command of a sovereign concerning all his subjects" . . . finally, he stresses that this in turn means that any sovereign must by definition be *legibus solutus* – totally "acquitted" from any obligation to obey the positive laws of the state' (1978: 289).
7 I am, of course, not referring here to all of 'Western philosophy' but those philosophies which are usually understood to be canonical.

8 Here I am mostly referring to Enlightenment and liberal philosophies. There have been some works that deal with the status of police power vis-à-vis sovereignty and law, but most do not go further than to say that police *exercise* or *administer* sovereign power. For example, Seri argues that police practices are where 'sovereign prerogatives are administered every day' (2012: 153). For reasons that will become clear throughout the book, though similar, this is not the position I am advancing when I say that police power is *an-archic*.

9 Hinsley writes, 'men were driven under the influence of the idea of sovereignty to seek the unity which they increasingly needed and desired, and of which the idea of sovereignty was itself a symbol, by claiming that political power was vested exclusively in one or the other separate factors in the dualism, in the People or in the Ruler' (1966: 134).

10 As Quentin Skinner notes, there are important shifts to take note of in the formation of the concept of the modern state; these in themselves revolve around 'the independence of each *regnum* or *civitas* from any external and superior power' (1978: 351) and also 'the supreme authority within each independent *regnum* should be recognised as having no rivals within its own territories as a law-making power and an object of allegiance' (1978: 351).

11 While I recognize that not *all* theories of sovereignty presuppose its indivisibility, I argue that it is important for the mythology of sovereignty being dealt with here – mobilized by thinkers such as Hobbes, Hegel and Schmitt and structured by its theological origins, which I will go on to discuss in detail.

12 The concept *Polizei* was first recorded in German statutes in 1464 (Knemeyer 1980: 12).

13 For detailed analysis of the development of 'police' as it occurred with the police state on the Continent, see Raeff (1983), Knemeyer (1980), Chapman (1970), for more on *Polizeiwissenschaft* see Small (1909).

14 As Tribe notes, however, this is contrasted to the Cameralism of the 1820s, due to the separation of state and civil society and separation of *Polizei* from being explicitly concerned with welfare and happiness (1995: 29).

15 The objects to which police ordinances were aimed at regulating were potentially inexhaustible and could include things like blasphemy, clothes, civil contracts, measures and weights, drunkenness, beggars, weapons and sale of wool (Dubber 2005: 70).

16 As Foucault tells us with reference to a French administrative compendium, police see to as broad a range of things as the following religion, health, morals, public safety, liberal arts, trade, the poor, in other words, he finds that most treatises on police in the seventeenth to eighteenth centuries, the 'police see to everything' (1979: 249).

17 That the term 'police' is lexically adjoined to the Greek *polis* and the Latin *politia* is pointed out by Knemeyer who finds that '"*Polizei*" signified not only the satisfactory regulation of the community but the community itself – in an exact analogy with the twin meaning the word possessed in Aristotelian ethics and politics' (1980: 179). As I am arguing, however, police occurs throughout literature alongside concerns of *oikonomia* – the significance of which will become clearer with an examination of *oikonomia* to follow.

18 Zartaloudis notes that Aristotle finds in the *oikos* three groups of relations: '(1) despotic relations between the father and slaves; (2) paternal relations between parents and children; and (3) marital relations between husband and wife. What unites these three types of relation under the term *oikonomia* is a paradigm that can be defined, Agamben suggests, as economic or managerial (in the sense of administrative management) and, as such, as a non-epistemic and non-political paradigm. Aristotle notes that this economic or managerial paradigm is not an episteme, but denotes a certain way of being, which implies decisions and dispositions that confront specific problems each time and that safeguard the functional order (taxis) of the different parts of the *oikos*. In this sense *oikonomia* is always praxiological and non-epistemic referring to particular activities' (Zartaloudis 2010: 56).

19 While I will go into more detail in the penultimate chapter, it is via the category of the signature that Agamben proposes order as itself *relational,* simultaneously revealing and suturing a split between transcendence and immanence, ontology and praxis (2011: 87–88). The signature, then, operates in its capacity as rendering intelligible certain propositions across different epochs and fields of knowledge. Thus something like order can be displaced from Aristotelian metaphysics to Christian theology and political philosophy across different time periods without intelligibility being lost. Indeed, the relationality that order points to is communicated in a way that renders the past intelligible to the present and vice versa.

20 See also Riedel, who writes that the 'evolution of modern society' precipitates the dissolving of the 'old substance of the household' (1984: 140).

21 In the UK, Black people are more than twice as likely to die in police custody, and more than five times as likely to have force used against them than white people (BBC 2020). In the United States, Black Americans are killed by police at more than twice the rate of white Americans (Washington Post 2022).

22 Here I am thinking of Benjamin's eighth thesis on the philosophy of history: 'The current amazement that the things we are experiencing are "still" possible in the twentieth century is *not* philosophical' (2005a).

23  Frank Wilderson formulates this issue as follows: 'Capital was kick-started by the rape of the African continent. This phenomenon is central to neither Gramsci nor Marx. The theoretical importance of emphasising this in the early twenty-first century is two-fold: first, "the socio-political order of the New World" was kick-started by approaching a particular body (a black body) with direct relations of force, not by approaching a white body with variable capital. Thus, one could say that slavery – the "accumulation" of black bodies regardless of their utility as labourers (Hartman; Johnson) through an idiom of despotic power (Patterson) – is closer to capital's primal desire than is waged oppression – the "exploitation" of unraced bodies (Marx, Lenin, Gramsci) that labour through an idiom of rational/symbolic (the wage) power: A relation of terror as opposed to a relation of hegemony. Secondly, today, late capitalism is imposing a renaissance of this original desire, direct relations of force (the prison industrial complex), the despotism of the unwaged relation, and this Renaissance of slavery, has once again, as its structuring image in libidinal economy, and its primary target in political economy, the black body' (2003: 229–30).

# Prologue

1  When one examines Smith's rejection of physiocratic doctrine, we can see that he is explicitly arguing *against* the idea that this idea of the 'natural order' should be transferred to the political (Smith 1976: 673–4). The idea that the 'natural order' should determine what form the political takes results in the idea that only a very specific form of government may be tolerated, lest disorder be provoked, is something that is contradicted for Smith by the wide range of governmental forms and economic progress in existence. If, as Smith believes, there is 'no necessary connection of the progress of a nation to a particular political form' (Tribe 2015: 57), then the idea that for Smith is an underlying metaphysic of (natural) order determines the political form societies take cannot be so readily maintained. In reality, wealth can be created and society prosper under a variety of political regimes, and thus there is no direct causal relationship between the order of *physis* and *nomos* that is usually posited – that is, that the order of *physis determines* or *limits* the forms and actions governments take.
2  Here more than a cursory reminder is made of the Hobbesian universe in which life appears as 'wild' and nature is no longer good, and, indeed 'life can no longer be separated from murder, nature from evil' and it is this that forms the basis of the necessity of the Leviathan.

3 As we will see in Chapters 3 and 6, the conception of nature as no longer being 'good' must also be seen in the context of a global idea of race that takes shape over this period.

4 I mention this tension in timelines not to refute Foucault but to draw out something that it gestures towards, that we cannot presume that political organization straightforwardly derives from a metaphysic of order in one direction, but rather that the reverse can also be true. I will expand on this later.

5 As Esposito writes, 'whereas in the sovereign regime life is nothing but the residue or the remainder left over, saved from the right of taking life, in biopolitics life encamps at the center of a scenario of which death constitutes the external limit or the necessary contour whereas in the first instance life is seen from the perspective opened by death, in the second, death acquires importance only in the light radiated by life' (2004: 34).

6 I write 'the juridical' instead of 'law' here, because as Ewald has noted, 'the norm, then, is not opposed to the law itself but to what Foucault would call "the juridical": the institution of law as the expression of the sovereign's power' (1990: 138).

7 In *The History of Sexuality* Foucault distinguishes between two slightly different, albeit interconnected, forms of biopower – disciplinary, which is aimed at individual bodies, and security, which is aimed at the level of the population (1984: 139). As Thomas Lemke has noted the instruments for security are distinct from discipline, concerned as they are with 'regulation and control' rather than 'discipline and supervision' (2011: 37). However, while these two forms of biopower are distinguishable it is also the case that they are intrinsically intertwined with each defining the other: 'discipline is not a form of individualization that is applied to already existing individuals, but rather it presupposes a multiplicity' (2011: 37). The two forms are also rendered indistinct, Lemke tells us, when one considers eighteenth-century *police* which was both a 'disciplinary apparatus and a state apparatus' (2011: 38). This further supports the claim being made in this book that police (as concerned with order) is always and necessarily a concern with articulating together two poles – the transcendent and the immanent, the universal and particular, individual and collective and thereby cannot be reduced to one.

8 This opposition between a negative form of politik and a positive form of *Polizei* is also articulated by Agamben; however, the distinction between the two, he argues, collapses under the Nazi regime:

'distinguishing between politics (politik) and police (Polizei), Von Justi assigned the first a merely negative task, the fight against the external and internal enemies of the state, and the second a positive one, the care and growth of the citizens' life. National Socialist biopolitics – and along with it, a good part of modern politics even outside the Third Reich – cannot be grasped if it is not understood as necessarily implying the disappearance of the difference between the two terms: the police now becomes politics, and the care of life coincides with the fight against the enemy' (1998: 147).

9  Lisa Herzog notes that the Scottish enlightenment more generally is credited with the idea that 'good purposes can be attained without good intentions' (2013: 25).

10 See, for example, Valverde who, in surveying the literature on police, writes that 'After Smith and with the spread of free trade ideas, both police science and police powers acquired a bad reputation in Britain' and his thought and liberal thought more generally 'broke with police logic' (2003: 236). See also Colin Gordon who writes that 'liberalism discards the police conception of order' (1991: 21) and Farmer who argues that the significance of Smith lies in the 'fact that he captures the moment at which the study of police power is beginning to be marginalized in Western legal thought' (2006: 161).

11 See Neocleous (2000) – Chapter two.

12 See, for example, Campesi who argues that it is supposedly with the advent of liberalism that government action is reduced to the execution of law (Campesi 2016: 163). It is now, Campesi argues, that police is finally subjected to 'the authority of the rule of law' (Campesi 2016: 161).

13 There are some who question the periodization narrative in which *Polizei* is replaced by 'the police' with little connecting the two: see, for example, Valverde (2003) and Novak (1996) who both agree that the premodern function of police is not, in some ways, 'external to common-law liberal regimes' (Valverde 2003: 236).

14 That the *Theory of Moral Sentiments* is not overturned or jettisoned by the later *Wealth of Nations* is evidenced by the fact that Smith continued to work on the former, revising and republishing it until his death (Tribe 2015: 157). In addition, as Raphael notes, according to 'Sir Samuel Romilly, he always considered the *Theory of Moral Sentiments* a much superior work to the *Wealth of Nations*' (1975: 85).

15 The largely German offshoot of neoliberalism, the Ordoliberals distinguished themselves from classical liberalism precisely on the question of order and how it arises. The Ordoliberals 'made it their task to translate the metaphysic of Ordo into a concrete political program' (Ptak 2009: 105). For Walter Eucken (an Ordoliberal and founder of the Freiburg School), Ordo represented an

'order, which accords with the essence of humans; this means an order in which proportion (measure) and balance exist' (Ptak 2009: 104). The Ordoliberals made explicit the link between the theological origins of the Ordo metaphysic that they were to draw upon for their aim of linking 'the order of the competitive market to a vision of the ordering of the whole of society' through what was called a 'Vitalpolitik' (Dean 2013: 178). Through this notion, the Ordoliberals sought to ensure the economy was linked back to an external, ethical order (Dean 2013: 179) that they found to be lacking in Adam Smith. As such, they promoted the idea that Smith was a laissez-faire liberal, something that a rigorous reading of Smith contradicts.

16  As Viner notes, this means by emphasizing the divine nature of order less, Smith is free to 'find defects in the order of nature without casting reflections on the workmanship of its author' (1927: 208).

17  What I would propose in turn is that while sovereign power is configured differently – a sovereign is no longer in a position to act directly on his subjects – we have not yet accounted for government; this, in itself, is intimately connected to the question of order. Government intervention and nature are not antithetical for Smith and thus the presumption that 'government' is expelled, eliminated, reduced or, indeed, subsumed under law cannot be maintained. It is precisely the problem of government that also cannot be addressed by focussing solely on the criticisms made of mercantilist policy. Indeed, the Wealth of Nations should not be read as a tract forbidding or ruling out government intervention in general but should be seen as a very specific attack on certain kinds of government intervention (Viner 1927: 218). Government intervention, when for the sake of public good and general welfare, can be part of the 'natural' order of things: 'the activities of government in the maintenance of justice are an essential part of the Order of Nature in its full development and [. . .] such activities are not interference with the system of natural liberty' (Viner 1976: 22).

18  Campesi's argument also follows this trajectory that police power had to be 'narrowed down' (2016: 146) given that 'The new art of government was grounded in a principle of rationality aimed at limiting government interference as far as possible' (2016: 152).

19  Indeed to think about police power primarily in terms of economy not only distorts the character of police power when it comes to 'order' but , more importantly, gives rise to accounts of police power that neglects what Black studies thinkers have called *gratuitous* violence that I discussed in the introduction, that is, violence that cannot be explained simply by reference to exploitation or discipline in capitalist terms.

20 Therefore, the 'natural' order that Foucault speaks of in relation to liberalism is clearly distinct from the 'natural' order of the classical episteme. This is what makes his claim that, in modernity, nature is 'wild once more' compatible with his thesis that there is a natural order to exchange and trade.

21 It is not only Foucault who reads police (*Polizei*) and liberalism as antithetical – see, for example, Radzinowicz, who claims that William Blackstone was 'an exponent of the liberal doctrine and of the liberal spirit' and as such did not recognize '"Police" as an institution. With all his conservatism, and largely because of it, the thing that mattered most to him was the concept of a State, patriarchal perhaps, but firmly grounded in the rule of law' (1956: 418).

22 Foucault is clear that 'from the seventeenth to the end of the eighteenth century, the word "police" had a completely different meaning from the one it has today' (2007: 312).

23 In this vein Mitchell Dean, taking his cue from Foucault, asserts that 'the notion and practice of *police* as a condition achieved within a well-governed polity in seventeenth and eighteenth century continental Europe cannot be understood through a twentieth century understanding of police as a force of officers charged with the maintenance of law and order' (1994: 28).

24 As Mark Neocleous writes, in medieval times, 'Social order was thus merely part of a wider universal order, natural and divinely ordained; social disorder was thus seen as unnatural and against divine law, but was prevented by the existence of a superior unifying order. Towards the end of the sixteenth and into the seventeenth century, however, the idea of order was gradually transformed, increasingly understood not as divine but as man-made. Concomitantly, social order was also increasingly seen as being structured politically' (2000: 7).

25 In Aristotle's analogy of the army when discussing order as the 'highest good', the good is found more in the leader for 'he does not depend on the order but it depends on him' (2004: 385).

26 When we look at Hobbes, we shall see that the idea of a natural order is evacuated with the state of nature, (humans are naturally violent) but Hobbes also holds that humans are naturally inclined to preserve their life, which means they 'naturally' tend to make laws and government.

27 On this, see Johnson (2014) Elden (2003) and Dean (1994).

28 As I note in Chapter 4 with regard to Derrida, police becomes 'the *dasein* of the polis' (2002: 278) and in Chapter 5 with regard to Rancière – police as something akin to the institutional status quo – there is a tendency to use the police concept in such a broad sense as to render it theoretically hollow.

29  To Veyne's image of channelling and smooth movement, facilitated by cops to guide people to safety, I would counter the controversial 'hard-stop' tactic used most famously in the case of Mark Duggan in Tottenham, London, in 2011. Alternatively, one merely has to glance at police violence in the United States, so frequently meted out on people stopped due to 'traffic violations'. In a recent study, Black drivers were shown to be around 20 per cent more likely to be stopped (NYU 2020). What these examples illustrate, therefore, is that for every example of smooth flows, there are countless examples of hard, violent stops, of police not so much enforcing the rules of the road as using violence against those who they deem have no place on the road to begin with.

# Chapter 1

1  The first recorded usage in England of the term 'police' according to the OED is 1714 (1989), while Leviathan was first published in 1651. The word police, however, was already in use in Europe.
2  See, for example, Riedel (1996) and Taminaux (1985).
3  See also Taminaux, who believes that the distinction between nature and convention was steadfastly held by the Greeks, only to be ruptured in modernity with Hobbes. Here again, Hobbes is seen as overturning the epistemological status of philosophy under the Greeks – remarking on its 'scientific' character (1985: 8).
4  This becomes clear when Hobbes dismisses the concept of tyranny, which 'signifieth nothing more, nor lesse than the name of Soveraignty, be it in one, or many men, saving that they use the former word, are understood to bee angry with them they call Tyrants; I think the toleration of a professed hatred of Tyranny, is a Toleration of hatred to Common-wealth in general, and another evill seed, not differing much from the former' (1996: 486).
5  As Whyte argues, 'the Hobbesian argument' regarding the violence of the state of nature 'represents the most powerful and evocative attempt in the history of liberal thought to derive sovereign authority from the fear of a lawless state' (2013: 63).
6  This exclusionary operation of the *polis,* whereby those who exist outside of the state are considered either more or less than human, is not, as we shall see, abandoned by Hobbes but is rather reformulated in his discussion of the covenant. Hobbes is emphatic that covenants with 'brute beasts is impossible' and immediately after, 'to make covenant with God, is impossible, but by

Mediation of such as god speaketh to, either by revelation supernaturall, or by his Lieutenants that govern under him' (1996: 14). Thus, Hobbes excludes both beasts and God from the covenant that forms, and by extension, the Leviathan itself.

7   This question is remarkably similar to a question Aristotle poses in *The Politics* which is as follows:

'but when the same population continues to dwell in the same territory, must we say that the state remains the same so long as there is continuity of race among that population, even though one generation of people dies and another is born – just as a river or spring is commonly said to be the same, although different water passes into and out of it all the time? Alternatively, ought we to speak of the population as being the same for the reasons stated, but say that the *state* is different? For the state is a kind of association – an association of citizens in a constitution; so when the constitution changes and becomes different in kind, the state also would seem necessarily not to be the same.... It is clear that the main criterion of the continued identity of a state ought to be its constitution' (1276a34 1992: 175).

Hobbes's main concern is the question: How can something that changes materially be regarded as the same? For Aristotle, however, the concern is how something that is composed of the same material can be different. Using the analogy of musical notes, which are 'fitted together differently, to produce either the Dorian or the Phrygian mode' (ibid.), Aristotle wants to emphasize that even though a population may remain the same, if the constitution changes the state cannot be regarded as the same state. In a sense, Hobbes inverts the Aristotelian question and in so doing foregrounds the question of order. What both have in common, however, is that the identity and endurance of the state is not fixed or inevitable but, rather, relies on the constitution (or law) in Aristotle's case and order in Hobbes's. Both of these occur as a result of action.

8   This corresponds to what Agamben identifies in the concept of Ordo: 'the incessant activity of government that presupposes and at the same time, continually heals the fracture between transcendence and immanence, God and the world' (2011: 90).

9   This is not to say that Aristotle's conception of the *polis* is lacking in activity. As Cornelius Castoriadis has argued, for the Greeks laws were not God-given, or eternal, on the contrary it is in Athens we find the first instance of a community collectively deliberating over laws, creating and changing them (1983: 94). It is, then, the continual activity of lawmaking that provides a community with its life

and endurance over time. For Hobbes, on the other hand, the specific content of laws themselves are unimportant (though they are a necessary feature of political life), rather it is the continual activity that constitutes 'order' that, without end, ensures the continuity of the commonwealth.

10  This issue is dealt with more extensively in Lamb, M. and Primera, G. (2019) 'Sovereignty between the Katechon and the Eschaton: Rethinking the Leviathan' *Telos*.

11  The importance of the *katechon* for Schmitt's philosophy of history should not be understated. As Schmitt argues in 1947: 'one must be able to name the *katechon* for every epoch of the past 1948 years. The position has never gone unoccupied, otherwise we would no longer exist' (quoted in Meier 2011: 161).

12  'The state', Schmitt emphatically writes 'after all, has been formed to end the kind of war that exists in a state of nature. A state is not a state unless it can put an end to that kind of war' (1996: 47).

13  This state of 'peace', however, as I have been arguing does not exclude violence.

14  As Hobbes writes: 'and this kind of Dominion, or Sovereignty, differeth from Sovereignty by Insititution onely in this, That men who choose their Sovereaign, do it for fear of one another, and not of him whom they Institute: But in this case, they subject themselves, to him they are afraid of. In both cases they do it for fear: which is to be noted by them, that hold all such Covenants, as proceed from fear of death, or violence, voyd: which if it were true, no man, in any kind of Commnwealth, could be obliged to Obedience' (1996: 138).

15  There is more than a cursory reminder here of Walter Benjamin's distinction between 'law-founding' and 'law-preserving' violence. I will discuss this in detail in the second part of this book.

16  In a similar way, Hegel also excludes state-founding violence as 'irrational' and unjustifiable. Of course, were these thinkers to legitimate state-founding violence the whole edifice of sovereignty would be under threat as the supreme power and the only legitimate user of violence.

17  Indeed, it is precisely this model of power – classical sovereignty as encapsulated by the figure of Leviathan – that Foucault argues (in contradistinction to his biopolitics) must be abandoned in order to understand power relations (ibid.). I shall return to this point, but for now it should be noted that this sovereign violence is as previously discussed not merely or only 'negative' and it is precisely in this ambiguity that the logic of police power finds its place.

18  Here what Agamben refers to as 'ordered power' and 'absolute power' (2011: 108) becomes helpful for thinking through the significance of Hobbes's idea that the sovereign is granted the authority to improvise. Absolute power is attributed to

the sovereign and to God, while ordered power is the power which exists in the world, in its day to day running. However, the distinction between the two is still present but made less clear when absolute power is seen as existing in those agents who can 'act beyond the law and against it' (2011: 108). Later in the book I shall examine the idea that it is police who by acting beyond the law and against it are invested with such absolute power.

19  The association of order with health and disorder as disease has a long lineage in Western political thought which has been traced as far back as Plato (Cavarero 2002: 103).

20  Agamben also notes the significance of disease for Hobbes who 'in his translation of Thucydides . . . had come across a passage in which the plague of Athens was defined as the origin of anomia (which he translates with licentiousness) and metabole (which he renders with revolution)' (2015: 38). Hobbes here continues the long-standing tradition of associating political ills with ill-health and disease.

21  Hobbes also adds that the state of nature can be seen not just in cases of states collapsing but also looking at 'the savage people in many places of America . . . have no government at all; and live at this day in a brutish manner' (1996: 89–90). As we will see the attempt to exclude 'natural' violence along racialized geographical lines is also found in Hegel – the state, then, is variously conceived by liberals and non-liberals alike as excluding 'barbaric' violence in the name of order.

22  As Kosseleck writes: 'to Hobbes history was a continuous alternation from civil war to the state, and from the state to civil war' (1987: 34).

23  Roberto Esposito makes the same point when he writes, 'The state of nature is not overcome once and for all by the civil, but it resurfaces again in the same figure of the sovereign, because it is the only one to have preserved natural right in a context in which all the others have given it up' (2010: 30).

24  Though Agamben does not put in terms of a 'signature' in the first volume of *Homo Sacer*, it is, I shall argue, through an understanding of order as a signature that we can see that order is not only that which sutures the split between a transcendent and immanent order but also, and crucially for my purposes here, it must also be seen as a suture to the *physis/nomos* divide. The oppositional distinction between *physis* and *nomos* is always already marked by an indistinction.

25  As previously discussed, this is the move from 'taking life and letting live' to making live and letting die (Foucault 2004: 241).

26  This raises the question about the distinction between Foucault and Agamben's understandings of biopolitics. While Foucault sees biopolitics as a discrete historical emergence at the beginning of modernity as I discussed in the prologue, Agamben 'on the other hand thinks the sequence of events known as Western history' as an encompassing phenomenon' (Schütz 2008: 115) rather than emphasizing a discontinuous discrete mode of politics.

27  See, for example, Ignatieff who argues that 'where all order in a state has disintegrated and its people have been delivered up to a war of all against all ... the only effective way to protect human rights is direct intervention, ranging from sanctions to the use of military force' (2001: 37).

28  This further bolsters the point that Hobbes has still not entirely broken with the classical tradition of the identification of people with the *polis*; indeed, as Castoriadis notes, 'the idea of a 'state' as an institution distinct and separated from the body of citizens would not have been understandable to a Greek' (1983: 101).

29  As Agamben argues the state of nature should 'rather could be understood as a principle internal to the State revealed in the moment in which the State is considered "as if it were dissolved"' (1998: 36).

30  For Riedel, the modern concept of civil society in fact begins with Hegel himself (1984: 147).

31  As Zartaloudis notes it is here that the modern stakes are reversed: it is not the individual or collective will or consciousness that gives reality to the state, but rather the state itself that realizes a 'moral idea' and that is, in this way, a *causa sui* (its *own* cause) (2010: 107).

# Chapter 2

1  As Riedel explains, the split between state and civil society that Hegel identifies and theorizes is a rupture with political philosophy that comes before: 'While the great tradition of political metaphysics from Aristotle to Kant names the state "civil society" because for them social life is already political – in the legal competence of the citizen, or *cives* as Kant, keeping to the Latin, explained it – and because the *status politicus* of the human world understood in these terms contains within itself the genuine "economic" and "social" element in the stratification of ruling and domestic classes, Hegel in contrast separates the political sphere of the state from the realm of "society" which has become "civil"' (1984: 139).

2 Hegel's critique is scattered throughout a number of works; however, the bulk of the critique can be found in *The Difference between Fichte and Schelling's System of Philosophy* and *Lectures on Natural Right and Political Science*.
3 This includes the translator of the *Philosophy of Right* T. M. Knox (1952: 360) and Riedel (1984: 152), as well as Foucault, who, as discussed, posits a more general break between a pre-modern and modern sense of 'police' – one as concerned with order and the other only concerned with the repression of disorder (2007: 354).
4 It is in the corporation that 'both the capability and livelihood are *recognized*, with the result that the corporation member needs no further *external evidence* to demonstrate his skill and his regular income and subsistence, i.e. the fact that he is *somebody*' (Hegel 2008: 225). This idea that an individual must demonstrate that he is 'somebody' in order to participate in civil and political life will be expanded on later. For now, it is worth noting that the corporation offers insight into what Hegel means by the universal. It is in the corporation that the 'skill' of an individual is made 'rational' insofar as the individual is able to elevate their activity for a 'common end' (2008: 226).
5 Hegel advocates a twofold approach so that right in civil society may be actualized: 'first, that contingent hindrances to one aim or another be removed, and undisturbed safety of the person and property be attained; and secondly that the securing of every single person's livelihood and welfare be treated and actualized as *right*, i.e. that *particular welfare* as such be so treated' (2008: 215). Security in Hegel then becomes, not merely security of the individual but security of the social totality, that is, the universal. The security of the individual is the condition for the social totality and vice versa.
6 Personality, Hegel writes, '[B]egins not with the subject's mere general consciousness of himself as an I concretely determined in some way or other, but rather with his consciousness of himself as a completely abstract I in which every concrete restriction and value is negated and without validity. In personality therefore, knowledge is knowledge of oneself as an object, but an object raised by thinking to the level of simple infinity and so an object that is purely self-identical' (2008: 54).
7 Frank Ruda makes this point when he writes: 'Here one can see what it means not to be under the legal commandment and to withdraw from the imperative to be a person: it means not only to fall out of the sphere of objectivity but also to fall out of the sphere of intersubjectivity. Not to be a person means not to realize one's freedom, to be unfree, a-social and thus to have no rights and no duties. For freedom as realized is always embedded into intersubjective relations that enable

this realization in the first place but only becomes effective through property relations' (Ruda 2011: 128).

8  I will return to this later, but for now it is important to note that even though the poor may not have rights because they don't have property, they still have the potential to have rights even if not actualized. Similarly, the rabble – though they might not want the universal to be stimulated in him, still has the potentiality for the universal to be actualized even if this is refused by the rabble individual. This is not the case for those constructed as not having the capacity for the universal in the first place. Thus the significance of what Hegel lays the groundwork for in the history of thought on law, violence and universality cannot be underestimated, given that it is here that universality is tied to modern European man, while 'negroes' are characterized by simple 'arbitrary' volition where there can be no political bond like the one found in the Hegelian state but only despotism (1975: 186).

9  Once again lawlessness is ascribed to a previous state of nature. The idea is reproduced that without the state, and in particular without police, an anarchic, 'natural' condition would reign. Interestingly, however, though Fichte sees this natural condition as 'previous' without the conditions he sets he believes we would 'continue' to live in it. This is a much more self-aware formulation of the temporality of the state of nature than we find in Hegel. I will return to this issue in Chapter 5.

10  In *Foundations of Natural Right*, Fichte goes into extensive detail about the ways in which the state can ensure no criminal can escape its grasp, wherein no transgression of the law may go unnoticed. In order to achieve this Fichte advocates a system in which 'everyone must always carry an identity card with him' (2000: 257). These 'identity cards' must be used not only when traveling from one locality to another but also must be used in the process of exchange: 'according to our suggestion, anyone who transfers a bill of exchange . . . would have to present his identity card in order to show that he is this particular person, where he can be found etc.' (Fichte 2000: 259). Bills of exchange function at this time as a type of currency, wherein the one who possesses a bill may either redeem its value with the issuer or use it as a form of payment. Thus 'the acknowledgment of debt therefore becomes a means of market exchange' (Chamayou 2013: 2). Each time the bill is handed over, the person who utilizes it must leave their name and signature on the back (Chamayou 2013: 3). When the bill is bought back to the person who wrote it in lieu of money, it is finally turned back into 'liquid currency' and thus the problem of fraud arises: if the person who originally wrote it is not identifiable or there is a forgery, the 'security of market exchange' is put

at risk (Chamayou 2013: 3). In pairing the use of bills of exchange with passports, Fichte has attempted to construct an autopoietic system of security.

11  In the Jena Lectures Hegel describes what he means by 'bad infinity' which is precisely the character of his critique of Fichte: 'Since the universal is here applied directly to the particular (in order that the particular may subsist), there arises the "bad infinity." [to aim at] a complete legislation in all its fullness is to set out on the same sort of thing as, for example, wanting to specify all colours' (2014: 143).

12  Coercion is seen not as something to be eliminated, rather, in transforming something contingent and irrational and subsuming it under right, it becomes necessary: 'that coercion is in its concept self-destructive is exhibited in reality by the fact that coercion is annulled by coercion; coercion is thus shown to be not only right under certain conditions but necessary, i.e. as a second act of coercion which is the annulment of one that has preceded' (Hegel 2008: 97).

13  While Fichte would not subscribe to Hegel's concept of the universal, the point to be made here is that for both there is a gap or moment of non-correspondence between two elements – that of the universal and particular, state and civil society for Hegel, and the government and citizens for Fichte, and it is here that the police come in.

14  This is clear in Hegel when he states: 'Of course every individual is from one point of view independent, but he is also a member of the system of civil society, and while everyone has the right to demand subsistence from it, it must at the same time protect him from himself. It is not simply starvation that is at issue; the further end in view is to prevent the formation of a pauperized rabble. Since civil society is responsible for feeding its members, it also has the right to press them to provide for their own livelihood' (Hegel 2008: 219).

15  Balibar recalls a claim made by Althusser that there could be '"no such thing as a Hegelian politics." From the first this thesis took its place, for Althusser, in the framework of a Machiavellian conception of politics as the reign of uncertainty, of the conflict between action and chance, that excludes necessity, or better, excludes predetermination of the kind that forms Hegelian teleology's "spiritual" horizon' (Balibar 2015: 29). In Hegel's discussion of police and sovereignty, however, uncertainty and chance certainly do take precedence, indeed as Hegel himself says – no 'objective' lines can be drawn.

16  There are very few exceptions to this; however, Mark Neocleous (1998) is a notable one.

17  Hegel wants to distance himself as far as possible from contract theories of the state as he makes clear in the *Philosophy of Right,* 'the state is not a contract at all

nor its fundamental essence the unconditional protection and guarantee of the life and property of individuals as such. On the contrary, it is that higher entity which even lays claim to this very life and property and demands its sacrifice' (2008: 103).

18   As Peperzak notes Hegel utilizes Aristotle's conception of 'second nature' to denote the civil or political state characterized by spirit: 'a "second" human nature does not emerge from a merely natural system of unhindered and conflicting forces, because there would not be a non-natural, i.e. spiritual intelligent and voluntary principle to negate the violence inherent to nature' (1995: 209). Once again, the confounding of the distinction between 'natural' and 'artificial' is circumvented by appealing to a 'second' nature one that could not be said to be strictly one or the other. As Peperzak sees it second nature 'is part of the spirit's actualization through naturalization, but we can also interpret it as part of the spiritualization of nature' (1995: 210).

19   Examples given by Hegel include Caesar and Napoleon (1952, §33).

20   The prevalence of this idea, especially with regard to police power, is examined and troubled via an engagement with the work of da Silva. For now it should be noted that that which is being posited as 'external' to states is often found at their core.

21   While Balibar sees in Hobbes and Hegel's characterizations of violence a difference between, on the one hand, a suppression of violence in Hobbes and a 'conversion' of violence in Hegel, I want to emphasize that for both the state of nature is a state of violence that must be held at bay by and through state-founding violence. Or, in other words, there is a natural 'disorder' that is presented in an oppositional relation to the 'order' engendered by the state.

22   This notion of externality cannot be taken for granted. As Andrew Benjamin writes when discussing Hegel's theory of sovereignty, 'What may appear to be outside the law is produced by the manner in which what counts as the law creates its own outside' (2015: 149).

23   On this point see, for example, Denise Ferreira da Silva *Toward A Global Idea of Race* where she identifies the racialized others who are explicitly 'outside of the trajectory of universal reason' (2007: 14).

24   Carl Schmitt of course theorizes the sovereign decision as being precisely 'groundless' and external to the law. I will return to this in the second part of this book.

25   While the monarch is and must be an individual for Hegel, this does not mean that they are to be thought of as *any* individual. In a similar vein to Hobbes, in their singularity as a person the monarch accomplishes the unity of the state. As Nancy writes: 'the monarch is thus the whole of the State – its "all at once" – as something

*extra*, that is to say, as some*one* whose personal unity accomplishes that of the State. (Everything sends us back thus to the axiom that unity in general is personal, and that the person is unitary.) The monarch is a man *in addition*, who is not to be numbered with other individuals but who on the contrary causes their *union* to exist as a *unity*. The monarch *is* the accomplishment of the relationship – as a relationship to itself' (Nancy 1982: 488).

26  See, for example, Pelczynski who writes, 'Apart from an obscure metaphysical argument about the personality of the state being fully actualized only in a concrete, natural person, Hegel can only justify his preference for monarchical sovereignty on the not very strong grounds of expediency' (1971: 231).

27  Revenge, like the violence of nature, is also for Hegel barbaric and uncivilized: 'amongst uncivilised peoples, revenge is undying . . . amongst the Arabs for instance it can be checked only by superior force or the impossibility of its satisfaction' (2008: 107).

28  Law in and of itself is not enough to guarantee the freedom of the individual for Hegel, it cannot secure by itself the subsumption of the particular under the universal and must therefore be supplemented by police power: 'there is a distinction between the monarch's decisions and their execution and application, or in general between his decisions and the continued execution or maintenance of past decisions, existing laws, regulations, organizations for the securing of common ends and so forth. This task of subsumption in general is comprised in the *executive power*, which also includes the power of the *judiciary* and the *police*' (2008: 277–8).

# Chapter 3

1  Neocleous cites the German liberal Eduard Lasker as an archetype of this line of thought: 'rule of law and rule of police are two different ways to which history points, two methods of development between which peoples must choose and have chosen. . . . The true man is the independent citizen. Every citizen should and must be independent, for each has to see to his own welfare. He has no other claim on the state than protection from injurious force' (2000: 29).

2  Benjamin echoes this sentiment in the *Origin of German Tragic Drama* when he writes that 'the attempt to find the origin of kingship in the state of creation is even encountered in legal theory' (1977: 85).

3  Schmitt refers frequently to a methodological approach that he has constructed – a 'sociology of concepts' which is 'concerned with establishing proof of two

spiritual but at the same time substantial identities. It is thus not a sociology of the concept of sovereignty when, for example, the monarchy of the seventeenth century is characterized as the real that is "mirrored" in the Cartesian concept of God. But it is a sociology of the concept of sovereignty when the historical-political status of the monarchy of that epoch is shown to correspond to the general state of consciousness that was characteristic of Western Europeans at the time, and when the juristic construction of the historical-political reality can find a concept whose structure is in accord with the structure of metaphysical concepts' (2005: 45).

4  Schmitt's idea of secularization differs from those he was in conversation with in Germany – Hans Blumenberg and Karl Löwith. Blumenberg sought to show that modernity was not the outcome of a secularization process against figures such as Löwith and Weber who tried to show the opposite. As Beatrice Hannsen writes, 'the precise connotations of the term secularization are as varied as the history of its usage in theology, philosophy and historiography, so that, as Hans Blumenberg has maintained, the term cannot purely be reduced to a common denominator – for example, the excision of transcendence' (2000: 54). However, this latter notion is precisely the way in which Schmitt characterizes the modern liberal state.

5  As Schmitt writes: 'The classical representative of this decisionist type is Thomas Hobbes' (Schmitt 2005: 33).

6  In Schmitt's own words: 'the precise details of an emergency cannot be anticipated, nor can one spell out what may take place in such a case, especially when it is truly a matter of an extreme emergency and of how it is to be eliminated' (Schmitt 2005: 6).

7  I will discuss this further in the second part of this chapter.

8  As I discussed in relation to Schmitt's reading of Hobbes, in order for sovereignty to function, the oppositional relation between anarchy and order must be operative. However, I will show in the following chapter how they implicate one another and are in fact indifferent.

9  This is not necessarily new or original to Schmitt – though he does have a particular way of characterizing it. As I discussed earlier with reference to Hegel and Marx, for Hegel it is only in times of exigency that sovereignty attains actuality – that the 'many powers of the state fuses into the concept of sovereignty' (Hegel 2008: 266). It is only at this point that 'ideality attains actuality' (Hegel 2008: 266). For Marx this means that sovereignty means nothing other than the decision of a singular will (1992: 81). It is this fusion of the many into the one – the absolute and irreducible point that cannot be derived

that Schmitt seeks to recapture out of what he perceives as its demise under liberalism.

10 One of the main recipients of Schmitt's attack on legal positivism is legal theorist Hans Kelsen, for whom the state was a hypostatization of the legal system. This, in Schmitt's view ignores the central questions of how and who realizes the law. For the legal positivists, there is a guiding assumption that a legal order already exists and all that is left is to aggregate individual interests – and in this sense: 'the state is confined exclusively to producing law. But this does not mean that it produces the content of law. It does nothing but ascertain the legal value of interests as it springs from the people's feeling or sense of right' (Schmitt 2005: 23).

11 Schmitt thus appears to vacillate between a discussion of the legal order and order in a metaphysical sense, though he does not make this explicit or explain how the two relate to each other in any substantial way.

12 On this point see Weber (1992) ,Martel (2010) and Agamben (2005).

13 The debate on sovereignty between Benjamin and Schmitt also passes through Hobbes as 'Schmitt explains that his influential book on Hobbes of 1938, which he himself characterized as his most significant, was intended as an answer to Benjamin's *origin of German tragic drama*: he said "Unfortunately my attempt to respond to Benjamin by examining a great political symbol (The Leviathan in the political thought of Thomas Hobbes) went unnoticed"' (Bredekamp 1999: 261).

14 As Benjamin writes: 'If history is secularized in this setting, this is an expression of the same metaphysical tendency which simultaneously led in the exact sciences to the infinitesimal method. In both cases chronological movement is grasped and analysed in a spatial image. The image of the setting or, more precisely, of the court becomes the key to historical understanding. For the court is the setting par excellence' (1977: 92).

15 Agamben argues that this is a translation error and that Benjamin in fact meant to say that the baroque knows an eschatology, but for Agamben, it's an empty one (2005: 56). However, to me, it seems the other characteristics of the baroque Benjamin identifies concerning time, order and nature indicate that he did, in fact, mean no eschatology. Indeed, it is the loss of redemption and *telos* that characterizes this period. As Koepnick argues: 'in the midst of a world devoid of transcendental values, a cosmos emptied of metaphysical security the trauerspiel shows political rulers who subscribe to unprecedented models of political sovereignty, concepts of pure politics that remove religious, moral or aesthetic concerns from the mechanics of domination and, therefore, explicitly endorse the differentiation of an autonomous sphere of politics' (1996: 280).

16  This catastrophe has been noted also by Agamben, who writes that 'the drastic redefinition of the sovereign function implies a different situation of the state of exception. It no longer appears as the threshold that guarantees the articulation between an inside and an outside, or between anomie and the juridical context, by virtue of a law that is in force in its suspension: it is, rather a zone of absolute indeterminacy between anomie and law, in which the sphere of creatures and the juridical order are caught up in a single catastrophe' (2005: 57).

17  As James Martel puts it 'in the sixteenth and seventeenth centuries, however, at least for a time, the objects of the world were relatively unarranged, not as subject to some grand order of meaning' (2010: 185).

18  As Susan Buck-Morss argues 'the Baroque poets saw in transitory nature an allegory for human history, in which the latter appeared, not as a divine plan or chain of events on a "road to salvation" but as death, ruin, catastrophe' (1989: 174).

19  Agamben agrees with Benjamin that modernity is characterized by the indistinguishability of the exception and norm, however modifies his account when he claims that 'it is important not to forget that the modern state of exception is a creation of the democratic-revolutionary tradition and not the absolutist one' (2005: 5). Whether or not one sees this as a characteristic of absolutism or not, however, both agree that the exception far from disappearing under the modern liberal state in fact coincides with the norm.

20  As Derrida has pointed out, 'critique' here 'does not simply mean negative evaluation, legitimate rejection or condemnation of violence, but judgment, evaluation, examination that provides itself with the means to judge violence' (2002: 265).

21  The word 'violence' is translated from the German *gewalt*. However, as is now well known, this translation doesn't capture its German counterpart well. The word *gewalt* 'contains an intrinsic ambiguity' (Balibar 2009: 101). It is not only that the word has connotations that its European equivalents simply do not (*violence* or *violenzia*, and *pouvoir*, *potere*, power . . . (Balibar 2009: 101)). It is also the case that it refers 'at the same time, to the negation of law and justice and to their realisation or the assumption of responsibility for them by an institution (generally the state)' (Balibar 2009: 101). The meaning is indeterminate, including both '*potestas and violentia*' (Tomba 2009: 126). For Balibar this 'signals the existence of a latent dialectic' or a 'unity of opposites' that is a constituent element of politics (2009: 101).

22  Benjamin endeavours to fashion a perspective that stands outside the juridical framework, outside of both natural and positive law, and for this to be

realized there must be a view of law that is 'historico-philosophical' (1978: 279). While Benjamin's concept of critique is indebted to Kant in the way it is presented as an alternative to a 'potentially interminable conflict between two antithetical positions, both of which are generated from an objective error or "transcendental illusion"' (Fenves 2010: 209). Nevertheless, Benjamin goes further than Kant in pushing the limits of critique outside of 'transcendentally secured criteria' (Caygill 1998: 34) and instead engages in a form of immanent critique in which the form of critique is found in the course of the critique itself. For Caygill this takes the form of a speculative critique in which it is acknowledged that 'both it [critique] and the work or object being judged are transformed by their encounter' (Caygill 1998: 34). In so doing, critique, in the hands of Benjamin is not an act of judgement exercised according to pre-given criteria or law, but the 'presentation of its immanent possibilities of transformation' (Caygill 1998: 46). The critique of violence is Benjamin's attempt then to exercise a speculative, immanent critique, whereby violence is judged not according to the laws that exits, but to situate in a 'broader experiential context' (Caygill 1998: 58) that would enable a reflection on the possibility of its transformation. It is through a *critique* of *gewalt* that Benjamin arrives at the concept of divine *gewalt*; the possibility of *gewalt* that is not only not legal but is also transformative.

23  In her discussion of the power of arrest, McBarnet argues that there has been a tendency (on the part of sociologists) to focus on the 'operation of discretion, rather than the legal structure in which it takes place' (1981: 35). While McBarnet accepts that there is a gap between the law and its application her insistence that discretion is still a legal power inscribed within the juridical order itself is an attempt to secure the 'internal nexus' between the law and its application. As we shall see, however, this nexus is not resolved by recourse to a concept such as discretion but only serves to point to the gap that exists between the law and its operation in the world.

24  In the absence of a decision found in the police, it is not, as with Derrida's judge the mechanical application of a rule, but rather the absence of decision points to the lack of determinate content, the lack of a legal metaphysical content that it refers back to. This again is why when considers the police, there is nothing intrinsic to encounter, a mythic, spectral substance without form.

25  The 'decision' that Benjamin here refers to is of course not to be confused with Schmitt's sovereign decision. Indeed, the presence of the 'metaphysical category' to which the law refers, that is, that a legal decision can and does refer to something outside of itself, does not apply to the sovereign decision which is

groundless. This is why, I argue, any consideration of police must grapple with the sovereign decision rather than the legal one.

26 Of course, this is highly reminiscent of what I discussed in Chapter 1 with regard to the relationship between violence and the state.

27 Many commentators on Benjamin's text have pointed out that the violence that exists at the heart of law is applicable not only to the positing of law, but applies to positing in general (see, for example, Derrida (2002), Hamacher (2000) and Duttman (1996)). In this move, from making a particular claim about law, to a general one pertaining to the structure of positing, Werner Hamacher finds a logic at work that sets in motion a declining cycle in which what is posited is eventually ruined by its reduction to a preservation (2000: 108-9). Positing in general contains within it, therefore, a destructive violence that must deny other positings, in order to preserve itself, and in this sense 'requires security ... because it is excessive and must maintain itself against other positings to which it remains exposed' (Duttmann 1996: 170). Despite the immanence of this cycle, Benjamin nevertheless conceives of a deposing violence that would interrupt this cycle, a violence he calls 'divine' (1978: 294).

28 In the case of the UK Robert Reiner has documented this phenomenon and cites the example of the *sub rosa* practice of stopping and questioning people in public. While this was not a power granted by any 'legislation or case law' the attempt to regulate the practice 'culminated in a de facto recognition of it' (2010: 220).

29 As Agamben demonstrates in *State of Exception* the question of the relation of the general and particular is not and cannot be one of mere subsumption of the particular under the general. This question, he argues, was in many ways foreclosed by Kant for whom in his theory of judgment, 'the relation between the particular case and the norm appears as a merely logical operation' (Agamben 2005: 39). As I have argued, this, far from being a logical operation, is one which requires an analysis of action as such. When confronted with a specific case there cannot be a mere application of the general rule given that there is always a moment of practical activity involved, one that in various ways, interprets or translates and thus modifies the general rule in the moment of its 'application'.

30 This is, for Thurschwell a point of contention between Agamben and Derrida on the 'question of whether the law must be viewed as politically irredeemable, and therefore something to be overcome in its entirety ... or rather whether one will agree with Derrida that a legitimate political praxis need not "suspect the juridical idea in itself"' (2005: 189).

31  As Agamben puts it: the presupposition here is that the state of exception entails a return to an original, pleromatic state in which the distinction among the different powers (legislative, executive, etc.) has not yet been produced. As we will see the state of exception constitutes rather a kenomatic state, an emptiness of law, and the idea of an originary indistinction and fullness of power must be considered a legal mythologeme analogous to the idea of a state of nature (and it is not by chance that it was precisely Schmitt who had recourse to this mythologeme) (Agamben 2005: 6).

# Chapter 4

1. Agamben's approach has been characterized as political ontology (see, e.g. Abbott, M. (2012)), which is, in part, an attempt to demonstrate the metaphysical grounds of political structures.
2. I will explore the *an-archic* character of police power at the end of this chapter, which shows that far from implementing a general law or sovereign will the activities of police are fundamentally 'groundless'.
3. As William Watkin points out, some of the confusion over the reception to *Homo Sacer* 1 stems from the fact that it 'was never intended to be read in isolation as his theory of politics' (2014: 210).
4. Indeed, it is, as I argued with regard to Hegel, with the splitting of state and civil society that the problem of police becomes even more urgent. Prior to this development, police had been the unmediated application of a sovereign will acting directly on its subjects, and thus police power could be characterized as an application of a transcendent will. While power is still here divided, it is once civil society is separated off as a distinct sphere requiring government that modern government acquires its decisive form.
5. This includes Hobbes for whom the 'right' and 'exercise' of sovereign power are split:

> 'we must distinguish between the right and the exercise of sovereign power; for they can be separated. For instance he who has the right but may be unwilling or unable to play a personal role in conducting trials, or deliberating issues. For there are occasions when Kings cannot manage affairs because of their age, or even though they can, they judge it more correct to content themselves with choosing ministers and counsellors, and to exercise their power through them. When right and exercise are

separated, the government of the commonwealth is like the ordinary government of the world, in which God the first mover of all things, produces natural effects through the order of secondary causes' (Hobbes 1996: 142).

6   As Jessica Whyte points out, this is particularly manifest in Rousseau's *Social Contract* who 'by positing the split between general and particular will as one between sovereignty and its execution, Rousseau is able to argue that sovereignty itself cannot be divided. . . . Sovereignty, for Rousseau is indivisible: "for either the will is general or it is not"' (2014: 175).

7   As Agamben demonstrates in *State of Exception* the question of the relation of the general and particular, he argues, was in many ways foreclosed by Kant in whose theory of judgment, 'the relation between the particular case and the norm appears as a merely logical operation' (2005: 39). As I argued in Chapter 4, this, far from being a logical operation, is one which requires an analysis of action as such. 'The law' when confronted with a specific case cannot merely 'apply' the general rule given that there is always a moment of practical activity involved, on that in various ways, interprets or translates and thus modifies the general rule in the moment of its 'application'.

8   Though Agamben does not cite Benjamin here, it is worth noting that Benjamin sees in the machinations of law a 'demonic ambiguity' (1978: 295) that he links to fate. It is via the concepts of fate and ambiguity that Benjamin exposes the way in which law, though it presents itself as being universal and with all equal who stand before it, actually produces fearful and guilt-ridden subjects marked by inequality, and for whom there is no certainty either in always knowing what the law prohibits (Benjamin refers to 'unmarked frontiers' (1978: 295)) or that if the law is transgressed whether or not one might be punished: 'for law preserving violence is a threatening violence. And its threat is not intended as the deterrent that uninformed liberal theorists interpret it to be. A deterrent in the exact sense would require a certainty that contradicts the nature of a threat and is not attained by any law, since there is always a hope of eluding its arm. This makes it all the more threatening, like fate, on which depends whether the criminal is apprehended' (1978: 285). As Alison Ross claims, Benjamin's notion of fate, identified as it is with the realm of the law, signifies the 'uncertainty' that reigns here and further in which the 'fear of punishment at every turn is overwhelming' (2015: 48).

9   On this point see Watkin who writes that 'the sovereign, the guarantor of norms is the power of the kingdom to refer to *The Kingdom and the Glory*, so that the *oikonomia*, the real distribution of power, can purport to possess a founding

legitimacy in the condition which, in truth, the conditioned actually produces' (2014: 15).

10  That order and *oikonomia* are intrinsically entwined becomes clear when Agamben writes: 'the being of God, as order, is structurally *ordinatio*, that is, praxis of government and activity that arranges [*dispone*] according to measure, number and weight. It is in this sense that the *dispositio* (which we should not forget is the Latin translation of *oikonomia*) of things in the order means nothing else but the *dispositio* of things in God himself. Immanent and transcendent order once again refer back to each other in a paradoxical coincidence, which can nevertheless be understood only as a perpetual *oikonomia*, as a continuous activity of government of the world, one that implies a fracture between being and praxis and, at the same time, tries to heal it' (2011: 89, emphasis in original).

11  This will become clearer following the discussion of what Agamben means by signature, but it is worth noting that while order does not have a singular meaning this does not mean that it can mean anything rather, as Watkin argues, 'it can develop an almost unlimited universe of references and be said in any number of different senses whilst remaining intelligible', and thus there is a 'consistency of meaning' (2014: 217) without one meaning being primary or essential.

12  Agamben's indebtedness to Benjamin for the category of the signature is made clear in *The Signature of All Things* where, in his explication of the concept, he writes, 'For Benjamin, especially from the time he begins to work on the Paris Arcades, history is the proper sphere of signatures. Here they appear under the names of "indices" ("secret," "historical," "temporal") or of "images" (*Bilder*), often characterized as "dialectical"' (2009a: 72).

13  Agamben, in agreement with Benjamin, argues that a sense of 'salvation in historical time is weakened or eliminated' which for Agamben means that 'the economy extends its blind and derisive dominion to every aspect of social life' (2012: 35).

14  This is discussed in Chapters 1–3.

15  On this point see Fatsis, L., and Lamb, M. (2022).

16  As will be recalled from the discussion of Hobbes, the logic that Hobbes ascribes to sovereignty is found in the manner in which police have the 'public will' as their transcendental legitimizing justification. For Hobbes, given that the sovereign's will is ultimately one's own, a logic is introduced for sovereign power which sees any action it takes as justified given its relation to the people. Here, on the other hand, police may use public sentiment and will as

justification for even brutal activity: in the name of 'public order' or 'public safety', and so on.

17 In this vein, we could speak of Jacques Rancière who uses police as a broad term designating not a 'social function but a symbolic constitution of the social' (2010: 36). For Rancière police is opposed to something he calls 'politics', where police refers to institutional state, electoral, party politics, and 'politics' is a disturbance that 'makes visible what had no business being seen and makes heard a discourse where once there was only place for noise' (1999: 30). For Rancière, however, the existence of police cannot be dispensed with altogether and indeed, there are 'worse and better police' orders (1999: 30–1). This is a very different conception of police order that I am working with here.

18 As I argued in the previous chapter, what Schmitt had given us access to, was the thought that the law annexes what is 'exterior' to it, that is anomie, or lawlessness via the exception in order to be rendered effective. In so doing this excluded element comes to be included within the law itself. Thus even when the law is 'suspended' in the state of exception, there remains, for Schmitt order (even though it is of an extraordinary kind). This means that for Schmitt even while law retreats, order remains under the state of exception. What is excluded is, then, not 'lawlessness' per se, which for Schmitt would be a condition of anarchy, but an extra-legally imposed order. What I argued was missing from Schmitt's account was any notion of police. In so doing, Schmitt unwittingly reproduces a view of liberal politics in which the 'transcendent' figure of sovereign decisionism is gradually pushed out in favour of an immanent form of governing by law. In this way, the personal decision located in a singular will of the sovereign disappears into the rule of law, precisely the argument I am challenging here.

19 I am not here concerned with the philosophy of anarchism per se, which, while important in its own right, is distinct from the an-archic core of state power (which it would want to overcome) as well as the 'an-archy' that is projected by the state into a future, past or other place where the state and police are not 'functional'. It is with these latter two concepts that the present work is concerned.

20 It could be said then that for Agamben 'the passage from potentiality to sovereignty is accomplished through the structure of the exception' (Gullí 2007: 146).

21 See also Dylan Rodríguez who writes: 'the (racial) formations of punishment and death inscribed on the various surfaces of the prison regime – from the nearby to the faraway – are in fact *generally unremarkable*' (2006: 10).

# Chapter 5

1 Important to note here is Aimé Césaire's *Discourse on Colonialism* that discusses Nazism in Europe via a conceptualization of the colonial boomerang: 'we must study how colonization works to *decivilize* the colonizer, to *brutalize* him in the true sense of the word, to degrade him, to awaken him to buried instincts, to covetousness, violence, race hatred, and moral relativism' (2000: 35), and furthermore, 'the bourgeoisie is awakened by a terrific boomerang effect: the gestapos are busy, the prisons fill up, the torturers standing around the racks invent, refine, discuss' (2000: 36). My purpose here is to neither explain nor examine Nazi Germany nor take issue with the presentation of Nazism that Césaire makes. I am rather examining the colonial boomerang argument as it has emerged in accounts of police power specifically, and how this may do more to obscure the nature of police power than enlighten.

2 The shock, of course, was not just at Gordon's innocence in terms of the protest but also, and very significantly, his status: 'much of the public distress about the Jamaica controversy had centred on the hanging of a Christian member of the assembly, with a trial that resembled a mockery of proper legal procedures' (Hall 1989: 185).

3 Not specifically mentioned here, but we can surmise was very much part of this reasoning, was the Haitian revolution suffusing the English with anxiety about rebellious Black subjects. *Fear* of conspiracy or revolt, was enough, in the eyes of Finalson and others, to justify not only martial law but the 'excessive' violence used by the English. Indeed, it did not matter that an uprising did not actually take place, or that those executed were not present at the initial protest that triggered the declaration of martial law.

4 For Frank Wilderson, 'the race of Humanism (White, Asian, South Asian and Arab) could not have produced itself without the simultaneous production of that walking destruction which became known as the black. Put another way, through chattel slavery the world gave birth and coherence to both the joys of domesticity and to its struggles of political discontent; and with these joys and struggles the Human was born, but not before it murdered the Black, forging a symbiosis between the political ontology of Humanity and the social death of Blacks' (2010: 20–1). Whiteness, and its construction through concepts like reason, universality, justice, the human and so on, was predicated on that which was not those things, that is, Black people. Many who critique Wilderson and Afropessimist thought more generally do so on the basis that race is 'ontologized' by which they mean taken out of the sphere of politics and power. Yet of course

this is to fundamentally misunderstand ontology which is, for Wilderson, as it is also for Agamben, political all the way down, though of course from different directions.

5   This is something attended to by Stuart Schrader who discusses how the idea that extremely repressive policing was used abroad only to boomerang back to the metropole doesn't apply to US police power which was being exercised repressively at home and then being exported around the world, constituting a police power that was (he argues, unlike the European exercise of colonial police power) not divided geographically between domestic and international.

6   See, for example, Bell who argues, 'All this suggests that English policing culture today is profoundly influenced by more militarised policing cultures tried and tested in Ireland and throughout the Empire. Since the disintegration of the Empire, it would seem that it is Northern Ireland which has provided the lead in influencing police culture on the mainland' (Bell 2013).

7   The complex but inextricable relationship between 'the ethical' and anti-Blackness is further illuminated by Calvin Warren who argues that 'ethics is a relationality between coherent ontologies that is predicated on fractured blackness, or the nonrelational landscape between the human and blacks' (2016: 64).

8   As discussed previously, Hobbes characterizes the state of nature not by 'continuous fighting' but an all-pervasive violent atmosphere that is like 'weather' (1996: 88). This weather is like da Silva's *what-is-known* something that is known and can therefore be pre-empted.

9   da Silva does not repeat the claim that 'the others of Europe have been placed outside of history and reason or claiming that they have been fixed in an earlier time or altogether outside time . . . the arsenal of the racial engulfs them by writing their difference as an effect of the play of productive reason' (2007: 166). This isn't about 'the spatializing of time' that critics of progress and development have utilized to explain why Europe's others are placed in Europe's 'past' (2007: 167), because while the question of the temporal is here interrogated and challenged, the question of the racial – how 'others' are produced is left unexplained.

10  I do not intend to collapse these categories into each other but rather point to the commonality that exists between them, that they all challenge a common-sense undertstanding of time.

## Concluding remarks

1. In a distinct but related line of argument, Frank Wilderson discusses how the 'inside/outside, civil society/black world' is distinguishable by 'the difference between those bodies that do not magnetize bullets and those that do' (2003a: 20).
2. As Agamben writes, 'just as there is never a pure sign without signature, neither is it possible ever to separate and move the signature to an originary position' (Agamben 2009: 79).

# References

Abbott, M. (2012), 'No Life Is Bare, the Ordinary Is the Exceptional: Giorgio Agamben and the Question of Political Ontology', *Parrhesia*, 14 (23): 23–36.

Abourhame, N. (2018), 'Of Monsters and Boomerangs: Colonial Returns in the Late Liberal City', *City: Analysis of Urban Change, Theory and Action*, 22 (1): 106–15.

Adorno, T. W. (1993), *Hegel: Three Studies*, Cambridge, MA: MIT Press.

Agamben, G. ([1995] 1998), *Homo Sacer: Sovereign Power and Bare Life*, Stanford, CA: Stanford University Press. (Homo Sacer I,1).

Agamben, G. ([1996] 2000), *Means Without End: Notes on Politics*, Minneapolis, MN: University of Minnesota Press.

Agamben, G. (2005), *State of Exception*, Chicago, IL: Chicago University Press. (Homo Sacer II,1).

Agamben, G. (2008), 'K', in J. Clemens et al. (eds), *The Work of Giorgio Agamben: Law, Literature, Life*, 13–28, Edinburgh: Edinburgh University Press.

Agamben, G. (2009a), *The Signature of All Things: On Method*, New York: Zone Books.

Agamben, G. (2009b), *What Is an Apparatus?: And Other Essays*, Stanford, CA: Stanford University Press.

Agamben, G. (2010), *The Sacrament of Language*, Cambridge: Polity Press.

Agamben, G. (2011), *The Kingdom and the Glory: For a Theological Genealogy of Economy and Government*, Stanford, CA: Stanford University Press. (Homo Sacer II,2).

Agamben, G. (2012), *The Church and the Kingdom*, London: Seagull Books.

Agamben, G. (2015), *Stasis: Civil War as a Political Paradigm*, Edinburgh: Edinburgh University Press.

Agamben, G. (2016), *The Use of Bodies*, Stanford, CA: Stanford University Press.

Aravamudan, S. (2009), 'Hobbes and America', in D. Carey and L. Festa (eds), *The Postcolonial Enlightenment: Eighteenth-Century Colonialism and Postcolonial Theory*, 37–64, Oxford: Oxford University Press.

Arendt, H. (2017), *The Origins of Totalitarianism*, London: Penguin Books.

Aristotle (1969), *Physics*, trans. H. G. Apostle, Bloomington, IN: Indiana University Press.

Aristotle (2004), *The Metaphysics*, trans. H. Lawson-Tancred, London: Penguin Books.

Aristotle (1992), *The Politics*, London: Penguin.

Aristotle (2013), *Politics*, trans. C. Lord, Chicago, IL: University of Chicago Press.

Ashcraft, R. (1972), 'Leviathan Triumphant: Thomas Hobbes and the Politics of Wild Men', in E. Dudley and M. E. Novak (eds), *The Wild Man Within: An Image in Western Thought from the Renaissance to Romanticism*, 141–83, Pittsburgh, PA: University of Pittsburgh Press.

Associated Press (2021), 'Drug Suspect Police Linked to Breonna Taylor Enters Plea', Available online: https://uk.movies.yahoo.com/drug-suspect-police-linked-breonna-182108383.html (accessed 15 May 2023).

Attell, K. (2015), *Giorgio Agamben: Beyond the Threshold of Deconstruction*, New York: Fordham University Press.

Avineri, S. (1972), *Hegel's Theory of the Modern State*, New York: Cambridge University Press.

Balibar, E. (2009), 'Reflections on *Gewalt*', *Historical Materialism*, 17: 99–125.

Balibar, E. (2015), *Violence and Civility: On the Limits of Political Philosophy*, New York: Columbia University Press.

Bauman, Z. (1992), *Intimations of Postmodernity*, London: Routledge.

BBC News (2020), 'George Floyd Death: How Many Black People Die in Police Custody in England and Wales', Available online: https://www.bbc.com/news/52890363 (accessed 1 October 2022).

Bell, E. (2013), 'Normalising the Exceptional: British Colonial Policing Cultures Come Home', *Memoire(s), Identité(s), Marginalité(s) Dans le Monde Occidental Contemporain*, 10.

Benjamin, A. (2005), 'Spacing as the Shared: Heraclitus, Pindar, Agamben', in A. Norris (ed), *Politics, Metaphysics and Death*, 145–73, Durham, NC: Duke University Press.

Benjamin, A. (2013), *Working with Walter Benjamin: Recovering a Political Philosophy*, Edinburgh: Edinburgh University Press.

Benjamin, A. (2015), *Towards a Relational Ontology: Philosophy's Other Possibility*, New York: State University of New York Press.

Benjamin, W. (1977), *The Origin of German Tragic Drama*, London: NLB.

Benjamin, W. (1978), 'Critique of Violence', in P. Demetz (ed), *Reflections*, 277–301, London: Harcourt Brace Jovanovich.

Benjamin, W. (2004), 'Fate and Character', in M. Bullock and M. W. Jennings (eds), *Walter Benjamin: Selected Writings Vol. 1: 1913–1926*, 201–7, Cambridge, MA: Harvard University Press.

Benjamin, W. (2005), 'On the Concept of History', Available online: https://www.marxists.org/reference/archive/benjamin/1940/history.htm (accessed 1 June 2016).

Bhattacharyya, G., et al. (2021), *Empire's Endgame: Racism and the British State*, London: Pluto Press.

Birnmaum, A. (2015), 'Variations of Fate', in B. Moran and C. Salzani (eds), *Towards the Critique of Violence: Walter Benjamin and Giorgio Agamben*, 91–109, London: Bloomsbury.

Blackstone, W. (2016), *Commentaries on the Laws of England: Book 1*, Oxford: Oxford University Press.

Blumenberg, H. (1983), *The Legitimacy of the Modern Age*, Cambridge, MA: MIT press.

Bobbio, N. (1993), *Thomas Hobbes and the Natural Law Tradition*, Chicago, IL: University of Chicago Press.

Bobbio, N. (2005), *Liberalism and Democracy*, London: Verso.

Bonefeld, W. (2013), 'Adam Smith and Ordoliberalism: On the Political Form of Market Liberty', *Review of International Studies*, 39 (2): 233–50.

Bonefeld, W. (2014), *Critical Theory and the Critique of Political Economy: On Subversion and Negative Reason*, London: Bloomsbury.

Breckman, W. (1999), *Marx, The Young Hegelians and the Origins of Radical Social Theory: Dethroning the Self*, Cambridge, MA: Cambridge University Press.

Bredekamp, H. (1999), 'From Walter Benjamin to Carl Schmitt, via Thomas Hobbes', *Critical Inquiry*, 25 (2): 247–66.

Brown, V. (1994), *Adam Smith's Discourse: Canonicity, Commerce and Conscience*, London: Routledge.

Buck-Morss, S. (1989), *The Dialectics of Seeing: Walter Benjmain and the Arcades Project*, Cambridge, MA: MIT Press.

Burchell, G. (1991), 'Peculiar Interests: Civil Society and Governing the System of Natural Liberty', in G. Burchell et al. (eds), *The Foucault Effect: Studies in Governmentality*, 119–51, London: Harvester Wheatsheaf.

Butler, J. (1993), 'Endangered/Endangering: Schematic Racism and White Paranoia' in R. Gooding-Williams (ed), *Reading Rodney King: Reading Urban Uprising*, 1–22, London : Routledge.

Campesi, G. (2016), *A Geneaology of Public Security: The Theory and History of Modern Police Powers*, Oxon: Routledge.

Castoriadis, C. (1984), *Crossorads in the Labyrinth*, Brighton: Harvester.

Castoriadis, C. (1983), 'The Greek Polis and the Creation of Democracy', *Graduate Faculty Philosophy Journal*, 9 (2): 79–115.

Caygill, H. (1989), *Art of Judgment*, Oxford: Blackwell.

Caygill, H. (1998), *The Colour of Experience*, London: Routledge.

Caygill, H. (2001), 'Perpetual Police? Kosovo and the Elision of Police and Military Violence', *European Journal of Social Theory*, 4 (1): 73–80.

Cavarero, A. (2002), *Stately Bodies: Literature, Philosophy and the Question of Gender*, Ann Arbor, MI: University of Michigan Press.

Césaire, A. (2000), *Discourse on Colonialism*, New York: Monthly Review Press.

Chamayou, G. (2013), 'Fichte's Passport – A Philosophy of the Police', *Theory and Event*, 16 (2): 1–16.

Chapman, B. (1970), *Police State*, New York: Praeger Publishers.

Chu, A. L. (2018), 'Black Infinity: Slavery and Freedom in Hegel's Africa', *The Journal of Speculative Philosophy*, 32 (3): 414–25.

Collins, S. L. (1989), *From Divine Cosmos to Sovereign State: An Intellectual History of Consciousness and the Idea of Order in Renaissance England*, Oxford: Oxford University Press.

Cover, R. M. (1986), 'Violence and the Word', *The Yale Law Journal*, 95 (8): 1601–29.

Crenshaw, K. and G. Peller (1993), 'Reel Time/Real Justice', in R. Gooding-Williams (ed), *Reading Rodney King/Reading Urban Uprising*, 56–73, New York: Routledge.

Cristi, R. (1998), *Carl Schmitt and Authoritarian Liberalism*, Cardiff: University of Wales Press.

Cropsey, J. (2001), *Polity and Economy: With Further Thoughts on the Principles of Adam Smith*, South Bend, IN: St. Augustine's Press.

D'Entreves, A. P. (1967), *The Notion of the State*, Oxford: Oxford University Press.

da Silva, D. F. (2001), 'Towards a Critique of the Socio-Logos of Justice: The *Analytics of Raciality* and the Production of Universality', *Social Identities*, 7 (3): 421–54.

da Silva, D. F. (2007), *Toward a Global Idea of Race*, Minneapolis, MN: University of Minnesota Press.

da Silva, D. F. (2009), 'No-Bodies: Law, Raciality and Violence', *Griffith Law Review*, 18 (2): 212–36.

da Silva, D. F. (2017a), 'Scene of Nature', in J. Desautels-Stein and C. Tomlins (eds), *Searching for Contemporary Legal Thought*, 275–89, Cambridge: Cambridge University Press.

da Silva, D. F. (2017b), 'The Banalization of Racial Events', *Theory and Event*, 20 (1): 61–5.

de la Durantaye, L. (2009), *Giorgio Agamben: A Critical Introduction*, Stanford, CA: Stanford University Press.

Davis, K. (2008), *Periodization and Sovereignty*, Philadelphia, PA: University of Pennsylvania Press.

Dean, M. (1994), *Critical and Effective Histories: Foucault's Methods and Historical Sociology*, London: Routledge.

Dean, M. (1999), *Governmentality: Power and Rule in Modern Society*, London: Sage Publications.

Dean, M. (2002), 'Liberal Government and Authoritarianism', *Economy and Society*, 31 (1): 37–61.

Dean, M. (2006), 'Military Intervention as "Police" Action?', in M. Dubber and M. Valverde (eds), *The New Police Science: The Police Power in Domestic and International Governance*, 185–207, Stanford, CA: Stanford University Press.

Dean, M. (2013), *The Signature of Power: Sovereignty, Governmentality and Biopolitics*, London: Sage Publications.

Denman, D. S. (2020), 'The Logistics of Police Power: Armored Vehicles, Colonial Boomerangs and Strategies of Circulation', *Society and Space*, 38 (6): 1138–56.

Derrida, J. (2002), 'Force of Law', in G. Andjar (ed), *Acts of Religion*, 230–98, London: Routledge.

Derrida, J. (2009), *The Beast and the Sovereign, Volume 1*, Chicago, IL: University of Chicago Press.

Dove, G. N. (1982), *The Police Procedural*, London: Popular Press.

Dreyfus, H. L. and P. Rabinow (1983), *Michel Foucault: Beyond Structuralism and Hermeneutics*, Chicago, IL: University of Chicago Press.

Dubber, M. (2005), *Police Power: Patriarchy and the Origins of American Government*, New York: Columbia University Press.

Dubber, M. (2006), 'The New Police Science and the Police Power Model of the Criminal Process', in M. Dubber and M. Valverde (eds), *The New Police Science: The Police Power in Domestic and International Governance*, 107–45, Stanford, CA: Stanford University Press.

Duttmann, A. G. (1996), 'The Violence of Destruction', in D. S. Ferris (ed), *Walter Benjamin: Theoretical Questions*, 165–84, Stanford, CA: Stanford University Press.

Elden, S. (2003), 'Plague, Panopticon, Police', *Surveillance and Society*, 1 (3): 240–53.

Esposito, R. (2004), *Bíos*, Minneapolis, MN: University of Minnesota Press.

Esposito, R. (2010), *Communitas: The Origin and Destiny of Community*, Stanford, CA: Stanford University Press.

Esposito, R. (2011), *Immunitas: The Protection and Negation of Life*, Cambridge: Polity Press.

Eucken, W. (1989), 'What Kind of Economic and Social System', in A. Peacock and H. Willgerodt (eds), *Germany's Social Market Economy: Origins and Evolution*, 27–43, New York: Palgrave Macmillan.

Ewald, F. (1990), 'Norms, Discipline and the Law', *Representations*, 30: 138–61.

Farmer, L. (2006), 'The Jurisprudence of Security: The Police Power and Criminal Law', in M. Dubber and M. Valverde (eds), *The New Police Science: The Police Power in Domestic and International Governance*, 145–63, Stanford, CA: Stanford University Press.

Fassin, D. (2013), *Enforcing Order: An Ethnography of Urban Policing*, Cambridge: Polity Press.

Fatsis, L. and M. Lamb (2022), *Policing the Pandemic: How Public Health becomes Public Order*, Bristol: Bristol University Press.

Fenves, P. (2010), *The Messianic Reduction: Walter Benjamin and the Shape of Time*, Stanford, CA: Stanford University Press.

Ferguson, A. (1996), *An Essay on the History of Civil Society*, Cambridge: Cambridge University Press.

Fichte, J. G. (1869), *The Science of Rights*, trans. A. E. Kroeger, Philadelphia, PA: Lippincott's Press.

Fichte, J. G. (2000), *Foundations of Natural Right*, Cambridge: Cambridge University Press.

Fitzpatrick, P. (1992), *The Mythology of Modern Law*, London: Routledge.

Fitzpatrick, P. (2001), *Modernism and the Grounds of Law*, Cambridge: Cambridge University Press.

Force, P. (2003), *Self-Interest before Adam Smith*, Cambridge: Cambridge University Press.

Forster, G. (2003), 'Divine Law and Human Law in Hobbes's "Leviathan"', *History of Political Thought*, 24 (2): 189–217.

Foucault, M. (1979), 'Omnes et Singulatim: Towards a Critique of Political Reason', Available online: https://tannerlectures.utah.edu/_documents/a-to-z/f/foucault81.pdf (accessed 20 January 2018).

Foucault, M. (1984), *The History of Sexuality Volume 1: The Will to Knowledge*, Hammondsworth: Penguin.

Foucault, M. (1987), 'Maurice Blanchot: The Thought from the Outside', in *Foucault Blanchot*, 7–61, New York: Zone Books.

Foucault, M. (1995), *Discipline and Punish: The Birth of the Prison*, New York: Vintage Books.

Foucault, M. (2002a), 'The Political Technology of Individuals', in J. D. Faubion (ed), *Essential Works of Foucault 1954–1984 Volume 3: Power*, 403–18, London: Penguin.

Foucault, M. (2002b), *The Order of Things*, London: Routledge.

Foucault, M. (2004), *Society Must be Defended: Lectures at the Collège De France 1975-76*, London: Penguin.

Foucault, M. (2007), *Security, Territory, Population: Lectures at the Collège De France 1977–1978*, Hampshire: Palgrave Macmillan.

Foucault, M. (2008), *The Birth of Biopolitics: Lectures at the Collège De France 1978–1979*, Hampshire: Palgrave Macmillan.

Franco, P. (1999), *Hegel's Philosophy of Freedom*, New Haven, CT: Yale University Press.

Friedman, M. (1951), 'Neoliberalism and its Prospects', Available online: https://miltonfriedman.hoover.org/friedman_images/Collections/2016c21/Farmand_02_17_1951.pdf (accessed 1 March 2016).

Friedrich, C. (1954), *The Philosophy of Hegel*, New York: Modern Library.
Gilroy, P. (1982), 'The Myth of Black Criminality', *Socialist Register*, 19: 47–56.
Golder, B. and P. Fitzpatrick (2009), *Foucault's Law*, Oxon: Routledge.
Gordon, C. (1991), 'Governmental Rationality: An Introduction', in G. Burchell et al. (eds), *The Foucault Effect: Studies in Governmentality*, 1–53, London: Harvester Wheatsheaf.
Gould, R. W. and M. J. Waldren (1986), *London's Armed Police*, London: Arms and Armour Press.
Graham, S. (2010), *Cities under Siege: The New Military Urbanism*, London: Verso Books.
Gray, B. M. (2022), 'Now It Is Always Now', *Political Theology* 1–15.
Gullì, B. (2007), 'The Ontology and Politics of Exception: Reflections of the Work of Giorgio Agamben', in M. Calarco and S. De Caroli (eds), *Giorgio Agamben: Sovereignty and Life*, 219–43, Stanford, CA: Stanford University Press.
Hall, B. (2005), 'Race in Hobbes', in A. Valls (ed), *Race and Racism in Modern Philosophy*, 43–57, New York: Cornell University Press.
Hall, C. (1989), 'The Economy of Intellectual Prestige: Thomas Carlyle, John Stuart Mill, and the Case of Governor Eyre', *Cultural Critique*, 12: 167–96.
Hall, S., et al. (2013), *Policing the Crisis: Mugging, the State, and Law and Order*, London: Red Globe Press.
Hamacher, W. (2000), 'Afformative, Strike', in A. Benjamin and P. Osborne (eds), *Walter Benjamin's Philosophy: Destruction and Experience*, 108–37, Manchester: Clinamen Press.
Hannsen, B. (2000), *Walter Benjamin's Other History: Of Stones, Animals, Human Beings and Angels*, Berkeley, CA: University of California Press.
Harney, S. and F. Moten (2015), 'Michael Brown', *Boundary 2*, 42 (4): 81–7.
Hartman, S. (2021), *Lose your Mother: A Journey along the Atlantic Slave Route*, London: Serpent's Tail.
Hayek, F. A. (1998), *Law, Legislation and Liberty*, London: Routledge.
Knox, T. M. and Hegel, G. W. F. (1952), *Hegel's Philosophy of Right*, trans. T. M. Knox, Oxford: Oxford University Press.
Hegel, G. W. F. (1975a), *Natural Law*, Philadelphia, PA: University of Pennsylvania Press.
Hegel, G. W. F. (1975b), *Lectures on the Philosophy of World History Introduction: Reason in History*, Cambridge: Cambridge University Press.
Hegel, G. W. F. (1977), *The Difference between Fichte's and Schelling's System of Philosophy*, New York: SUNY Press.
Hegel, G. W. F. (1995a), *Lectures on the History of Philosophy Vol.3: Medieval and Modern Philosophy*. Lincoln, NE: University of Nebraska Press.
Hegel, G. W. F. (1995b), *Lectures on Natural Right and Political Science*, trans. J. M. Stewart and P. Hodgson, Berkeley, CA: University of California Press.

Hegel, G. W. F. (2008), *Outlines of the Philosophy of Right*, Oxford: Oxford University Press.

Hegel, G. W. F. (2014), 'Jena Lectures 1803/1804', in P. Ifergan (ed), *Hegel's Discovery of the Philosophy of Spirit: Autonomy, Alienation and the Ethical Life: The Jena Lectures 1802–1806*, 116–56, New York: Palgrave Macmillan.

Herzog, L. (2013), *Inventing the Market: Smith, Hegel and Political Theory*, Oxford: Oxford University Press.

Hill, L. (2001), 'The Hidden Theology of Adam Smith', *European Journal of the History of Economic Thought*, 8 (1): 1–29.

Hinsley, F. H. (1966), *Sovereignty*, London: Watts.

Hobbes, T. (1969), *Elements of Law*, London: Frank Cass and Company Limited.

Hobbes, T. (1976), *Thomas White's De Mundo Examined*, trans. H. W. Jones, Bradford: Bradford University Press.

Hobbes, T. (1978), *Man and Citizen*, Hemel Hempstead: Harvester Press.

Hobbes, T. (1983), *De Cive*, Oxford: Clarendon Press.

Hobbes, T. (1996), *Leviathan*, Cambridge: Cambridge University Press.

Hobbes, T. (1998), *On the Citizen*, ed. and trans. Richard Tuck, Cambridge: Cambridge University Press.

Honneth, A. (2010), *The Pathologies of Individual Freedom: Hegel's Social Theory*, Princeton, NJ: Princeton University Press.

House of Commons Library (2022), 'Child Q and the Law on Strip Search', Available online: https://commonslibrary.parliament.uk/child-q-and-the-law-on-strip-search/ (accessed 15 May 2023).

Hussain, N. (2019), *The Jurisprudence of Emergency: Colonialism and the Rule of Law*, Ann Arbor, MI: University of Michigan Press.

Ignatieff, M. (2001), *Human Rights as Politics and Idolatry*, Princeton, NJ: Princeton University Press.

Ilting, K.-H. (1971), 'The Structure of Hegel's Philosophy of Right', in Z. Pelczynski (ed), *Hegel's Political Philosophy*, 90–111, Cambridge: Cambridge University Press.

Jackson, Z. I. (2020), *Becoming Human: Matter and Meaning in an Antiblack World*, New York: New York University Press.

Johnson, A. (2014), 'Foucault: Critical Theory of the Police in a Neoliberal Age', *Theoria*, 61 (141): 5–29.

Kafka, F. (1999), 'Before the Law', in N. N. Glatzer (ed), *Franz Kafka: The Complete Short Stories*, 3–5, London: Vintage.

Kantorowicz, E. (1957), *The King's Two Bodies: A Study in Mediaeval Political Theology*, Princeton, NJ: Princeton University Press.

King, P. (1974), *The Ideology of Order: A Comparative Analysis of Jean Bodin and Thomas Hobbes*, London: George Allen & Unwin.

Klockars, C. B. (1985), *The Idea of Police*, Beverly Hills, CA: Sage.
Knemeyer, F. L. (1980), 'Polizei', *Economy and Society*, 9 (2): 12–32.
Koepnick, L. P. (1996), 'The Spectacle, the "Trauerspiel" and the Politics of Resolution: Benjamin Reading the Baroque Reading Weimar', *Critical Inquiry*, 22 (2): 268–91.
Koselleck, R. (1987), *Critique and Crisis*, Cambridge, MA: MIT Press.
Kotsko, A. (2010), 'Dismantling the Theo-Political Machine: On Agamben's Messianic Nihilism', in A. P. Smith and D. Whistler (eds), *After the Postsecular and the Postmodern: New Essays in Continental Philosophy of Religion*, 209–25, Newcastle: Cambridge Scholars Publishing.
Kotsko, A. (2013), 'Genealogy and Political Theology', *Political Theology*, 14 (1): 107–14.
Laird, J. (1942), 'Hobbes on Aristotle's "Politics"', *Proceedings of the Aristotelian Society*, 43: 1–20.
Lemke, T. (2011), *Bio-Politics: An Advanced Introduction*, New York: New York University Press.
Liska, V. (2015), 'Benjamin and Agamben on Kafka, Judaism and the Law', in B. Moran and C. Salzani (eds), *Towards the Critique of Violence: Walter Benjamin and Giorgio Agamben*, 201–15, London: Bloomsbury.
Locke, J. (1993), *Two Treatises of Government*, London: Everyman.
Löwith, K. (1957), *Meaning in History*, Chicago, IL: University of Chicago Press.
Lukács, G. (1975), *The Young Hegel: Studies in the Relations between Dialectics and Economics*, London: Merlin Press.
Luther, T. C. (2009), *Hegel's Critique of Modernity: Reconciling Individual Freedom and the Community*, Plymouth: Lexington Books.
Macfie, A. (1971), 'The Invisible Hand of Jupiter', *Journal of the History of Ideas*, 32 (4): 595–9.
Major-Poetzel, P. (1983), *Michel Foucault's Archaeology of Western Culture: Toward a New Science of History*, Chapel Hill, NC: University of North Carolina Press.
Marcuse, H. (1955), *Reason and Revolution: Hegel and the rise of Social Theory*, London: Routledge.
Martel, J. (2007), *Subverting the Leviathan: Reading Thomas Hobbes as a Radical Democrat*, New York: Columbia University Press.
Martel, J. (2010), 'Walter Benjamin, Sovereignty and the Eschatology of Power', in C. Barbour and G. Pavlich (eds), *After Sovereignty: On the Question of Political Beginnings*, 180–93, Oxon: Routledge.
Martinot, S. and J. Sexton (2003), 'The Avant-garde of White Supremacy', Available online: https://www.ocf.berkeley.edu/~marto/avantguard.htm (accessed 1 February 2019).

Marx, K. (1942), 'Karl Marx on India', *New International*. Available online: https://www.marxists.org/history/etol/newspape/ni/vol08/no06/marx.htm (accessed 1 March 2020).

Marx, K. (1992a), 'A Contribution to the Critique of Hegel's Philosophy of Right', in *Karl Marx: Early Writings*, trans. R. Livingstone and G. Benton, 243–59, London: Penguin.

Marx, K. (1992b), 'Critique of Hegel's Doctrine of the State', in *Karl Marx: Early Writings*, 57–199, London: Penguin.

Mbembe, A. (2003), 'Necropolitics', *Public Culture*, 15 (1): 11–40.

McBarnet, D. (1981), *Conviction: The Law, the State and the Construction of Justice*, Basingstoke: Palgrave Macmillan.

McCall, T. (1996), 'Momentary Violence', in D. S. Ferris (ed), *Walter Benjamin: Theoretical Questions*, 185–209, Stanford, CA: Stanford University Press.

Meier, H. (2011), *The Lesson of Carl Schmitt: Four Chapters on the Distinction between Political Theology and Political Philosophy*, Chicago, IL: University of Chicago Press.

Mirabeau, M. (1963), 'Miscellaneous Extracts', in J. Meek (ed), *The Economics of Physiocracy*, 65–72, London: George Allen & Unwin Ltd.

Menke, B. (2015), 'Techniques of Agreement, Diplomacy, Lying', in B. Moran and C. Salzani (eds), *Towards the Critique of Violence: Walter Benjamin and Giorgio Agamben*, 19–39, London: Bloomsbury.

Mills, C. (1999), *The Racial Contract*, Ithaca, NY: Cornell University Press.

Montesquieu, C. (2001), *The Spirit of the Laws*, Kitchener, ON: Batoche Books.

Moran, B. and C. Salzani (2015), 'Introduction: On the *Actuality* of "Critique of Violence"', in B. Moran and C. Salzani (eds), *Towards the Critique of Violence: Walter Benjamin and Giorgio Agamben*, 1–19, London: Bloomsbury.

Nancy, J.-L. (1982), 'The Jurisdiction of the Hegelian Monarch', *Social Research*, 49 (2): 481–516.

Neocleous, M. (1996), *Administering Civil Society: Towards a Theory of State Power*, Basingstoke: Macmillan.

Neocleous, M. (1998a), 'Policing and Pin-Making: Adam Smith, Police and the State of Prosperity', *Policing and Society*, 8 (4): 425–49.

Neocleous, M. (1998b), 'Policing the System of Needs: Hegel, Political Economy and the Police of the Market', *History of European Ideas*, 24 (1): 43–58.

Neocleous, M. (2000), *The Fabrication of Social Order*, London: Pluto Press.

Neocleous, M. (2006), 'Theoretical Foundations of the "New Police Science"', in M. Dubber and M. Valverde (eds), *The New Police Science: The Police Power in Domestic and International Governance*, 17–42, Stanford, CA: Stanford University Press.

Neocleous, M. (2014), 'The Monster and the Police', *Radical Philosophy*, 185: 8–18.

Novak, W. (1996), *The People's Welfare: Law and Regulation in Nineteenth Century America*, Chapel Hill, NC: University of North Carolina Press.

NYU (2020), 'Research Shows Black Drivers More Likely To Be Stopped by Police', Available online: nyu.edu/about/news-publications/news/2020/may/black-drivers-more-likely-to-be-stopped-by-police.html (accessed 5 October 2022).

Simpson, J. and E. Weiner, eds. (1989), *Oxford English Dictionary*, 2nd edn, Oxford: Clarendon Press.

Palaver, W. (1995), 'Hobbes and the *Katechon*: The Secularization of Sacrificial Christianity', *Contagion: Journal of Violence, Mimesis and Culture*, 2: 57–74.

Pasquino, P. (1991), 'Theatricum Politicum: The Genealogy of Capital – Police and the State of Prosperity', in G. Burchell et al. (eds), *The Foucault Effect: Studies in Governmentality*, 105–19, London: Harvester Wheatsheaf.

Patterson, O. (1982), *Slavery and Social Death*, Cambridge, MA: Harvard University Press.

Pearce, R. H. (1965), *The Savages of America: A Study of the Indian and the Idea of Civilization*, Baltimore, MD: The Johns Hopkins Press.

Pelczynski, Z. A. (1971), 'The Hegelian Conception of the State', in Z. A. Pelczynski (ed), *Hegel's Political Philosophy: Problems and Perspectives*, 1–30, Cambridge: Cambridge University Press.

Pelczynski, Z. A. (1971a), 'Hegel's Political Philosophy: Some Thoughts on its Contemporary Relevance', in Z. A. Pelczynski (ed), *Hegel's Political Philosophy: Problems and Perspectives*, 230–43, Cambridge: Cambridge University Press.

Pelczynski, Z. A. (1984), 'Political Community and Individual Freedom in Hegel's Philosophy of State', in Z. A. Pelczynski (ed), *The State and Civil Society: Studies in Hegel's Political Philosophy*, 55–76, Cambridge: Cambridge University Press.

Peperzak, A. (1995), 'Hegel and Hobbes Revised', in A. B. Collins (ed), *Hegel on the Modern World*, 199–219, New York: State University of New York Press.

Pestoulas, C. (2001), *Hayek's Liberalism and its Origins*, London: Routledge.

Pocock, G. J. A. (1972), 'Time, History and Eschatology in the Thought of Thomas Hobbes', in G. J. A. Pocock (ed), *Politics, Language and Time: Essays on Political Thought and History*, 148–202, London: Methuen & Co.

Prozorov, S. (2014), *Agamben and Politics: A Critical Introduction*, Edinburgh: Edinburgh University Press.

Ptak, R. (2009), 'Neoliberalism in Germany: Revisiting the Ordoliberal Foundations of the Social Market Economy', in P. Mirowski and D. Plehwe (eds), *The Road from Mont Pelerin: The Making of the Neoliberal Thought Collective*, 98–139, London: .

Radzinowicz, L. (1956), *A History of English Criminal Law and its Administration*, vol. 3, London: Stevens and Sons Limited.

Raeff, M. (1975), 'The Well-Ordered Police State and the Development of Modernity in Seventeenth and Eighteenth-Century Europe: An Attempt at a Comparative Approach', *The American Historical Review*, 80 (5): 1221–43.

Raeff, M. (1983), *The Well-Ordered Police State*, New Haven, CT: Yale University Press.

Rancière, J. (1999), *Dis-Agreement*, Minneapolis, MN: University of Minnesota Press.

Rancière, J. (2010), *Dissensus*, London: Continuum.

Raphael, D. D. (1975), 'The Impartial Spectator', in A. S. Skinner and T. Wilson (eds), *Essays on Adam Smith*, 83–100, Oxford: Clarendon Press.

Rasch, W. (2004), *Sovereignty and its Discontents: On the Primacy of Conflict and the Structure of the Political*, London: Birkbeck Law Press.

Reiner, R. (2010), *The Politics of the Police*, Oxford: Oxford University Press.

Riedel, M. (1984), *Between Tradition and Revolution: The Hegelian Transformation of Political Philosophy*, Cambridge: Cambridge University Press.

Riedel, M. (1996), 'Paradigm Evolution in Political Philosophy: Aristotle and Hobbes', in R. Lilly (ed), *The Ancients and the Moderns*, 101–15, Bloomington, IN: Indiana University Press.

Robinson, C. (2016), *The Terms of Order*, Chapel Hill, NC: University of North Carolina Press.

Rodríguez, D. (2006), '(Non) Scenes of Captivity: The Common Sense of Punishment and Death', *Radical History Review*, 96: 9–32.

Ross, A. (2015), 'The Ambiguity of Ambiguity in Benjamin's "Critique of Violence"', in B. Moran and C. Salzani (eds), *Towards the Critique of Violence: Walter Benjamin and Giorgio Agamben*, 39–57, London: Bloomsbury.

Ruda, F. (2011), *Hegel's Rabble: An Investigation into Hegel's Philosophy of Right*, London: Bloomsbury.

Rüstow, A. (1942), 'General Social Laws of the Economic Disintegration and Possibilities of Reconstruction', in Afterword to Röpke, W., *International Economic Disintegration*, 267–83, London: William Hodge.

Seri, G. (2012), *Seguridad: Crime, Police Power and Democracy in Argentina*, New York: Continuum.

Schecter, D. (2000), *Sovereign States or Political Communities?* Manchester: Manchester University Press.

Schmitt, C. (1996), *The Leviathan in the State Theory of Thomas Hobbes: Meaning and Failure of a Political Symbol*, London: Greenwood Press.

Schmitt, C. (2003), *The Nomos of the Earth in the International Law of the Jus Publicum Europeaum*, New York: Telos Press.

Schmitt, C. (2005), *Political Theology: Four Chapters on the Concept of Sovereignty*, Chicago, IL: University of Chicago Press.

Schmitt, C. (2007), *The Concept of the Political*, Chicago, IL: University of Chicago Press.
Schmitt, C. (2014), *Dictatorship*, Cambridge: Polity Press.
Scholze-Stubenrecht, W. and J. B. Sykes, eds. (1997), *The Oxford-Duden German Dictionary*, Oxford: Clarendon Press.
Schrader, S. (2019), *Badges without Borders: How Global Counterinsurgency Transformed American Policing*, Berkeley, CA: University of California Press.
Schütz, A. (2008), 'The Fading Memory of Homo Non Sacer', in J. Clemens et al. (eds), *The Work of Giorgio Agamben: Law, Literature, Life*, Edinburgh: Edinburgh University Press.
Sharpe, C. (2016), *In the Wake: On Blackness and Being*, Durham, NC: Duke University Press.
Skinner, Q. (1978), *The Foundations of Modern Political Thought. Volume 2: The Age of Reformation*, Cambridge: Cambridge University Press.
Skinner, Q. (1999), 'Hobbes and the Purely Artificial Person of the State', *The Journal of Political Philosophy*, 7 (1): 1–29.
Small, A. W. (1909), *The Cameralists: The Pioneers of German Social Polity*, Chicago, IL: University of Chicago Press.
Smith, A. (1964), *Lectures on Justice, Police, Revenue and Arms*, New York: Sentry Press.
Smith, A. (1976), *An Inquiry into the Nature and the Causes of the Wealth of Nations (Vol. 1 and Vol. 2)*, Oxford: Oxford University Press.
Smith, A. (1978), *Lectures on Jurisprudence*, Oxford: Oxford University Press.
Smith, A. (1980a), 'The History of Ancient Physics', in W. P. D. Wightman and J. C. Bryce (eds.), *Essays on Philosophical Subjects*, 106–18, Oxford: Clarendon Press.
Smith, A. (1980b), 'The History of Astronomy', in W. P. D. Wightman and J. C. Bryce (eds), *Essays on Philosophical Subjects*, 5–33, Oxford: Clarendon Press.
Smith, A. (2002), *The Theory of Moral Sentiments*, Cambridge: Cambridge University Press.
Smith, C. (2006), *Adam Smith's Political Philosophy: The Invisible Hand and Spontaneous Order*, Oxon: Routledge.
Smith, S. B. (1989), *Hegel's Critique of Liberalism: Rights in Context*, Chicago, IL: University of Chicago Press.
Soanes, C. and A. Stevenson (2006), *Concise Oxford English Dictionary*, Oxford: Oxford University Press.
Sorell, T. (1986), *Hobbes*, London: Routledge.
Spragens, T. A. (1973), *The Politics of Motion: The World of Thomas Hobbes*, Lexington, KY: University of Kentucky Press.
Springborg, P. (1995), 'Hobbes' Biblical Beasts: Leviathan and Behemoth', *Political Theory*, 23 (2): 353–75.

Strauss, L. (1952), *The Political Philosophy of Hobbes*, Chicago, IL: University of Chicago Press.

Tarizzo, D. (2011), 'The Untamed Ontology', *Angelaki*, 16 (3): 53–61.

Tarizzo, D. (2017), *Life: A Modern Invention*, Minneapolis, MN: University of Minnesota Press.

Taminaux, J. (1985), *Dialectic and Difference: Finitude in Modern Thought*, London: Palgrave Macmillan.

Temple-Smith, R. (2007), 'Adam Smith's Treatment of the Greeks in *The Theory of Moral Sentiments*: The Case of Aristotle', in G. Cockfield et al. (eds), *New Perspecitves on Adam Smith's The Theory of Moral Sentiments*, 29–47, Cheltenham: Edward Elgar.

Thurschwell, A. (2005), 'Cutting the Branches for Akiba: Agamben's Critique of Derrida', in A. Norris (ed), *Politics, Metaphysics, and Death: Essays on Giorgio Agamben's Homo Sacer*, 173–98, Durham, NC: Duke University Press.

Tomba, M. (2009), 'Another Kind of *Gewalt*: Beyond Law Re-Reading Walter Benjamin', *Historical Materialism*, 17: 126–44.

Toscano, A. (2011), 'Divine Management: Critical Remarks on Giorgio Agamben's the Kingdom and the Glory', *Angelaki*, 16 (3): 125–36.

Trafford, J. (2022), *The World as Police*, Unpublished.

Tribe, K. (1995), *Strategies of Economic Order: German Economic Discourse 1750–1950*, Cambridge: Cambridge University Press.

Tribe, K. (1988), *Governing Economy: The Reformation of German Economic Discourse 1750–1840*, Cambridge: Cambridge University Press.

Tribe, K. (2015), *The Economy of the Word: Language, History and Economics*, Oxford: Oxford University Press.

Valverde, M. (2003), 'Police Science, British Style: Pub Licensing and Knowledges of Urban Disorder', *Economy and Society*, 32 (2): 234–52.

Veyne, P. (1997), 'Foucault Revolutionizes History', in A. I. Davidson (ed), *Foucault and His Interlocutors*, 146–83, Chicago, IL: University of Chicago Press.

Viner, J. (1927), 'Adam Smith and Laissez Faire', *Journal of Political Economy*, 35 (2): 198–232.

Viner, J. (1976), *The Role of Providence in the Social Order*, Princeton, NJ: Princeton University Press.

Vivenza, G. (2001), *Adam Smith and the Classics: The Classical Heritage in Smith's Thought*, Oxford: Oxford University Press.

Waddington, P. A. J. (1998), *Policing Citizens: Police, Power and the State*, Oxon: Routledge.

Wang, J. (2018), *Carceral Capitalism*, Cambridge, MA: MIT Press.

Warren, C. (2016), 'Black Time: Slavery, Metaphysics, and the Logic of Wellness', in S. C. Colbert et al. (eds), *The Psychic Hold of Slavery: Legacies in American Expressive Culture*, 55–69, New Brunswick, NJ: Rutgers University Press.

*Washington Post* (2022), 'Fatal Force', Available online: https://www.washingtonpost.com/graphics/investigations/police-shootings-database/ (accessed 1 October 2022).

Watkin, W. (2014), *Agamben and Indifference: A Critical Overview*, London: Rowman & Littlefield.

Watkin, W. (2015), 'Agamben, Benjamin and the Indifference of Violence', in B. Moran and C. Salzani (eds), *Towards the Critique of Violence: Walter Benjamin and Giorgio Agamben*, 139–53, London: Bloomsbury.

Weber, S. (1992), 'Taking Exception to Decision: Walter Benjamin and Carl Schmitt', *Diacritics*, 22 (3/4): 5–18.

Weber, S. (2008), *Benjamin's-Abilities*, Cambridge, MA: Harvard University Press.

Weheliye, A. G. (2014), *Habeas Viscus: Racializing Assemblages, Biopolitics, and Black Feminist Theories of the Human*, Durham, NC: Duke University Press.

Westphal, K. (1993), 'The Basic Context and Structure of Hegel's Philosophy of Right', in F. C. Beiser (ed), *The Cambridge Companion to Hegel*, 234–64, Cambridge: Cambridge University Press.

Whyte, J. (2013), *Catastrophe and Redemption: The Political Thought of Giorgio Agamben*, Albany, NY: State University of New York Press.

Whyte, J. (2014), '"The King Reigns but He Doesn't Govern": Thinking Sovereignty and Government with Agamben, Foucault and Rousseau', in T. Frost (ed), *Giorgio Agamben: Legal, Political and Philosophical Perspectives*, 143–61, London: Routledge.

Wightman, W. P. D. (1975), 'Adam Smith and the History of Ideas', in A. S. Skinner and T. Wilson (eds), *Essays on Adam Smith*, 44–68, Oxford: Clarendon Press.

Wilderson, F. (2003a), 'The Prison Slave as Hegemony's (Silent) Scandal', *Social Justice*, 30 (2): 18–27.

Wilderson, F. (2003b), 'Gramsci's Black Marx: Whither the Slave in Civil Society?', *Social Identities*, 9 (2): 225–40.

Wilderson, F. (2010), *Red, White and Black: Cinema and the Structure of U.S. Antagonisms*, Durham, NC: Duke University Press.

Wilderson, F. and P. Douglass (2013), 'The Violence of Presence: Metaphysics in a Blackened World', *The Black Scholar*, 43 (4): 117–23.

Williams, R. (1997), *Hegel's Ethics of Recognition*, Berkeley, CA: University of California Press.

Young, J. T. (2002), 'Adam Smith and the Physiocrats: Contrasting Views of the Laws of Nature', *History of Economic Ideas*, 10 (3): 7–28.

Zartaloudis, T. (2010), *Giorgio Agamben: Power, Law and the Uses of Criticism*, London: Routledge.

Zartaloudis, T. (2015), 'Violence Without Law? On Pure Violence as Destituent Power', in B. Moran and C. Salzani (eds), *Towards the Critique of Violence: Walter Benjamin and Giorgio Agamben*, 169–87, London: Bloomsbury.

# Index

Abbott, Matthew   14
absolutism police   114–15
administration of justice   71–3
Africans   87–89, 92
Agamben, G.   2–4, 8, 10–11, 13–14, 21, 23, 62, 64
   *auctoritas vs. potestas*   118–19
   on collateral effects   121–5
   division of power, characterization of   118–21
   on exceptionality   105, 134–7
   on force-of-law   112–13
   *Homo Sacer* project   117–18
   *Kingdom and the Glory, The*   7, 117–18, 127
   on multitude *vs.* people   64–5
   *oikonomia*   118–21
   ontology *vs.* praxis   10, 12, 120–1
   and police   116–37
   political ontology   14
   on potentiality   134–7
   *Sacrament of Language, The*   126–7
   signature of order   125–32
   'Sovereign Police'   2, 117
   on sovereignty *vs.* government   11, 117–18
   state of exception   21, 98, 105, 112, 117–18, 134–7, 154, 158, 165, 187 n.19, 189 n.29, 190 n.31, 191 n.7, 193 n.18
   *State of Exception*   119, 189 n.29, 191 n.7
   state of nature   152–3
Alexander of Aphrodisias   121–2
anachronism   45–6, 132–4
analogy   55
analytics of raciality   139–44
an-archy
   and disorder   133
   of order   116–37
   of police power   14–17, 132–4
   relationality, dissolution of   133

anti-blackness police power   14–18, 155–60
anti-Black paradigm   91
anti-Black violence   14–18, 151, 155–60, 162
*arché* (archaeology)   126–7
Arendt, Hannah   142–3
arguments   17–19
Aristotle   8, 10, 20, 47–8, 91
   hegemony in political philosophy   46
   on living *vs.* living well   56–62
   man as *zoon politikon*, conception of   46, 49–53
   motion, idea of   54–6
   nature   49–53
   order, conception of   39, 51–3
   *Politics, The*   49, 51–2, 176 n.7
   on teleology   54–6
   *telos*   57
   transcendence *vs.* immanence   10–11
artificial person   60, 67
artificial *vs.* natural violence   49–53
*auctoritas vs. potestas*   118–19
autonomy   34
Avineri, S.   82

Balibar, E.   87, 182 n.15, 183 n.21
baroque era   101–4
Benjamin, Andrew   91, 105
Benjamin, Walter   1, 15, 18–19, 96
   baroque era analysis   101–4
   on contingency   102–3
   *Critique of Violence*   96, 105–7
   emergency *vs.* norm   105
   German *Trauerspiel*, analysis of   101–4
   law-preserving *vs.* law-founding violence   109–10
   on modernity from secularization   101–2
   *Origin of German Tragic Drama*   96, 101–5

on police and its violence 108–10
Schmitt's notion of sovereignty,
    critique of 96, 101–5
on transcendence 102
Bhattacharyya, G. 146
biopolitics 20, 23
    Foucault's view on 27–32, 64
    modernity with 28
biopower 171 n.7
Black people 87–9, 92, 150–3, 169 n.21
Blackstone, William 3, 6
Bodin, Jean 156–7
British police power 148–9
Brown, Michael 1, 34

capitalism 16
Carlyle, Thomas 45
catastrophe 103
Cavarero, Adriana 46–7
Caygill, H. 11–12, 55, 188 n.22
Chauvin, Derek 14
Christian theology 120–1
civil society 6, 34, 68–9
    administration of 69, 71–4
    enforces contracts in 75
    poverty in 69, 74–5
civil war 156
civitas 168 n.10
coercion 88–91
collateral effects 121–5
colonial power 144–50
*Commentaries on the Laws of England*
    (Blackstone) 3
Common-wealths 50, 56, 58–9
compulsion 80–1
consciousness 140
continental *vs.* overseas
    imperialism 142–3
contingency 102–3
Crenshaw, K. 15
*Critique of Violence*
    (Benjamin) 96, 105–7
cultural difference 149

da Silva, Denise Ferreira 18–19, 21,
    91, 138–60
    analytics of raciality 139–44
    on anti-Black violence 155–60
    on colonial boomerangs 144–50
    concept of racial 152

exteriority, notions of 139
    on police violence 138–9, 144–50
    on state of nature 150–5
    on time 155–60
Davis, Kathleen 156
*De Cive* (Hobbes) 49, 56, 152
de Menezes, John Charles 149
Derrida, Jacques 45–6, 48, 108–10
    on act of judgment 111–12
    on force-of-law 111–12
despotism 151
Diallo, Amadou 16, 153–4
disciplinary power 20, 29–32
disease of disorder 64
(dis)order 25, 31–2, 34, 37–8, 54–6
    appearance of 25
    of nature 53
    repressing 23
division of power 118–21
Douglass, Patrice 16–17
Dreyfus, H. L. 27–30, 39
Duggan, Mark 149

economy 36–7
emergency 90–1, 103–5
*Empire's Endgame* (Bhattacharyya) 146
equality 53
Esposito, Roberto 31–2
essential order 25–6
ethical life 80
European territory, police power in 138,
    141–7, 152, 154–9
exceptionality 105, 134–7
exploitation violence 16–17
expulsion thesis 31
externality 80–1
Eyre, Edward John 145–6

*Fabrication of Social Order, The*
    (Neocleous) 7
Falk, Francesca 62
Fassin, Didier 153
fate 122–3, 191 n.8
fear
    of an-archy 67
    of death 56, 58
    and sovereign/sovereignty 45–67
feudalism 156
Fichte, J. G. 20, 69, 77–85
    Hegel's critique of 78–81

police 20, 69, 77–85
　on police laws *vs.* civil laws 77–8
Fitzpatrick, P. 31
Floyd, George 14
force-of-law 98, 111–15
　Agamben's perspective on 112–13
　Derrida's views on 111–12
Foucault, Michael 2–3, 20, 58–9
　archaeology 24–29
　on biopolitics 20, 23, 27–32, 64, 141
　on discipline 20, 29–32
　*History of Sexuality Volume 1,*
　　*The* 30, 171 n.7
　interrogation of order 23–4
　on modern power 29–32
　order 24–32, 38–41
　*Order of Things, The* 23–31, 39
　*Political Technology of*
　　*Individuals, The* 29
　racism, treatment of 141–2
　in relation to life 27
　*Security, Territory, Population* 55–6
　on security 20
　*Society Must be Defended* 30–1, 141, 144
　on sovereign power 59
　Weheliye's analysis of race 141–3
　works on police and order 22–41
*Foucault's Law* (Golder and Fitzpatrick) 31
freedom 83, 89
　individual 70–2
　and violence 87–89, 92
Friedrich, C. 70

German *Trauerspiel* 101–4, 106
*gewalt* 107
Gilroy, Paul 162
goal 57
God 8–9, 11, 65–6, 96–7, 99–100, 103, 118–19, 121–2
Golder, B. 31
good life 56–62
Gordon, George William 143–4
government/governmentality 2, 7–10, 121–5
　*vs.* an-archy 52–3
　as collateral effect 122–5
　free men *vs.* household in opposition 8

managerial form of 8
　of world 122
Graham, Stephen 146
gratuitous violence 16, 172 n.19
Gray, Biko Mandela 15, 158
Greeks 46–7, 91
　vain philosophy 47
grid of intelligibility 140
Gulf War 146–7

Hannsen, Beatrice 101
Harney, Stefano 1
Hartman, Saidiya 157
Hegel, G. W. F. 18, 20–1, 104–5
　Africa and African people,
　　characterizations of 87–9, 92
　on civil society 68–9
　on coercion 88–9
　emergency 90–1
　on Fichte's police 78–81
　*Lectures on the Philosophy of*
　　*History* 85–6
　personality, account of 76–7
　*Philosophy of Right* 68–74, 80, 85, 90, 182 n.17
　on police (*Polizei*) 68, 72–85
　on police-power 81–5
　property, account of 76–7
　secret police points, advocacy of 81
　state 70–2, 83–5
　theorization of sovereignty 85–91
　on times of peace *vs.* situations of exigency 89–90
*History of Sexuality Volume 1, The*
　(Foucault) 30, 171 n.7
Hobbes, T. 4, 7, 20, 33, 35, 45–67, 68, 84–7, 91, 97, 104–5, 132–3, 140, 151–2, 163–5
　Aristotle's thought, reductive presentation of 67
　artificial *vs.* natural violence 49–53
　civil state 48
　criticisms of Aristotle 49–53
　*De Cive* 49, 56, 152
　idea of order 46–67
　'Kingdome divided in it selfe cannot stand' 4
　Leviathan 64, 67
　life with order 55–6
　on living *vs.* living well 56–62

on man   49–53
motion, idea of   54–6
on natural law   58
political philosophy   57
on sovereignty   45–67
state 'natural' violence   49–53
theory of representation   60
theory of state with police   45–67
'This great Authority being Indivisible'   4
Hobbesian universe   57, 171 n.2
*Homo Sacer* project   117–18
human artifice   38–9
humanity   87–8
Hussain, Nasser   143–6

imperialism   142–3
injustice/injury   59

Jackson, Zakiyyah Iman   88
John of Salisbury   3
Justi, Von   6
justice   8, 15, 29, 32, 52, 112
    administration of   71–3
    operative   60
    police for   32–3

Kaba, Chris   14, 149
Kantorowicz, Ernst   3
*katechon*   57
King, Rodney   15, 147
*Kingdom and the Glory, The* (Agamben)   7, 117–18, 127
knowledge   24–5
Knox, T. M.   72, 74
Koepnick, L. P.   103–4, 186 n.15

Laird, J.   50
law-positing violence   109–10
law-preserving *vs.* law-founding violence   109–10
laws   2–4, 75, 105
    force of   111–15
    and police   19, 95–6
    police laws *vs.* civil laws   77–8
    and racism   141–4
    in service of order   55
*Lectures on Jurisprudence* (Smith)   32–3
legal positivism   99, 101

Lemke, Thomas   171 n.7
Leviathan   45–6, 48–50, 53, 56–9, 62–7, 130, 165, 170 n.2, 177 n.17, 186 n.13
    artificial creation of   46
liberalism   18, 21, 29, 33, 35, 37, 73, 99–101
life   29–30
    ethical   80
    good   56–62
    with order   55–6
    for political power   30
    sovereignty and   56
    of state   54–6
living   56–62
living well   56–62
*logos*   53
*Lose Your Mother* (Hartman)   157
Lukács, G.   79–80

man
    *vs.* animals   52–3
    Hobbes on   52–3
    natural equality   53
    as *zoon politikon*   46, 49–53
martial law in Jamaica   143–6
Martinot, S.   1, 159–60
Marx, Karl   89–90, 144
Mbembe, Achille   3
metaphysical violence   16–17
military urbanism   146
Mills, Charles   150–1
modernity   17, 22, 64
    with biopolitics   28–32
    institutions as transition to   29
    level of power as transition to   29–32, 47
    life and   39–30
    police power in   2, 21, 95–6
    raciality and   140–4
    from secularization   101–2
Moten, Fred   1
motion   54–6
multitude *vs.* people   64–5

natural law   58, 154–5
natural order   13, 32–6, 41, 48
natural organism   67
natural violence   61, 86
nature   26–7, 85–91

# Index

Neocleous, Mark   7, 22–3, 45–7
*nomos* of *raison d'état*   37
Northern Ireland   148–9

*Oekonomie* (*oikonomia*)   6–14, 131, 169 n.17, 192 n.10
   and power   118–21
   relation   169 n.18
ontology *vs.* praxis   10, 12, 120–1
order of *physis*   26–7, 38–9
*Order of Things, The* (Foucault)   23–4, 27–31, 39
order/ordering   7–8, 11, 32–41
   an-archy of   116–37
   for Christian theology   129–30
   conception of   25
   essential   25–6
   Foucault, Michael on   24–32, 38–5
   immanent   120
   level of   23
   life with   55–6
   metaphysics of   32–6, 38–9, 41
   motion of government   55–6
   natural   32–6, 41, 48
   *physis/nomos*   26–7, 38–41
   of polis   47
   positive power   30
   represent   25–6
   signature of   125–32
   of state   55–6
   transcendent   120
   transforming   25
   understanding of   22
Ordoliberals   35, 172 n.15
*Origin of German Tragic Drama* (Benjamin)   96, 101–5
*Origins of Totalitarianism, The* (Arendt)   142–3

Patterson, Orlando   17
peace   109
Pelczynski, Z. A.   70, 184 n.26
Peller, G.   15
personality   76–7
*Philosophy of Right* (Hegel)   68–74, 80, 85, 90, 182 n.17
*physis* as order   26–7, 38–9
plague   62–3
police (*Polizei*)   5–14, 32–41, 81–5, 169 n.17

   for administration of justice   71–3
   Agamben's   116–37
   Benjamin's   108–10
   contemporary society, role in   20
   corporation and   72–3
   definition of   45
   during eighteenth century   5–6
   exceptionality and   134–7
   Fichte's views on   20, 69, 77–85
   Hegel's views on   68–92
   as institution   14
   killings   1–2
   and law   19, 95–6
   liberal view of   33
   modern   73
   ordinances   11–12
   and political theology   118–19
   politics (politik) *vs.*   171 n.8
   potentiality   134–7
   as public authority   72
   regulations   34
   science of   5–6
   sovereign   5–12
   understanding of   22
   violence   2–3, 109–10, 138–9, 144–50
police brutality   140–4
police laws *vs.* civil laws   77–8
police militarization   148–9
police order   21, 68–92
police power   1–2, 17–19, 77, 81–5, 95–6, 116–17
   analytics of raciality   140–4
   an-archic character of   14–17, 132–4
   anti-blackness   14–17
   da Silva on   138–9, 144–50
   in European territory   138, 141–7, 152, 154–9
   to law   2, 21
   logic of   2
   in modernity   2, 21, 95–6
   periodization of   149
   race difference and   21, 140–4
   Smith's conceptualization of   32–8
   to sovereignty   2–4, 21
   unbounded   21
police state   20, 29
political animal *vs.* wolf   49–53
political economy   12, 22, 32, 36–7, 99, 170
political ontology   14, 17, 150

political philosophy   97,
    169 n.19, 179 n.1
  Aristotle's   46, 66
  geometric   38
  Hobbes's   57
  mathematical   38
  Western   1, 7, 114
*Political Technology of Individuals, The*
    (Foucault)   29
political theology   118–19
*Political Theology* (Schmitt)   98–9, 101–2
political thinking   27
*Politics, The* (Aristotle)   49, 51–2, 176 n.7
*politik*   32
*Polizeigewalt*   113
*Polizeiwissenschaft*   5–6, 20, 35
positive law   167 n.6
potentiality   134–7
poverty in civil society   69, 74–5
power
  disciplinary   30–2
  division of   118–21
  negative   31, 38
  and *oikonomia*   118–21
  of ordering   31
  police   1–2, 17–19, 77, 81–5
  positive   34
  sovereign   4, 32, 55–62, 64–7, 84,
    90, 92–6, 99, 101, 103–4, 115,
    117, 119–20, 124–5, 129–35,
    147, 151–2, 154–5, 164–5,
    167 n.4, 168 n.8, 173 n.17,
    190 n.5, 192 n.16
  splitting of   62–6
praxis *vs.* ontology   10, 12, 120–1
primordial violence   86
productive power   69
property   76–7
providence   9–12, 65, 87, 120–3
public will   67
punishment   90–1

Quesnay's economic Table   25–6

Rabinow, P.   27–30, 39
race difference   140–4, 149–50
race injustice   140–4
race war   142
raciality, analytics of   139–44
racial power   140–4

racism   140–4, 149–50
recognition   82–5
regnum   168 n.10
represent order   25–26
Riedel, M.   73, 179 n.1
Robinson, Cedric   38–9
Rodney, Azelle   149
Roman law   76
Ruda, Frank   75
rule of law   50, 100

*Sacrament of Language, The*
    (Agamben)   126–7
safety   56
Schmitt, Carl   45, 57, 67, 96, 101–5, 114,
    119, 124–6, 129, 135–6, 165,
    177 nn.11–12, 183 n.24, 184 n.3,
    185 nn.4, 6
  Benjamin's critique of notion of
    sovereignty   96, 101–5
  on contingency   102–3
  exception, theorization of   96–9
  on liberalism   99–101
  police state   99
  on political concepts   96–7
  *Political Theology*   98–9, 101–5
  political topology   99
  reading of Hobbes   57
  on secularization   96, 99, 101–3, 126,
    130, 156, 185 n.4
  sovereignty,
    conceptualization of   96–101
  thesis   57–8
  on transcendence   102
Schrader, Stuart   147
science of police   5–6
secret police points   81
secularization   96, 99, 101–3, 126, 130,
    156, 185 n.4
security   69
*Security, Territory, Population*
    (Foucault)   55–6
self-defence   150, 153–5
Sexton, Jared   1, 159–60
Sharpe, Christina   157
signature of order   125–32
situations of exigency   89–90
Skinner, Quentin   60
slavery   156–8
Smith, Adam   20, 25, 32–3, 170 n.1

*Lectures on Jurisprudence* 32–3
notion of nature 35–6
police power,
    conceptualization of 32–8
    from *polizei* to police 32–8
*Theory of Moral Sentiments* 35–6, 172 n.14
*Wealth of Nations* 33–6, 172 n.14
social control 41, 96, 108, 132
social death 17
*Society Must be Defended* (Foucault) 30–1, 141, 144
'Sovereign Police' (Agamben) 2, 117
sovereign/sovereignty 2–4, 10, 13
    Benjamin's critique of Schmitt's notion of 96
    and fear 45–67
    Hegel's theorization of 85–91
    Hobbes on 45–67
    life and 56
    police 5–14
    power 4, 55–62, 64–7, 84, 90, 92–6, 99, 101, 103–4, 115, 117, 119–20, 124–5, 129–35, 147, 151–2, 154–5, 164–5, 167 n.4, 168 n.8, 173 n.17, 190 n.5, 192 n.16
    *raison d'être* of 47
    Schmitt's conceptualization of 96–101
    theorizations of 92
    transcendent pole of 10
splitting of power 62–6
state
    absolutism of 45
    as ethical community 70–1
    Hegelian 70–2
    as organism 70–1
    political 70–1
    power 34–5
state of exception 21, 98, 105, 112, 117–18, 134–7, 154, 158, 164, 187 n.19, 189 n.29, 190 n.31, 191 n.7, 193 n.18
*State of Exception* (Agamben) 118, 189 n.29, 191 n.7
state of nature 18, 40, 50, 52–3, 58–9, 61–2, 67, 84–5, 87–8, 92, 106, 124, 133, 135–6, 150–5, 162, 166, 175 n.5, 177 n.12, 178 nn.22, 24, 179 n.30, 183 n.21

Strauss, Leo 56
subjects of necessitas 91
symbolics of blood 143
system of natural liberty 36

Tarizzo, David 28, 29
technologization 100–1
teleology 16, 54–6
*Theory of Moral Sentiments* (Smith) 35–6, 172 n.14
theory of representation 60
time 155–60
times of peace 89–90
Toscano, Alberto 125–6
total state 99
Trafford, James 152
transcendence 102
    *vs.* immanence 10–11
transforming order 25
transgressive act 17
*Trauerspiel* (German) 101–4, 106
Tribe, Keith 35
Trinity 8–9

unity 65
universality 69, 73, 75, 87–9, 120, 139–41, 155, 161, 164, 181 n.8
US policing 147
utility 30

vain philosophy 47
value 30
Viner, J. 36, 173 n.16
violence 49–53, 85–91, 187 n.21
    anti-Black 14–17
    artificial *vs.* natural 49–53
    Benjamin's critique of 105–7
    of contingency 88–9
    of exploitation *vs.* metaphysical 16–17
    and freedom 87–9, 92
    gratuitous 172 n.19
    Hegel's theorization of 85–91
    law-preserving *vs.* law-founding 109–10
    natural 61, 86
    police 2–3, 109–10
    primordial 86
    against savagery 88–9
    of state of nature 58, 61–2, 87, 150–5

Wang, Jackie 161
Warren, Calvin 15–16, 19, 158
Watkin, William 126–8, 190 n.3, 192 n.9
*Wealth of Nations* (Smith) 33–6, 172 n.14
Weber, Samuel 103
Weheliye, Alexander 141–2

white supremacy 14–17, 159–60
Wilderson, Frank 16–17, 19, 89, 170 n.23
Willmott, Simon 153

Zartaloudis, T. 105, 124, 169 n.18, 179 n.32

www.ingramcontent.com/pod-product-compliance
Lightning Source LLC
Chambersburg PA
CBHW052108300426
44116CB00010B/1574